✳ *Listening to Your Life*

❋ *Listening to Your Life*

DAILY MEDITATIONS WITH
Frederick Buechner

Compiled and edited by George Connor

HarperOne
An Imprint of HarperCollins*Publishers*

Acknowledgment is made for permission to reprint material from the following sources: Excerpts from *The Book of Bebb,* copyright © 1971, 1972, 1974, 1977, 1979 by Frederick Buechner; from *Brendan,* copyright © 1987 by Frederick Buechner; from *The Final Beast,* copyright © 1965 by Frederick Buechner, from *Godric,* copyright © 1980 by Frederick Buechner, reprinted by permission of Atheneum Publishers, an imprint of Macmillan Publishing Company. From *The Faces of Jesus* by Frederick Buechner, copyright © 1989 by Stearn Publishers, Ltd., reprinted by permission of Stearn Publishers, Ltd.

HarperCollins books may be purchased for educational, business, or sales promotional use. For information, please e-mail the Special Markets Department at SPsales@harpercollins.com.

HarperCollins Web site: http://www.harpercollins.com

HarperCollins®, 📖®, and HarperOne™ are trademarks of HarperCollins Publishers.

TEXT DESIGN BY NAOMI SCHIFF

Library of Congress Cataloging-in-Publication Data

Buechner, Frederick.
   Listening to your life : daily meditations with Frederick Buechner / compiled by George Connor.
     p. cm.
   Includes bibliographical references and index.
   ISBN 978–0–06–069864–5
   1. Meditations.   2. Devotional calendars.   I. Connor, George.
II. Title.
BV4832.2.B8274   1992
242'.2—dc20   92–52653

16 17 18 RRD(H) 60 59 58 57 56 55 54 53

For Janet Gilbert

Contents

Introduction ◆ ix

About This Book ◆ xiii

January ◆ 1

February ◆ 29

March ◆ 59

April ◆ 85

May ◆ 111

June ◆ 143

July ◆ 173

August ◆ 199

September ◆ 233

October ◆ 263

November ◆ 291

December ◆ 313

Books by Frederick Buechner ◆ 343

Sources by Book ◆ 345

Sources by Day ◆ 347

Index by Title ◆ 353

Introduction

WHAT FOLLOWS ARE three hundred and sixty-six quotations culled from various books I have written over the past nearly thirty years, fiction and non-fiction both, one quotation for every day of the calendar plus one extra thrown in for leap year. Out of the goodness of his heart my friend George C. Connor, Professor Emeritus of the University of Tennessee in Chattanooga, agreed to do the culling for me, and my gratitude to him knows no bounds. I can only imagine how it would have been if I had had to go back over all those pages myself.

I remember reading an anecdote somewhere about Ralph Waldo Emerson at a point in his life when, according to *The Oxford Companion to American Literature*, he had "gradually slipped into a serene senility in which his mind finally became a calm blank." Apparently the old Brahmin happened to pick up a volume of his own essays one day and after he had finished browsing through it for a while remarked something to the effect that although he couldn't place the young fellow who wrote them, he thought that all in all they showed promise. Sweet are the uses of serene senility. With my own wits still more or less about me, how would I have reacted to a similar browse if George Connor hadn't taken the task on for me? Would I have been able to extract three hundred and sixty-six passages that I considered worth enshrining in a volume like this? Would I have found the books promising, or would I have cringed at them the way you can cringe at letters you wrote long ago, wondering how on earth you could ever have been so callow and wrong-headed, so alternately glib and pontifical? Or maybe it would have been a combination of both, with some parts striking me as promising and other parts making me cringe if only at the thought of how much better I might have written them if I had just known then some of the things I have come to know since. If I hadn't said this. If I had said that. But thanks to my friend, I was spared having to read the twenty-odd books themselves and can only guess at what my reaction would have been if he hadn't spared me.

There is a little of everything here—bits of novels, of sermons, lectures, autobiographical ruminations, a kind of theological ABCs called *Wishful Thinking* and its successor *Whistling in the Dark,* a collection of thumbnail sketches of biblical characters called *Peculiar Treasures,* and so on. I have not read the three hundred and sixty-six cullings straight through from January 1st to December 31st, nor of course is that the way a book like this is ever supposed to be read by anybody, but dipping in here and there I suppose I have read more or less all of them at one time or another. In a way it seems to me less my book than it does George Connor's. There is no denying that I wrote all the passages in it, but because they were chosen by him and arranged by him according to his own scheme and for the purpose of focusing on certain things that to him seemed more apt than others or more literarily felicitous or what-have-you, I find myself looking at the whole with something approaching Emerson's senescent detachment. I find that there is little if anything here that I would not still be willing to sign my name to despite the fact that some of the passages were written so long ago that I have a hard time remembering very clearly what it was like, on the inside anyway, to be the man who wrote them. I would undoubtedly say some things in different ways if called upon to say them again today, but the things themselves still represent pretty much who I am and what I believe. I am a writer who frets endlessly about style as well as content—it has to sound right and look right as well as in some sense, one always hopes, to *be* right—but I don't recall finding many places here where I let my concern for effect take precedence over my attempt to be as true as I could reasonably manage to be to the truth of whatever I was trying to get across. I suppose there are some where I got carried away by my own rhetoric, but at least there are fewer than there might have been. George Connor has a good ear.

There are a lot of books like this floating around these days, and I own several of them myself. I keep them on my bedside table and am most apt to look at them at night just before I switch off the light. I open to the quotation for whatever day it happens to be and hope that it will turn out to be a good one to go to sleep on. Sometimes it is, and sometimes it isn't. The good ones, for me, are the ones that almost uncannily hit on something that I have been thinking about, often without realizing that I have. They are the ones that sound like a friend talking, like somebody who has been more or less where I have been and felt something more or less like what I have been feeling—about life, about myself, about the people I love and the people I am unable to love, about God. They are not so much the ones that tell me something new that will keep me awake, puzzling over it, as the ones that will help me see something as familiar as my own face in a new way, with a new sense of its depth and preciousness and mystery.

Above all, I guess, the good ones, for me, are the ones that one way or another suggest that although the night is coming, it is not darkness but light that is the end of all things. I can only hope that the reader will find at least a few like that buried among all these pages. And that they will bring good dreams.

About This Book

FREDERICK BUECHNER spent a week on the campus of the University of Tennessee at Chattanooga in November 1986 as a participant in one of the programs in observance of the university's centennial year. As chairman of the committee for that program, I was his escort and almost constant companion for that week; I believe that on one public occasion he called me his manager. One happy result—the happiest for me— was that Frederick Buechner and I became friends. We discovered that we look at the world in much the same way; we have many of the same sympathies and, yes, many of the same dislikes. Making new friends is not easy as one grows older, and I look on that week as a gift of grace.

When I was asked to serve as editor of this book of meditations, I readily agreed, both as an act of homage and as a self-indulgence. My admiration for Frederick Buechner as a writer is virtually without limit. If there is a writer with a more felicitous style now working in the English language, I do not know who it is.

As an editor, I have tried to be as unobtrusive as possible. Where an introduction to one of the meditations seemed necessary, I have made it as brief as possible. Where there was no title for the selection being used, I have provided one, using as often as possible a word or phrase from the text itself.

There are very minor changes here and there from the original text (e.g., a transitional phrase removed, a name or another noun substituted for a pronoun) without the usual scholarly indication that such a change has been made. All of us involved in the book, certainly including Frederick Buechner with whose consent the changes were made, agreed at the outset that we ought not to clutter up the text with footnotes, ellipses, brackets, and the like. But where a lengthy portion has been left out of a passage, I have used an ellipsis. The source for each passage can be found in the back of the book along with a listing of passages from each book used.

I want finally to thank several persons to whom I am indebted for generous help, beginning with Frederick Buechner himself, who was infinitely patient in answering my queries. I have been helped enormously also by my own parish, St. Peter's Episcopal Church in Chattanooga, especially by Hallie Warren, the rector; Patsy Phillips, parish secretary; and the members of the Bishop Barth Bible Class, who spent three sessions discussing the plans for the book and giving me useful suggestions.

George Connor

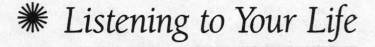 *Listening to Your Life*

 *January*

Life Itself Is Grace ✳ January 1

Listen to your life.
All moments are key moments.

I DISCOVERED THAT IF you really keep your eye peeled to it and your ears open, if you really pay attention to it, even such a limited and limiting life as the one I was living on Rupert Mountain opened up onto extraordinary vistas. Taking your children to school and kissing your wife goodbye. Eating lunch with a friend. Trying to do a decent day's work. Hearing the rain patter against the window. There is no event so commonplace but that God is present within it, always hiddenly, always leaving you room to recognize him or not to recognize him, but all the more fascinatingly because of that, all the more compellingly and hauntingly. . . . If I were called upon to state in a few words the essence of everything I was trying to say both as a novelist and as a preacher, it would be something like this: Listen to your life. See it for the fathomless mystery that it is. In the boredom and pain of it no less than in the excitement and gladness: touch, taste, smell your way to the holy and hidden heart of it because in the last analysis all moments are key moments, and life itself is grace.

If God Speaks ✳ January 2

IF GOD SPEAKS anywhere, it is into our personal lives that he speaks. Someone we love dies, say. Some unforeseen act of kindness or cruelty touches the heart or makes the blood run cold. We fail a friend, or a friend fails us, and we are appalled at the capacity we all of us have for estranging the very people in our lives we need the most. Or maybe nothing extraordinary happens at all—just one day following another, helter-skelter, in the manner of days. We sleep and dream. We wake. We work. We remember and forget. We have fun and are depressed. And into the thick of it, or out of the thick of it, at moments of even the most humdrum of our days, God speaks. But what do I mean by saying that God speaks?

◆ ◆ ◆

He speaks not just through the sounds we hear, of course, but through events in all their complexity and variety, through the harmonies and disharmonies and counterpoint of all that happens. As to the meaning of what he says, there are times that we are apt to think we know. Adolf Hitler dies a suicide in his bunker with the Third Reich going up in flames all around him, and what God is saying about the wages of sin seems clear enough. Or Albert Schweitzer renounces fame as a theologian and musician for a medical mission in Africa, where he ends up even more famous still as one of the great near-saints of Protestantism; and again we are tempted to see God's meaning as clarity itself. But what is God saying through a good man's suicide? What about the danger of the proclaimed saint's becoming a kind of religious prima donna as proud of his own humility as a peacock of its tail? What about sin itself as a means of grace? What about grace, when misappropriated and misunderstood, becoming an occasion for sin? To try to express in even the most insightful and theologically sophisticated terms the meaning of what God speaks through the events of our lives is as precarious a business as to try to express the meaning of the sound of rain on the roof or the spectacle of the setting sun. But I choose to believe that he speaks nonetheless, and the reason that his words are impossible to capture in human language is of course that they are ultimately always incarnate words. They are words fleshed out in the everydayness no less than in the crises of our own experience.

Alphabet of Grace ✳ *January 3*

LIFE ITSELF CAN BE thought of as an alphabet by which God graciously makes known his presence and purpose and power among us. Like the Hebrew alphabet, the alphabet of grace has no vowels, and in that sense his words to us are always veiled, subtle, cryptic, so that it is left to us to delve their meaning, to fill in the vowels, for ourselves by means of all the faith and imagination we can muster. God speaks to us in such a way, presumably, not because he chooses to be obscure but because, unlike a dictionary word whose meaning is fixed, the meaning of an incarnate word is the meaning it has for the one it is spoken to, the meaning that becomes clear and effective in our lives only when we ferret it out for ourselves.

Listen for Him ✳ *January 4*

THE QUESTION IS not whether the things that happen to you are chance things or God's things because, of course, they are both at once. There is no chance thing through which God cannot speak—even the walk from the house to the garage that you have walked ten thousand times before, even the moments when you cannot believe there is a God who speaks at all anywhere. He speaks, I believe, and the words he speaks are incarnate in the flesh and blood of our selves and of our own footsore and sacred journeys. We cannot live our lives constantly looking back, listening back, lest we be turned to pillars of longing and regret, but to live without listening at all is to live deaf to the fullness of the music. Sometimes we avoid listening for fear of what we may hear, sometimes for fear that we may hear nothing at all but the empty rattle of our own feet on the pavement. But *be not affeard*, says Caliban, nor is he the only one to say it. "Be not afraid," says another, "for lo, I am with you always, even unto the end of the world." He says he is with us on our journeys. He says he has been with us since each of our journeys began. Listen for him. Listen to the sweet and bitter airs of your present and your past for the sound of him.

No Time Lost? ✳ January 5

Godric is speaking:

A ILRED, I KNOW hours well enough," I said. "Stick a twig into the soil and watch the shadow turn. That's hours. Or take old Wear out there. Let him rise another inch or two, and either we'll grow gills or shipwreck sure. That's hours for you. It's inch by inch and hour by hour to death. It's hours gone and hours still to go. No puzzle there. A child can count it out. But what is time itself, dear friend? What is the sea where hours float? Am I daft, or is it true there's no such thing as hours past and other hours still to pass, but all of them instead are all at once and never gone? Is there no time lost that ever was? Is there no time yet to come that's not here now?"

Epiphany ✳ January 6

T HE GIFTS THAT THE three Wise Men, or Kings, or Magi, brought to the manger in Bethlehem cost them plenty but seem hardly appropriate to the occasion. Maybe they were all they could think of for the child who had everything. In any case, they set them down on the straw—the gold, the frankincense, the myrrh—worshiped briefly, and then returned to the East where they had come from. It gives you pause to consider how, for all their great wisdom, they overlooked the one gift that the child would have been genuinely pleased to have someday, and that was the gift of themselves and their love.

◆ ◆ ◆

The foolishness of the wise is perhaps nowhere better illustrated than by the way the three Magi went to Herod the Great, King of the Jews, to find out the whereabouts of the holy child who had just been born King of the Jews to supplant him. It did not even strike them as suspicious when Herod asked them to be sure to let him know when they found him so he could hurry on down to pay his respects.

Luckily for the holy child, after the three Magi had followed their star to the manger and left him their presents, they were tipped off in a dream to avoid Herod like the plague on their way home.

Herod was fit to be tied when he realized he'd been had and ordered the murder of every male child two years old and under in the district. For all his enormous power, he knew there was somebody in diapers more powerful still. The wisdom of the foolish is perhaps nowhere better illustrated.

Life Is With ✸ *January 7*

THE TEMPTATION IS always to reduce life to size. A bowl of cherries. A rat race. Amino acids. Even to call it a mystery smacks of reductionism. It is *the* mystery.

As far as anybody seems to know, the vast majority of things in the universe do not have whatever life is. Sticks, stones, stars, space—they simply *are*. A few things *are* and are somehow aware of it. They have broken through into Something, or Something has broken through into them. Even a jellyfish, a butternut squash. They're in it with us. We're all in it together, or it in us. Life is *it*. Life is *with*.

After lecturing learnedly on miracles, a great theologian was asked to give a specific example of one. "There is only one miracle," he answered. "It is life."

Have you wept at anything during the past year?

Has your heart beat faster at the sight of young beauty?

Have you thought seriously about the fact that someday you are going to die?

More often than not do you really listen when people are speaking to you instead of just waiting for your turn to speak?

Is there anybody you know in whose place, if one of you had to suffer great pain, you would volunteer yourself?

If your answer to all or most of these questions is No, the chances are that you're dead.

Our Pilot, Our Guide ✳ January 8

The following passage is taken from a seminary commencement address:

CHRIST IS OUR employer as surely as the general contractor is the carpenter's employer, only the chances are that this side of Paradise we will never see his face except mirrored darkly in dreams and shadows, if we're lucky, and in each other's faces. He is our general, but the chances are that this side of Paradise we will never hear his voice except in the depth of our own inner silence and in each other's voices. He is our shepherd, but the chances are we will never feel his touch except as we are touched by the joy and pain and holiness of our own life and each other's lives. He is our pilot, our guide, our true, fast, final friend and judge, but often when we need him most, he seems farthest away because he will always have gone on ahead, leaving only the faint print of his feet on the path to follow. And the world blows leaves across the path. And branches fall. And darkness falls: We are, all of us, Mary Magdalene, who reached out to him at the end only to embrace the empty air. We are the ones who stopped for a bite to eat that evening at Emmaus and, as soon as they saw who it was that was sitting there at the table with them, found him vanished from their sight. Abraham, Moses, Gideon, Rahab, Sarah are our brothers and sisters because, like them, we all must live *in faith,* as the great chapter puts it with a staggering honesty that should be a lesson to us all, "not having received what was promised, but having seen it and greeted it from afar," and only from afar. And yet the country we seek and do not truly find, at least not here, not now, the heavenly country and homeland, is there somewhere as surely as our yearning for it is there; and I think that our yearning for it is itself as much a part of the truth of it as our yearning for love or beauty or peace is a part of those truths. And Christ is there with us on our way as surely as the way itself is there that has brought us to this place. It has brought us. We are here. He is with us—that is our faith—but only in unseen ways, as subtle and pervasive as air.

Praise, Praise ✳ *January 9*

Godric is speaking:

"PRAISE, PRAISE!" I croak. Praise God for all that's holy, cold, and dark. Praise him for all we lose, for all the river of the years bears off. Praise him for stillness in the wake of pain. Praise him for emptiness. And as you race to spill into the sea, praise him yourself, old Wear. Praise him for dying and the peace of death.

In the little church I built of wood for Mary, I hollowed out a place for him. Perkin brings him by the pail and pours him in. Now that I can hardly walk, I crawl to meet him there. He takes me in his chilly lap to wash me of my sins. Or I kneel down beside him till within his depths I see a star.

Sometimes this star is still. Sometimes she dances. She is Mary's star. Within that little pool of Wear she winks at me. I wink at her. The secret that we share I cannot tell in full. But this much I will tell. What's lost is nothing to what's found, and all the death that ever was, set next to life, would scarcely fill a cup.

A Crazy, Holy Grace ✳ January 10

A CRAZY, HOLY GRACE I have called it. Crazy because whoever could have predicted it? Who can ever foresee the crazy how and when and where of a grace that wells up out of the lostness and pain of the world and of our own inner worlds? And holy because these moments of grace come ultimately from farther away than Oz and deeper down than doom, holy because they heal and hallow. "For all thy blessings, known and unknown, remembered and forgotten, we give thee thanks," runs an old prayer, and it is for the all but unknown ones and the more than half-forgotten ones that we do well to look back over the journeys of our lives because it is their presence that makes the life of each of us a sacred journey. We have a hard time seeing such blessed and blessing moments as the gifts I choose to believe they are and a harder time still reaching out toward the hope of a giving hand, but part of the gift is to be able, at least from time to time, to be assured and convinced without seeing, as Hebrews says, because that is of the very style and substance of faith as well as what drives it always to seek a farther and a deeper seeing still.

There will always be some who say that such faith is only a dream, and God knows there is none who can say it more devastatingly than we sometimes say it to ourselves, but if so, I think of it as like the dream that Caliban dreamed. Faith is like the dream in which the clouds open to show such riches ready to drop upon us that when we wake into the reality of nothing more than common sense, we cry to dream again because the dreaming seems truer than the waking does to the fullness of reality not as we have seen it, to be sure, but as by faith we trust it to be without seeing. Faith is both the dreaming and the crying. Faith is the assurance that the best and holiest dream is true after all. Faith in *something*—if only in the proposition that life is better than death—is what makes our journeys through time bearable.

Your Own Journey ✳ *January 11*

These two paragraphs conclude the introduction to The Sacred Journey:

WHAT I PROPOSE TO do now is to try listening to my life as a whole, or at least to certain key moments of the first half of my life thus far, for whatever of meaning, of holiness, of God, there may be in it to hear. My assumption is that the story of any one of us is in some measure the story of us all.

For the reader, I suppose, it is like looking through someone else's photograph album. What holds you, if nothing else, is the possibility that somewhere among all those shots of people you never knew and places you never saw, you may come across something or someone you recognize. In fact— for more curious things have happened—even in a stranger's album, there is always the possibility that as the pages flip by, on one of them you may even catch a glimpse of yourself. Even if both of those fail, there is still a third possibility which is perhaps the happiest of them all, and that is that once I have put away my album for good, you may in the privacy of the heart take out the album of your own life and search it for the people and places you have loved and learned from yourself, and for those moments in the past—many of them half forgotten—through which you glimpsed, however dimly and fleetingly, the sacredness of your own journey.

Rinkitink ❋ January 12

Buechner discusses the beginning of his fascination with the Land of Oz:

FOR REASONS THAT I can only guess at now, no one I came to know during that first year in Oz left a deeper mark on me than a plump, ebullient king named Rinkitink. He was a foolish man in many ways who laughed too much and talked too much and at moments of stress was apt to burst into unkingly tears; but beneath all that, he gave the impression of remarkable strength and resilience and courage even, a good man to have around when the chips were down. He and his young friend Prince Inga of Pingaree came into possession of three magic pearls—a blue one that conferred such strength that no power could resist it; a pink one that protected its owner from all dangers; and a pure white one that could speak words of great wisdom and helpfulness. "Never question the truth of what you fail to understand," the white pearl said when Rinkitink consulted it for the first time, "for the world is filled with wonders." It was great wisdom indeed, and has proved greatly helpful many times since.

For the First Time ❋ January 13

IN ANY CASE, OF all the giants who held up my world, Naya [Buechner's maternal grandmother] was perhaps chief, and when I knew she was coming to Georgetown for a visit that day, I wanted to greet her properly. So what I did at the age of six was prepare her a feast. All I could find in the icebox that seemed suitable were some cold string beans that had seen better days with the butter on them long since gone to wax, and they were what I brought out to her in that fateful garden. I do not remember what she said then exactly, but it was an aside spoken to my parents or whatever grown-ups happened to be around to the effect that she did not usually eat much at three o'clock in the afternoon or whatever it was, let alone the cold string beans of another age, but that she would see what she could do for propriety's sake. Whatever it was, she said it drily, wittily, the way she said everything, never dreaming for a moment that I would either hear or understand, but I did hear, and what I came to understand for the first time in my life, I suspect—why else should I remember it?—was that the people you love have two sides to them. One is the side they love you back with, and the other is the side that, even when they do not mean to, they can sting you with like a wasp. It was the first ominous scratching in the walls, the first telltale crack in the foundation of the one home which perhaps any child has when you come right down to it, and that is the people he loves.

Alive and Changing ✳ January 14

G OD SPEAKS TO US through our lives, we often too easily say. *Something* speaks anyway, spells out some sort of godly or godforsaken meaning to us through the alphabet of our years, but often it takes many years and many further spellings out before we start to glimpse, or think we do, a little of what that meaning is. Even then we glimpse it only dimly, like the first trace of dawn on the rim of night, and even then it is a meaning that we cannot fix and be sure of once and for

all because it is always incarnate meaning and thus as alive
and changing as we are ourselves alive and changing.

Humanly Best ✳ January 15

After Buechner's father's death, the family moved to Bermuda,
rather to Grandma Buechner's disapproval:

"Y OU SHOULD STAY AND face reality," she wrote, and in terms
of what was humanly best, this was perhaps the soundest
advice she could have given us: that we should stay and,
through sheer Scharmann endurance, will, courage, put our
lives back together by becoming as strong as she was herself.
But when it comes to putting broken lives back together—
when it comes, in religious terms, to the saving of souls—the
human best tends to be at odds with the holy best. To do for
yourself the best that you have it in you to do—to grit your
teeth and clench your fists in order to survive the world at its
harshest and worst—is, by that very act, to be unable to let
something be done for you and in you that is more wonderful
still. The trouble with steeling yourself against the harshness
of reality is that the same steel that secures your life against
being destroyed secures your life also against being opened
up and transformed by the holy power that life itself comes
from. You can survive on your own. You can grow strong on
your own. You can even prevail on your own. But you cannot
become human on your own. Surely that is why, in Jesus' sad
joke, the rich man has as hard a time getting into Paradise as
that camel through the needle's eye because with his credit
card in his pocket, the rich man is so effective at getting for
himself everything he needs that he does not see that what
he needs more than anything else in the world can be had
only as a gift. He does not see that the one thing a clenched

fist cannot do is accept, even from *le bon Dieu* himself, a helping hand.

Remember ✳ January 16

WHEN YOU REMEMBER me, it means that you have carried something of who I am with you, that I have left some mark of who I am on who you are. It means that you can summon me back to your mind even though countless years and miles may stand between us. It means that if we meet again, you will know me. It means that even after I die, you can still see my face and hear my voice and speak to me in your heart.

For as long as you remember me, I am never entirely lost. When I'm feeling most ghost-like, it's your remembering me that helps remind me that I actually exist. When I'm feeling sad, it's my consolation. When I'm feeling happy, it's part of why I feel that way.

If you forget me, one of the ways I remember who I am will be gone. If you forget me, part of who I am will be gone.

"Jesus, remember me when you come into your kingdom," the good thief said from his cross (Luke 23:42). There are perhaps no more human words in all of Scripture, no prayer we can pray so well.

The Power of Language ✳ January 17

Buechner is remembering his Lawrenceville school years:

AT THE SAME TIME I happened to have for an English teacher an entirely different sort of man. He had nothing of the draughtsman about him, no inclination to drill us in anything, but instead a tremendous, Irishman's zest for the blarney and wizardry of words. I had always been a reader and loved words for the tales they can tell and the knowledge they can impart and the worlds they can conjure up like the Scarecrow's Oz and Claudius' Rome; but this teacher, Mr. Martin, was the first to give me a feeling for what words are, and can do, in themselves. Through him I started to sense that words not only convey something, but *are* something; that words have color, depth, texture of their own, and the power to evoke vastly more than they mean; that words can be used not merely to make things clear, make things vivid, make things interesting and whatever else, but to make things happen inside the one who reads them or hears them. When Gerard Manley Hopkins writes a poem about a blacksmith and addresses him as one who "didst fettle for the great gray drayhorse his bright and battering sandal," he is not merely bringing the blacksmith to life, but in a way is bringing us to life as well. Through the sound, rhythm, passion of his words, he is bringing to life in us, as might otherwise never have been brought to life at all, a sense of the uniqueness and mystery and holiness not just of the blacksmith and his great gray drayhorse, but of reality itself, including the reality of ourselves. Mr. Martin had us read wonderful things—it was he who gave me my love for *The Tempest,* for instance—but it was a course less in literature than in language and the great power that language has to move and in some measure even to transform the human heart.

So Much to Read ✳ January 18

And Princeton:

I TOOK GERMAN LIKE medicine, hoping that it might land me in Intelligence when my time came instead of the Infantry, and almost flunked it despite artful cribbing from Rainer

Maria Rilke in my German compositions. I took medieval history, I no longer remember why, and out of it all, the one thing that stuck by me was Saint Francis of Assisi and his Canticle to the Sun. *"Laudato sie, misigniore,"* he sang—praise to thee, *misigniore,* for Brother Sun, for Sister Moon, and though there was much in it that reminded me of the creaking baritone in the Tryon church where I sometimes went with Naya, there was a passion to it that was new to me and a mystery too because it was not just Brother Sun and Sister Moon that he was giving praise for in his canticle but Sister Death too, of all things, death no less than life as sister and friend. I had heard before of praising God, but the madness of Saint Francis' praise was new to me, the madness of throwing away everything he ever had or ever hoped to have for love of the creation no less than of the creator, of making a marvelous and holy fool of himself by tramping out into the fields to tell swallows and skylarks and red-winged blackbirds that they ought to praise God too for the air that bore them up and for their nests in the high trees.

I took creative writing, too—wondering, as I still do, what other kind of writing there is—and wrote poems about Saint Francis, about flying kites in Bermuda on Good Friday, about war and love, but in all of them I think my chief interest was less in trying to tell some kind of truth, if only a truth about myself or what I had seen, than in trying to make an effect. "You have a way with words," my instructor, the critic R. P. Blackmur, told me, and although at the time it was like getting the Pulitzer Prize, it seems to me now that there was also a barb to his remark. I wrote poems with punch lines, had a way of making words ring out and dance a little, but there was little if any of my life's blood in my poems. I was writing for my teachers, for glory. I had not yet started trying to write either out of myself very much or for myself, partly, of course, because I had only a very dim sense of who that self was, and what with both the war and my eighteenth birthday bearing down on me hard, there was precious little time to find out. We had the sense—all of us, I think—that our time was running out, and that was why we tried to fill it as full as we did with whatever came to hand, why in the face of death it was a time with so much life in it. There was so much to do, so much to be, so much to read. John Donne I read especially, and William Blake, and T. S. Eliot, more carried away with the sound of their voices than with what they said—the stammering intensity of Donne, the toying, crazy innocence of Blake, and Eliot so weary and civilized and under control, the wisest old possum of them all.

A Wider World ❋ January 19

"WITHIN THE CENTER of my ring / I found myself, and that was everything," the poem says. Whatever my twenty-year-old self was, it was the pivot on which the circle of my life revolved. I do not think that I was a more selfish person than most. Through such unhappiness as I had known myself, I had a feeling for the unhappiness of others, and at least to those I liked I had it in me to be a good friend. But I was, as I have said, centered on myself. The tree, the cloud, the sun—I knew there was a wider world beyond myself and my small circle: the world that Saint Francis praised God for, the world that had marked with such sadness and pity and weariness the face of Jesus in Da Vinci's study. And I knew that somewhere out there, or deep beneath, there might well be God for all I knew. But all of that seemed very remote, mysterious and unreal compared with the immediate and absorbing reality of myself. And though I think I knew even then that finding that self and being that self and protecting and nurturing and enjoying that self was not the "everything" I called it in the poem, by and large it was everything that, to me, really mattered. That, in any event, was the surface I floated on and in many ways float on still as to one degree or another we all of us both do and must lest otherwise we get lost or drown in the depths. But to lose track of those depths to the extent that I was inclined to—to lose track of the deep needs beyond our own needs and those of our closest friends; to lose track of the deep mystery beyond or at the heart of the mystery of our separate selves—is to lose track also of what our journey is a journey toward and of the sacredness and high adventure of our journey. Nor, if we have our eyes, ears, hearts open at all, does life allow us to lose track of the depths for long.

The Need to Praise ✳ *January 20*

T HE NEXT WINTER I sat in Army fatigues somewhere near Anniston, Alabama, eating my supper out of a mess kit. The infantry training battalion that I had been assigned to was on bivouac. There was a cold drizzle of rain, and everything was mud. The sun had gone down. I was still hungry when I finished and noticed that a man nearby had something left over that he was not going to eat. It was a turnip, and when I asked him if I could have it, he tossed it over to me. I missed the catch, the turnip fell to the ground, but I wanted it so badly that I picked it up and started eating it anyway, mud and all. And then, as I ate it, time deepened and slowed down again. With a lurch of the heart that is real to me still, I saw suddenly, almost as if from beyond time altogether, that not only was the turnip good, but the mud was good too, even the drizzle and cold were good, even the Army that I had dreaded for months. Sitting there in the Alabama winter with my mouth full of cold turnip and mud, I could see at least for a moment how if you ever took truly to heart the ultimate goodness and joy of things, even at their bleakest, the need to praise someone or something for it would be so great that you might even have to go out and speak of it to the birds of the air.

When a Man Leaves Home ✸ January 21

The ghost of St. Cuthbert is talking with Godric; Glythwin is a rabbit:

THE NIGHT I DIED, they waved lit torches to and fro from that high ledge behind you there to tell my monks on Lindisfarne the news. Would you believe it, though? There was not one of them awake. So Glythwin sank his teeth into the abbot's toe. You should have seen the jig he did with one foot tucked beneath him like a stork!"

"You say that you were dead, and yet you saw?" I said.

"Not only saw but laughed," he said, "till tears ran down."

"Would I be right that you're a ghost then, Father, and you haunt this place?"

"Ah well, and if it comes to that," he said, "your shadow fell here long before your foot, and that's a kind of haunting too. Farne had long been calling you, I mean, before you heard at last and came."

"I heard no call, Father," I said. "I came here as a stranger, and I came by chance."

"Was it as a stranger and by chance you wept?" he said, then let me wonder at his words a while before he spoke again. "When a man leaves home, he leaves behind some scrap of his heart. Is it not so, Godric? . . . It's the same with a place a man is going to. Only then he sends a scrap of his heart ahead."

A Power from Beyond Time ✸ January 22

BEYOND TIME IS THE phrase that I have used to describe this leg of my journey because it was then that I think I first began to have a pale version of the experience that Saint Paul describes in his letter to the Philippians. "Work out your own salvation with fear and trembling," he writes, "for God is at work in you both to will and to work for his good pleasure."

I was a long way from thinking in terms of my own salvation or anybody else's, but through the people I met like the drunken boy at the Nass and the black man at the head of the line, through the courses I happened to take and the books I happened to read, through such events as eating that muddy turnip in Alabama, through my revulsion at my own weaknesses as well as through such satisfaction as I had in my own strengths, it seems to me now that a power from beyond time was working to achieve its own aim through my aimless life in time as it works through the lives of all of us and all our times.

Something Better and Truer ✸ January 23

THERE WAS THE DAY I signed the contract for that first novel that I had started in college, for instance. It was a major event for me, needless to say—the fulfillment of my wildest dreams of literary glory. But of the actual signing itself in the offices of Alfred Knopf—who was there and what was said and how I felt—I remember nothing. What I remember instead is leaving the publisher's office afterwards and running into somebody in the building whom I had known slightly at college. He was working as a messenger boy, he told me. I was, as I thought, on the brink of fame and fortune. But instead of feeling any pride or sense of superior accomplishment by the comparison, I remember a great and unheralded rush of something like sadness, almost like shame. I had been very lucky, and he had not been very lucky, and the pleasure that I might have taken in what had happened to me was all but lost in the realization that nothing comparable, as far as I could see, had happened to him. I wanted to say something or do something to make it up to him, but I had no idea how or what and ended up saying nothing of any consequence at all, least of all anything about the contract that I had just signed. We simply said goodbye in the lobby, he going his way and I mine, and that was that. All I can say now is that something small but unforgettable happened inside me as the result of that chance meeting—some small flickering out of the truth that, in the long run, there can be no real joy for anybody until there is joy finally for us all—and I can take no credit for it. It was nothing I piously thought my way to. It was no conscious attempt to work out my own salvation. What I felt was something better and truer than I was, or than I am, and it happened, as perhaps all such things do, as a gift.

Another Moment ✱ January 24

A ND THEN, FROM wherever it is that they come from, there came another moment. Not long after *A Long Day's Dying* was published, a man I scarcely knew asked me to have lunch with him. He was one of the ministers who came regularly to preach at the Lawrenceville chapel and whose sermons had a sort of witty, sardonic liveliness to them. All through lunch I remember wondering why it was that he had sought me out. He was some twenty years older than I was, and we had nothing in common as far as I knew, had never exchanged more than a few words before. I have long since forgotten what we talked about, but it seems to me that he told me a good deal about himself and his work, and I mainly just listened, drawing lines on the white tablecloth with my fork as I wondered when he would get to the point if indeed there was any point. Then at some moment during the conversation, I became aware that the subject had switched from him to me. I was highly thought of as a writer, he said. There were a lot of people who took my words seriously and were influenced by them. Had I ever considered, he said—and though I cannot remember his words, I remember his tone of voice which was dry and slightly mocking in a way that left you uncertain whether it was you he was mocking or himself. He was a complicated sort of man with a little black moustache who spoke in a way that struck me as concealing more about him than it revealed. Had I ever considered, he said, putting my gift with words to work for—God, did he say? Or the Church? Or Christ? I no longer remember how he put it exactly, and he made no great thing of it but passed on soon to other matters so that I do not to this day know whether this was what he had asked me to lunch to say or not. I no longer remember what I answered him either or what impression his words made on me except that they took me entirely by surprise. No, I must have told him. I had never considered such a thing. And that was the end of it except that out of all the events that took place during those five years of teaching at Lawrenceville, it is one of the few that I remember distinctly, like an old photograph preserved by accident between the pages of a book.

Shattering Revelation ❊ January 25

MY MOTHER'S APARTMENT by candlelight was haven and home and shelter from everything in the world that seemed dangerous and a threat to my peace. And my friend's broken voice on the phone was a voice calling me out into that dangerous world not simply for his sake, as I suddenly saw it, but also for my sake. The shattering revelation of that moment was that true peace, the high and bidding peace that passeth all understanding, is to be had not in retreat from the battle, but only in the thick of the battle. To journey for the sake of saving our own lives is little by little to cease to live in any sense that really matters, even to ourselves, because it is only by journeying for the world's sake—even when the world bores and sickens and scares you half to death—that little by little we start to come alive. It was not a conclusion that I came to in time. It was a conclusion from beyond time that came to me. God knows I have never been any good at following the road it pointed me to, but at least, by grace, I glimpsed the road and saw that it is the only one worth traveling.

Great Laughter ✳ January 26

PART OF THE FARCE was that for the first time in my life that year in New York, I started going to church regularly, and what was farcical about it was not that I went but my reason for going, which was simply that on the same block where I lived there happened to be a church with a preacher I had heard of and that I had nothing all that much better to do with my lonely Sundays. The preacher was a man named George Buttrick, and Sunday after Sunday I went, and sermon after sermon I heard. It was not just his eloquence that kept me coming back, though he was wonderfully eloquent, literate, imaginative, never letting you guess what he was going to come out with next but twitching with surprises up there in the pulpit, his spectacles a-glitter in the lectern light. What drew me more was whatever it was that his sermons came from and whatever it was in me that they touched so deeply. And then there came one particular sermon with one particular phrase in it that does not even appear in a transcript of his words that somebody sent me more than twenty-five years later so I can only assume that he must have dreamed it up at the last minute and ad-libbed it—and on just such foolish, tenuous, holy threads as that, I suppose, hang the destinies of us all. Jesus Christ refused the crown that Satan offered him in the wilderness, Buttrick said, but he is king nonetheless because again and again he is crowned in the heart of the people who believe in him. And that inward coronation takes place, Buttrick said, "among confession, and tears, and great laughter."

It was the phrase *great laughter* that did it, did whatever it was that I believe must have been hiddenly in the doing all the years of my journey up till then. It was not so much that a door opened as that I suddenly found that a door had been open all along which I had only just then stumbled upon. After church, with a great lump still in my throat, I walked up to 84th Street to have Sunday dinner with Grandma Buechner. She sat in her usual chair with the little Philco silent at her side and a glass of sherry in her hand, and when I told her something of what had happened, I could see that she was as much bemused as pleased by what I had said. I have forgotten her words, but the sense of her answer was that she was happy for me that I had found whatever it was that I had found. *Le bon Dieu.* You could never be sure what he was up to. If there was a *bon Dieu* at all. Who could say? Then old Rosa came listing in to say *Essen ist fertig, Frau Büchner,* and we went in to lunch.

Beyond All Understanding ✳ January 27

FAITH. HOPE. LOVE. Those are their names of course, those three—as words so worn out, but as realities so rich. Our going-away presents from beyond time to carry with us through time to lighten our step as we go. And part at least of the wisdom of the third one is, as Rinkitink heard it, "Never question the truth of what you fail to understand, for the world is filled with wonders." Above all, never question the truth beyond all understanding and surpassing all other wonders that in the long run nothing, not even the world, not even ourselves, can separate us forever from that last and deepest love that glimmers in our dusk like a pearl, like a face.

Unforeseen ✳ January 28

"MY OWN HEART LET me more have pity on," Gerard Manley Hopkins wrote . . . and then he goes on: "Leave comfort root-room; let joy size / At God knows when to God knows what; whose smile / 's not wrung, see you: unforeseen times rather." Nor is it only the joy of God and the comfort of God that come at unforeseen times. God's coming is always unforeseen, I think, and the reason, if I had to guess, is that if he gave us anything much in the way of advance warning, more often than not we would have made ourselves scarce long before he got there.

King Lear ✳ January 29

THERE WOULD BE a strong argument for saying that much of the most powerful preaching of our time is the preaching of the poets, playwrights, novelists because it is often they better than the rest of us who speak with awful honesty about the absence of God in the world and about the storm of his absence, both without and within, which, because it is unendurable, unlivable, drives us to look to the eye of the storm. I think of *King Lear* especially with its tragic vision of a world in which the good and the bad alike go down to dusty and, it would seem, equally meaningless death with no God to intervene on their behalf, and yet with its vision of a world in which the naked and helpless ones, the victims and fools, become at least truly alive before they die and thus touch however briefly on something that lies beyond the power of death. It is the worldly ones, the ones wise as the world understands wisdom and strong in the way the world understands strength, who are utterly doomed. This is so much the central paradox of *Lear* that the whole play can be read as a gloss if not a homily on that passage in First Corinthians where Paul expresses the same paradox in almost the same terms by writing, "God chose what is foolish in the world to shame the wise. God chose what is weak in the world to shame the strong. God chose what is low and despised in the world, even things that are not, to bring to nothing things that are" (1 Corinthians 1:27–28), thus pointing as Shakespeare points to the apparent emptiness of the world where God belongs and to how the emptiness starts to echo like an empty shell after a while until you can hear in it the still, small voice of the sea, hear strength in weakness, victory in defeat, presence in absence.

I think of Dostoevski in *The Brothers Karamazov* when the body of Alyosha's beloved Father Zossima begins to stink in death instead of giving off fragrance as the dead body of a saint is supposed to, and at the very moment where Alyosha sees the world most abandoned by God, he suddenly finds the world so aflame with God that he rushes out of the chapel where the body lies and kisses the earth as the shaggy face of the world where God, in spite of and in the midst of everything, is.

Lear *Among the Young* ✳ *January 30*

Poor naked wretches, wheresoe'er you are,
That bide the pelting of this pitiless storm,
How shall your houseless heads and unfed sides,
Your loop'd and window'd raggedness, defend you
From seasons such as these?

(III. IV. 35 ff)

OUT OF THE SILENCE of a high-school classroom the tragic word is spoken, and, if the teacher is right in his conjectures, it is also heard. The poor naked wretches of the world are all of them, everybody. They did not know it before, but they know it now because they have heard it spoken. Without the word, they might never have guessed it, or, if they had guessed it, it would have been for them only one more unspoken thing among many other unspoken things that they carried around inside the worlds they were. Once spoken, the word of their nakedness and wretchedness is a shattering word. They are young and full of lunch and full of hope and clothed in the beauty that it is to be young, and thus of all people they are in a way the least naked, the least wretched; but the word out of the old play tells them for a moment otherwise. It speaks in a way they cannot avoid hearing for themselves, which is the awesome power of words because, although there are times when they shield us from reality, at other times they assail us with it. The play tells them that life is a pitiless storm and that they are as vulnerable to it as Lear himself, not just in the sense that youth grows old and beauty fades but in the sense that youth and beauty themselves are vulnerable—their heads are houseless, their youth itself a looped and windowed raggedness and as inadequate to the task of sheltering them as their teacher's middle-aged urbanity is to the task of sheltering him. The word out of the play strips them for a moment naked and strips their teacher with them and to that extent Shakespeare turns preacher because stripping us naked is part of what preaching is all about, the tragic part.

So Now at Last ✳ January 31

Long after Roger Mouse's death, Godric bids him a proper goodbye:

WHEN FRIENDS SPEAK overmuch of times gone by, often it's because they sense their present time is turning them from friends to strangers. Long before the moment came to say goodbye, I think, we said goodbye in other words and ways and silences. Then when the moment came for it at last, we didn't say it as it should be said by friends. So now at last, dear Mouse, with many, many years between: goodbye.

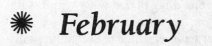

February

The Face of Christ ✳ February 1

I ENTERED UNION Theological Seminary in the fall of 1954. If anyone had told me as little as a year or so earlier that I was going to do such a thing, I would have been no less surprised than if I had been told I was going to enter the Indianapolis 500. The preceding year I had become in some sense a Christian, though the chances are I would have hesitated to put it like that, and I find something in that way of expressing it which even now makes me feel uncomfortable. "To become a Christian" sounds like an achievement, like becoming a millionaire. I thought of it rather, and think of it still, more as a lucky break, a step in the right direction. Though I was brought up in a family where church played virtually no role at all, through a series of events from childhood on I was moved, for the most part without any inkling of it, closer and closer to a feeling for that Mystery out of which the church arose in the first place until, finally, the Mystery itself came to have a face for me, and the face it came to have for me was the face of Christ. It was a slow, obscure process . . . and the result of it was that I ended up being so moved by what I felt that I found it inadequate simply to keep it inside myself like a secret but had to do something about it.

More Than Intellect Involved ✳ February 2

COLLEGE FOR ME had been a Renaissance sampling of whatever happened to catch my fancy—medieval history and creative writing, literary criticism and American architecture, Russian and German in addition to Greek—a random accumulating of riches for no motive more far-reaching than simply to enrich myself. Seminary, on the other hand, was my Reformation. Such skills of reading, writing, understanding, as I had picked up during my disheveled and war-interrupted college career I gathered together and directed toward a more or less single end. I wanted to learn about Christ—about the Old Testament, which had been his Bible, and the New Testament, which was the Bible about him; about the history of the church, which had been founded on the faith that through him God had not only revealed his innermost nature and his purpose for the world, but had released into the world a fierce power to draw people into that nature and adapt them to that purpose, the church that not even the assorted barbarities and blunders of its ragged two thousand years had ever quite managed finally to discredit or destroy; about the theological systems that the passion of his original followers, and of Saint Paul in particular, had been distilled into. No intellectual pursuit had ever aroused in me such intense curiosity, and much more than my intellect was involved, much more than my curiosity aroused. In the unfamiliar setting of a Presbyterian church, of all places, I had been moved to astonished tears which came from so deep inside me that to this day I have never fathomed them. I wanted to learn more about the source of those tears and the object of that astonishment. I wanted to know, and be known by, people who knew greatly more about Christ than I did, were greatly closer to him than I was, greatly more aware of what they were about and of what he was about in them. Maybe above everything, I wanted to *do* something for him; and since—as writer, reader, teacher—most of my doing in the past had involved paper and pen, books and study, a seminary seemed the proper place to do it.

Reinhold Niebuhr ✳ February 3

IN THE LAST ANALYSIS, I have always believed, it is not so much their subjects that the great teachers teach as it is themselves. In some box in the attic, or up over the garage, I must still have notes on the lectures I heard given by Niebuhr,

Tillich, and the rest of them. It would be possible to exhume them and summarize some of what struck me most. But though much of what these teachers said remains with me still and has become so much a part of my own way of thinking and speaking that often I sound like them without realizing it, it is they themselves who left the deeper mark.

I see Reinhold Niebuhr, for instance, in a beret with the wind ballooning out his raincoat as he walks his poodle along Riverside Drive. A stroke had left his speech slightly indistinct at times and one arm less than fully functional, but he always gave me the impression of great energy and wit, great involvement in the events of his time. He had been Roosevelt's adviser. He was Auden's friend. There seemed to be no phase of human history that he didn't have at his fingertips, no eminence that he couldn't have attained in any field where he'd chosen to attain it; but it was to the church that he gave himself in all its shabbiness as well as all its glory, to his students, to the work of Christ, whom he served with all his urbanity and shrewdness—that tamed cynic, as he called himself, his bad arm tucked in against his chest and his speech slurred. It was the glittering breadth of his knowledge that I remember best, his gift for applying the insights of the Christian faith to the whole spectrum of politics, economics, international affairs. He was bald, owlish-looking, with deep frown-lines, a deep-cut, sardonic mouth. He had a nose quick to sniff out the irony and ambivalence of things in general and of piety in particular, an eye sharp to perceive that the children of darkness are apt to be not only wiser but often more appealing and plausible than the children of light.

James Muilenburg ✳ February 4

BUT FOR ME, AS for most of us studying there in those days, there was no one on the faculty who left so powerful and lasting an impression as James Muilenburg. He was an angular man with thinning white hair, staring eyes, and a nose and chin which at times seemed so close to touching that they gave him the face of a good witch. In his introductory Old Testament course, the largest lecture hall that Union had was always packed to hear him. Students brought friends. Friends brought friends. People stood in the back when the chairs ran out. Up and down the whole length of the aisle he would stride as he chanted the war songs, the taunt songs, the dirges of ancient Israel. With his body stiff, his knees bent, his arms scarecrowed far to either side, he never merely taught the Old Testament but *was* the Old Testament. He would be Adam, wide-eyed and halting as he named the beasts—"You are . . . an elephant . . . a butterfly . . . an ostrich!"—or Eve, trembling and afraid in the garden of her lost innocence, would be David sobbing his great lament at the death of Saul and Jonathan, would be Moses coming down from Sinai. His face uptilted and his eyes aghast, he would be Yahweh himself, creating the heavens and the earth, and when he called out, "Let there be *light!*" there is no way of putting it other than to say that there would *be* light, great floods of it reflected in the hundreds of faces watching him in that enormous room. In more or less these words, I described him in a novel later, and when I showed him the typescript for his approval, he was appalled because it seemed to confirm his terrible fear that he was making a fool of himself. And, of course, if it hadn't been for his genius, for the staggering sincerity of his performance, he might almost have been right. It was a measure of folly as well as of strength and courage, I suppose, to let himself come so perilously close to disaster.

"Every morning when you wake up," he used to say, "before you reaffirm your faith in the majesty of a loving God, before you say *I believe* for another day, read the *Daily News* with its record of the latest crimes and tragedies of mankind and then see if you can honestly say it again." He was a fool in the sense that he didn't or couldn't or wouldn't resolve, intellectualize, evade, the tensions of his faith but lived those tensions out, torn almost in two by them at times. His faith was not a seamless garment but a ragged garment with the seams showing, the tears showing, a garment that he clutched about him like a man in a storm.

Opening of a Door ✳ February 5

MUILENBURG WAS A fool, I suppose, in the sense that he was an intimate of the dark, yet held fast to the light as if it were something you could hold fast to; in the sense that he wore his heart on his sleeve even though it was in some ways a broken heart; in the sense that he was as absurdly himself before the packed lecture hall as he was alone in his office; a fool in the sense that he was a child in his terrible candor. A fool, in other words, for Christ. Though I was no longer at Union when he gave his final lecture there, I am told that a number of students from the Jewish seminary across the street attended it and, before entering the great room, left their shoes in the corridor outside to indicate that the ground on which they stood with him was holy ground.

◆ ◆ ◆

As a scholar, he knew plenty and demanded plenty from his students. He was uncompromising in his insistence, especially, upon the necessity of exposing the Bible to all the modern instruments of literary and historical criticism and refused ever to sacrifice, or to let any of us sacrifice, scholarly integrity to the demands and presuppositions of conventional religiosity. In order to impress upon his students what he felt to be the crucial importance of this approach, he assigned us the task of writing what was known to fame as the Pentateuch Paper. In it we were to expound and support by close textual analysis the hypothesis that the first five books of the Old Testament could not be a single work written by Moses, as traditionally supposed, but were a composite work consisting of some four or more documents, each of which had its own style, theological outlook, and polemical purpose. The paper came as the climax of Muilenburg's introductory course, but the shadow it cast was a long one, and from the earliest weeks it loomed less as a paper than as a rite of passage. It had to be very long. It had to be very good. It had to hold water. And I remember still the acute apprehension with which I launched into it, the first paper I had written for anybody about anything since college. It turned out to be the opening of a door.

Vast Diversity ✳ February 6

WHAT I BEGAN TO SEE was that the Bible is not essentially, as I had always more or less supposed, a book of ethical principles, of moral exhortations, of cautionary tales about exemplary people, of uplifting thoughts—in fact, not really a religious book at all in the sense that most of the books you would be apt to find in a minister's study or reviewed in a special religion issue of the *New York Times* book section are religious. I saw it instead as a great, tattered compendium of writings, the underlying and unifying purpose of all of which is to show how God works through the Jacobs and Jabboks of history to make himself known to the world and to draw the world back to himself.

For all its vast diversity and unevenness, it is a book with a plot and a plot that can be readily stated. God makes the world in love. For one reason or another the world chooses to reject God. God will not reject the world but continues his mysterious and relentless pursuit of it to the end of time. That is what he is doing by choosing Israel to be his special people. That is what he is doing through all the passion and poetry and invective of the prophets. That is why history plays such a crucial part in the Old Testament—all those kings and renegades and battles and invasions and apostasies—because it was precisely through people like that and events like those that God was at work, as, later, in the New Testament, he was supremely at work in the person and event of Jesus Christ. Only "*is* at work" would be the more accurate way of putting it because if there is a God who works at all, his work goes on still, of course, and at one and the same time the biblical past not only illumines the present but becomes itself part of that present, part of our own individual pasts. Until you can read the story of Adam and Eve, of Abraham and Sarah, of David and Bathsheba, as your own story, Muilenburg said, you have not really understood it. The Bible, as he presented it, is a book finally about ourselves, our own apostasies, our own battles and blessings; and it was the discovery of that more than of the differences between the Yahwist, Elohist, Deuteronomic, and Priestly sources of the Pentateuch that constituted the real reward of writing that apocalyptic paper.

Among the Poor ✳ February 7

As a seminary student, Buechner was assigned to work part-time in an East Harlem parish. Here he is commenting on the regular parish staff members:

THEY HAD CAUGHT something from Christ, I thought. Something of who he was and is flickered out through who they were. It is not easy to describe. It was compassion without sentimentality as much as anything else, I think—a lucid, cool, grave compassion. If it had a color, it would be a pale, northern blue. They never seemed to romanticize the junkies and winos and deadbeats and losers they worked among, and they never seemed to let pity or empathy distort the clarity with which they saw them for no more if no less than what they were. Insofar as they were able to approach loving them, I got the impression that they did so not just in spite of everything about them that was neither lovely nor lovable but right in the thick of it. There was a kind of sad gaiety about the way they went about their work. The sadness stemmed, I suppose, from the hopelessness of their task—the problems were so vast, their resources for dealing with them were so meager—and the gaiety from a hope beyond hope that, in the long run if not the short, all would in some holy and unimaginable way be well. If, as I suspect, they looked at me and at the others who worked there only part-time as less committed than they, farther away from where the real battle was being fought, then I can say only that, of course, they were right. But they seemed less to hold the difference against us than simply to mark it and leave it for us to come to terms with as best we could.

What they make me think of, looking back, is the passage in Mark where Jesus tells the rich young ruler that if he really wants to be perfect, then he must sell everything he has and give it to the poor, whereupon what the rich young ruler does is turn on his heel and walk sorrowfully away because he has great possessions. Jesus made no attempt to hold him there, shouted no reproaches or entreaties after him, simply let him go as the parish let me go, but you feel that the look in his eye as he watched him disappearing down the road was as full of compassion for the young man himself as for the poor whom the young man could not bring himself to serve fully. And they make me think, too, of how, in the same passage, Jesus bridles at the rich young ruler's addressing him as "good Teacher." "No one is good but God alone," Jesus says, and surely that is what the parish staff would I think have said too. At their strongest and saintliest, I believe, they knew that in the last analysis they weren't really a spiritual elite, not really better than other people. They were just luckier.

How Far Do You Go? ✳ February 8

WHEN YOU FIND something in a human face that calls out to you, not just for help but in some sense for yourself, how far do you go in answering that call, how far *can* you go, seeing that you have your own life to get on with as much as he has his? As for me, I went as far as that windy street corner up around 120th Street and Broadway, and I can see him standing there as in some way he is standing there still, and as I also am standing there still. He is alone and making the best of it with his thin, church-rummage overcoat flapping around his legs. His one free hand is raised in the air to wave good-bye. It was the last time. "Here and there in the world and now and then in ourselves," Tillich said, "is a New Creation." This side of glory, maybe that is the best we can hope for.

Decision ✳ February 9

MUCH AS I HAD enjoyed teaching my students there how to read such classroom staples as *Macbeth, Ethan Frome, The Red Badge of Courage,* and how to write the English language with some measure of clarity and skill, it seemed to me in the last analysis to be icing on the cake. A boy could learn all I knew about reading and writing and still have little understanding of himself or his own life, have nothing to hold on to, to believe in, when the chips were down. As far as the decision for or against belief in God was concerned, most of the time he had little idea even what the issues were because no one had ever made the effort to discuss them with him. If he rejected Christianity, it was usually such a caricature of it that I would have rejected it myself, and if he accepted it, the chances were he knew equally little about what he was accepting. Compared to the teaching of other subjects, the teaching of religion at most schools I had any knowledge of tended to be cursory—a course that met only once a week for half a year, say, usually with very little work required in it and taught by people from other departments who had no real training in the area themselves. The very fact that it was relegated to such an obscure corner of the curriculum was itself, of course, a way of telling students that it was not a subject that much mattered. At Exeter, on the other hand, I would have the chance to set up some rigorous, academically respectable courses in the subject and to try to establish them as an enterprise no less serious, relevant, and demanding than the study of American history or physics. Even though it was not a form of ministry that I had ever considered, I decided to give it a try.

"Cultured Despisers" ✳ February 10

After his ordination, Buechner was invited to join the faculty of Phillips Exeter.

I WAS ORDAINED as an evangelist, but *apologist,* I suppose, would have been, and continues to be, the more appropriate word. My job, as I saw it, was to defend the Christian faith against its "cultured despisers," to use Schleiermacher's phrase. To put it more positively, it was to present the faith as appealingly, honestly, relevantly, and skillfully as I could. In this sense my more skeptical faculty colleagues were of course justified in suspecting my lack of objectivity. The deck I used was as stacked as the deck of any teachers who want their students to catch fire from whatever subject they are teaching. Tillich, Barth, C. S. Lewis—I had my students read the most provocative and persuasive theologians I knew. And on the grounds that, even in the hands of masters, such ideas as sin and salvation, judgment and grace, tend, as ideas, to sound cerebral and remote, I tried to put flesh on the theological bones by having them read also works of fiction and drama where those same ideas appear in human form—where grace, for instance, is the power by which Graham Greene's whiskey priest becomes a kind of saint despite all his shortcomings and seedy ineffectuality; where King Lear is saved in the sense of being made aware of the poor, naked wretches of the world, made compassionate, alive, and human at last through his sufferings on the stormy heath; where sin more than Smerdyakov's villainy is what destroys the father of the brothers Karamazov as a human being, that old buffoon estranged by his own self-loathing not just from his sons but from everybody else including both himself and God. Koestler's *Darkness at Noon*, Miller's *Death of a Salesman*, Joyce's *Portrait of the Artist as a Young Man*, Lagerkvist's *Barabbas*—they were so bright and so verbal, most of those boys, that there was almost no reading that I couldn't assign them. My frustration was, rather, in discovering that although many modern writers have succeeded in exploring the depths of human darkness and despair and alienation in a world where God seems largely absent, there are relatively few who have tried to tackle the reality of whatever salvation means, the experience of Tillich's New Being whereby, even in the depths, we are touched here and there by a power beyond power to heal and make whole. Sin is easier to write about than grace, I suppose, because the territory is so familiar and because, too, it is of the nature of grace, when we receive it, to turn our eyes not inward, where most often writers' eyes turn, but outward, where there is a whole world of needs to serve far greater than the need simply for another book. I was too occupied with my job to think much about the next novel I myself might write, but it occurred to me that, if and when the time ever came, it would be the presence of God rather than his absence that I would write about, of death and dark and despair as not the last reality but only the next to the last.

THE OTHER PART OF my experience as a Christian that I tried to deal with in *The Final Beast* was the experience of prayer, and . . . I drew directly from an event in my own life. A year or so before writing the book, I took two or three days off to attend a series of seminars on prayer conducted by an Episcopal laywoman named Agnes Sanford, who was recommended to me by a friend as a fascinating and deeply spiritual woman who had had remarkable success as a faith healer. "Spiritual" was another of those words that I always choked on a little, and faith-healing was something I associated with charlatans and the lunatic fringe; but since my friend had only recently left the college chaplaincy to become a Jungian analyst, I couldn't dismiss him as easily taken in, so I decided to accept his recommendation and go.

I saw Agnes Sanford first in the dingy front hall of the building where the talks were to take place, and after no more than a few minutes' conversation with her, I felt as sure as you can ever be in such matters that if there was such a thing as the Real Article in her line of work, then that was what she was. She was rather short and on the plump side with a breezy matter-of-factness about her which was the last thing I would have expected. She had far more the air of a college dean or a successful businesswoman than of a Mary Baker Eddy or Madam Blavatsky. She seemed completely without pretensions, yet just as completely confident that she knew what she was talking about. She had an earthy sense of humor.

◆ ◆ ◆

The most vivid image she presented was of Jesus standing in church services all over Christendom with his hands tied behind his back and unable to do any mighty works there because the ministers who led the services either didn't expect him to do them or didn't dare ask him to do them for fear that he wouldn't or couldn't and that their own faith and the faith of their congregations would be threatened as the result. I recognized immediately my kinship with those ministers. A great deal of public prayer seemed to me a matter of giving God something that he neither needed nor, as far as I could imagine, much wanted. In private I prayed a good deal, but for the most part it was a very blurred, haphazard kind of business—much of it blubbering, as Dr. Muilenburg had said his was, speaking words out of my deepest needs, fears, longings, but never expecting much back by way of an answer, never believing very strongly that anyone was listening to me or even, at times, that there was anyone to listen at all.

That was the whole point, Agnes Sanford said. You had to expect. You had to believe. As in Jesus' parables of the Importunate Friend and the Unjust Judge, you had to keep at it. It took work. It took practice, was in that sense not unlike the Buddhist Eightfold Path. More than anything else, it took faith. It was faith that unbound the hands of Jesus so that through your prayers his power could flow and miracles could happen, healing could happen, because where faith was, healing always was too, she said, and there was no power on earth that could prevent it. Inside us all, she said, there was a voice of doubt and disbelief which sought to drown out our prayers even as we were praying them, but we were to pray down that voice for all we were worth because it was simply the product in us of old hurts, griefs, failures, of all that the world had done to try to destroy our faith. More even than our bodies, she said, it was these hurtful memories that needed healing. For God, all time is one, and we were to invite Jesus into our past as into a house that has been locked up for years—to open windows and doors for us so that light and life could enter at last, to sweep out the debris of decades, to drive back the shadows. The healing of memories was like the forgiveness of sins, she said. Prayer was like a game, a little ridiculous the way she described it, but we were to play it anyway—praying for the healing both of ourselves and others—because Jesus told us to and because most of the other games we played were more ridiculous still and not half so useful.

We were to believe in spite of not believing. That was what faith was all about, she told us. "Lord, I believe; help thou mine unbelief," said the father of the sick son (Mark 9:24), and though it wasn't much, Jesus considered it enough. The boy was healed. Fairy-tale prayers, she called them. Why not? Jesus prayers. The language of the prayer didn't matter, and her own language couldn't have been plainer or her prayers more unliterary and down-to-earth. Only the faith mattered. All of this she spoke with nothing wild-eyed or dramatic about her, but clearly, wittily, less like a mystic than like the president of a rather impressive club. And you could also get too much praying, too much religion, she said, and when that happened, the thing to do was just to put it aside for a while as she did and do something else. She herself read murder mysteries, she said. Or just collapsed.

What's Good About Religion? ✹ February 12

FOR A WHILE THE dean's office made an exception to the rule about required church. The edict was handed down that a student might attend a religious discussion group instead, and those groups were scheduled to take place before church in order to prevent boys from attending only so they could get a little more sleep on Sunday mornings. For that reason only the most radical dissenters attended, and it was one of those—a lean, freckle-faced senior—who turned to me once, thin-lipped with anger, and said, "So what's so good about religion anyway?" and I found myself speechless. I felt surely there must be something good about it. Why else was I there?

But for the moment I couldn't for the life of me think what it was. Maybe the truth of it is that religion the way he meant it—a system of belief, a technique of worship, an institution—doesn't really have all that much about it that is good when you come right down to it, and perhaps my speechlessness in a way acknowledged as much.

Unless you become like a child, Jesus said, you will never enter the Kingdom of Heaven, and maybe part of what that means is that in the long run what is good about religion is playing the way a child plays at being grown up until he finds that being grown up is just another way of playing and thereby starts to grow up himself. Maybe what is good about religion is playing that the Kingdom will come, until—in the joy of your playing, the hope and rhythm and comradeship and poignance and mystery of it—you start to see that the playing is itself the first-fruits of the Kingdom's coming and of God's presence within us and among us.

Peace of the Mountain ✳ February 13

WHEN WE FIRST started living in Vermont all year round in 1967, I was reluctant to believe that it would be our last move and that our house would be the one I would die in, but I have long since concluded that this will probably be the case and accept it with comparative equanimity. And I long ago concluded something else, too. The first few years we were there, the children were still little, and our problems with them, like theirs with us, seemed little too. They were healthy and happy, and so were we. Like everybody else they had their troubles at school, but basically they liked it well enough. They had their friends, and we had our friends, but the richest part of our lives seemed to be the part we had together—the picnics by the gentian pond, the sledding in winter, the summer trips. We were a world very much to ourselves up there on our mountain, and by and large all was well with us. But down below there was another world where, by and large, all was not well. Friends got sick and died there. Accidents happened to people we knew. Children not much older than ours got into all sorts of grief. Couples got divorced, and men lost their jobs. And farther away still, Vietnam happened, assassinations happened, Watergate happened, until there were times when it seemed to me as though the world below was a stormy sea with waves all around us as high as the hills we were encircled by, and the little patch of mountain where we lived was the only place left anywhere that was safe and dry. What I concluded then—less in a way to mar our peace than to deepen my sense of it—was that the day would come when the wild waves would wet us too, and the winds would lash us, and the great beast browsing its way up from below would raise its head and notice us at last. I concluded that even in Paradise, maybe especially in Paradise, the dark times come.

A Memorable Woman ✳ February 14

AND PART OF ME will always be homesick, too, for a person I came to know, also in Manchester, during those same years. When the Baptist church, of which she was a member, was without a minister one winter, I took the services every Sunday for a few months, and that was how we met. She was a woman well on into her seventies, very thin, very stooped. She had been married a number of times, and for years, as a widow, had been living alone, on welfare, in the one small apartment left inhabitable in a house that had been gutted by fire a few years earlier. Shaking hands at the church door after the service one Sunday morning, I had said to her—neither expecting nor much caring about an answer—"How are you?"

and she looked up at me out of her wry, beleaguered old face and said, "As well as can be expected." Just that and no more, then made her way down the steps and out into the cold.

I am as deaf as the next one and usually deafer when it comes to calls for help, but I was all she had by way of a minister just then, after all, and I was not so literary and detached and specialized as not to know that every once in a while, if only to keep their hands in, Christians are supposed to be Christs to each other for Christ's sweet sake, so I steeled myself and went to call on her one winter afternoon. I expected the worst, of course, because that is my nature. I expected a long, dreary monologue. I expected plenty of complaints with some tears to go with them. I expected to feel awkward and inadequate. I expected to be bored and hoped to get away as soon as I decently could. And I couldn't possibly have been more wrong on every count. None of the things I expected to happen happened, and none of the things I expected to feel did I feel, neither on that first day I went to see her nor on all the other days I went to see her from that time on until finally, around Saint Valentine's day some seven or eight years later, she died, and I conducted her burial service before a little knot of family and friends under a gray Vermont sky with the wind flapping my black robe around my ankles.

Call to Prayer ❋ February 15

BECAUSE THE WORD that God speaks to us is always an incarnate word—a word spelled out to us not alphabetically, in syllables, but enigmatically, in events, even in the books we read and the movies we see—the chances are we will never get it just right. We are so used to hearing what we want to hear and remaining deaf to what it would be well for us to hear that it is hard to break the habit. But if we keep our hearts and minds open as well as our ears, if we listen with patience and hope, if we remember at all deeply and honestly, then I think we come to recognize, beyond all doubt, that, however faintly we may hear him, he is indeed speaking to us, and that, however little we may understand of it, his word to each of us is both recoverable and precious beyond telling. In that sense autobiography becomes a way of praying, and a book like this, if it matters at all, matters mostly as a call to prayer.

Unmemorable Moments ✳ February 16

WHEN IT CAME TO my work, my ministry, writing books was not the only form it took. I continued to preach from time to time—at fancy places like Yale and Princeton and unfancy places like the small Congregational church in Rupert, where the thirty or so people who came of a Sunday and the creaking old organ and the swept and dusted shabbiness gave me often a richer sense of a place where God had been truly spoken to and heard than many a more Gothic and grander. I taught Sunday school in the deserted bar of an inn in Dorset and helped with religion conferences elsewhere. When some of the local churches were without a minister for one reason or another, I took weddings and funerals and christenings. Every once in a while, people with problems who had never found their way to a church found their way to me precisely because I had no church and for that reason seemed to them more approachable. And I kept on trying to pray the way Agnes Sanford had taught me because I was helpless to do otherwise. So both at work and at play, life went on in many places other than the room where I wrote, in other words; there were memorable moments and unmemorable moments, and as far as my sense of being trapped is concerned, it was the unmemorable ones, the apparently random and everyday ones, that turned out to be the key moments, the key that let me out of the trap at last.

Words ✳ February 17

WORDS—ESPECIALLY religious words, words that have to do with the depth of things—get tired and stale the way people do. Find new words or put old words together in combinations that make them heard as new, make you yourself new, and make you understand in new ways. "Blessed are the meek" are the words of the English translators—words of great beauty and power—but over the years they have become almost too familiar to hear any more. *"Heureux sont les debonnaires"* are the French words—Blessed are the debonair—and suddenly new beauty, new power, flood in like light. Blessed is Fred Astaire in white tie and tails. Blessed is Oliver Hardy in rusty black suit and derby hat as he picks his dapper way toward the unseen banana peel on the sidewalk. Blessed is my old friend as she tries to let me win at Aggravation, rattling her dice in the cup which the pills that keep her alive come in. Arrange the alphabet into words that are true in the sense that they are true to what you experience to be true. If you have to choose between words that mean more than what you have experienced and words that mean less, choose the ones that mean less because that way you leave room for your hearers to move around in and for yourself to move around in too.

Enter Leo Bebb ✳ February 18

I WAS READING a magazine as I waited my turn at a barber shop one day when, triggered by a particular article and the photographs that went with it, there floated up out of some hitherto unexplored subcellar of me a character who was to dominate my life as a writer for the next six years and more. He was a plump, bald, ebullient southerner who had once served five years in a prison on a charge of exposing himself before a group of children and was now the head of a religious diploma mill in Florida and of a seedy, flat-roofed stucco church called the Church of Holy Love, Incorporated. He wore a hat that looked too small for him. He had a trick eyelid that every once in a while fluttered shut on him. His name was Leo Bebb.

I had never known a man like Leo Bebb and was in most ways quite unlike him myself, but despite that, there was very little I had to do by way of consciously, purposefully inventing him. He came, unexpected and unbidden, from a part of myself no less mysterious and inaccessible than the part where dreams come from; and little by little there came with him a whole world of people and places that was as heretofore unknown to me as Bebb was himself. I have no doubt that, as in my earlier novels, I had to do more hard work than I now remember. I had to figure out names for people that seemed to suit them and to explore possible relationships between them. I had to search my memories of the South where they lived so I could get the look and the feel of it more or less right and the country way they some of them had of talking. I had to worry about plot, about what scenes to put in and what scenes to let the readers imagine for themselves. All of that. But in the case of *Lion Country* especially—the first of the four novels I wrote about Bebb—what I found myself involved in was a process much less of invention than of discovery. I had never written a book that seemed so much "on the house." It floated up out of my dreaming so charged with a life of its own that there was a sense in which almost all I had to do was sit back and watch it unfold. Instead of having to force myself to go back to it every morning as I had with novels in the past, I could hardly wait to go back to it; and instead of taking something like two years to write as the earlier ones had, it was all done in just short of three months.

Certainties ✳ February 19

THERE ARE TIMES when I suspect the world may come to an end before most of us are ready to—which would have the advantage at least of our not having to leave, one by one, while the party is still going strong—but most of the time I believe that the world will manage somehow to survive us, and that has its advantages too. I suppose Judy and I will keep on living in Vermont because after all these years it's hard to imagine living anywhere else, and as long as the dreams keep being dreamed, I suppose I will go on writing books. They never reach as wide a public as I would like— too religious for secular readers, I suspect, and too secular for religious ones—but in the end justice is almost always done in literary matters, I believe, and if they are worth enduring, they will endure. Who can say? Humanly speaking, in fact, who can say for sure about anything? And yet there are some things I would be willing to bet maybe even my life on.

That life is grace, for instance—the givenness of it, the fathomlessness of it, the endless possibilities of its becoming transparent to something extraordinary beyond itself. That— as I picked up somewhere in Jung and whittled into the ash stick I use for tramping around through the woods some-times—*vocatus atque non vocatus Deus aderit,* which I take to mean that in the long run, whether you call on him or don't call on him, God will be present with you. That if we really had our eyes open, we would see that all moments are key moments. That he who does not love remains in death. That Jesus is the Word made flesh who dwells among us full of grace and truth. On good days I might add a few more to the list. On bad days it's possible there might be a few less.

Art ✳ February 20

"AN OLD SILENT pond. / Into the pond a frog jumps. / Splash! Silence again." It is perhaps the best known of all Japanese haiku. No subject could be more humdrum. No language could be more pedestrian. Basho, the poet, makes no comment on what he is describing. He implies no meaning, message, or metaphor. He simply invites our attention to no more and no less than just this: the old pond in its watery stillness, the kerplunk of the frog, the gradual return of the stillness.

In effect he is putting a frame around the moment, and what the frame does is enable us to see not just something about the moment but the moment itself in all its ineffable ordinariness and particularity. The chances are that if we had been passing by when the frog jumped, we wouldn't have noticed a thing or, noticing it, wouldn't have given it a second thought. But the frame sets it off from everything else that distracts us. It makes possible a second thought. That is the nature and purpose of frames. The frame does not change the moment, but it changes our way of perceiving the moment. It makes us NOTICE the moment, and that is what Basho wants above all else. It is what literature in general wants above all else too.

From the simplest lyric to the most complex novel and densest drama, literature is asking us to pay attention. Pay attention to the frog. Pay attention to the west wind. Pay attention to the boy on the raft, the lady in the tower, the old man on the train. In sum, pay attention to the world and all that dwells therein and thereby learn at last to pay attention to yourself and all that dwells therein.

The painter does the same thing, of course. Rembrandt puts a frame around an old woman's face. It is seamed with wrinkles. The upper lip is sunken in, the skin waxy and pale. It is not a remarkable face. You would not look twice at the old woman if you found her sitting across the aisle from you on a bus. But it is a face so remarkably *seen* that it forces you to see it remarkably just as Cézanne makes you see a bowl of apples or Andrew Wyeth a muslin curtain blowing in at an open window. It is a face unlike any other face in all the world. All the faces in the world are in this one old face.

Unlike painters, who work with space, musicians work with time, with note following note as second follows second. Listen! says Vivaldi, Brahms, Stravinsky. Listen to this time that I have framed between the first note and the last and to these sounds in time. Listen to the way the silence is broken into uneven lengths between the sounds and to the silences themselves. Listen to the scrape of bow against gut, the rap of stick against drumhead, the rush of breath through reed and wood. The sounds of the earth are like music, the old song goes, and the sounds of music are also like the sounds of the earth, which is of course where music comes from. Listen to the voices outside the window, the rumble of the furnace, the creak of your chair, the water running in the kitchen sink. Learn to listen to the music of your own lengths of time, your own silences.

Literature, painting, music—the most basic lesson that all art teaches us is to stop, look, and listen to life on this planet, including our own lives, as a vastly richer, deeper, more mysterious business than most of the time it ever occurs to us to suspect as we bumble along from day to day on automatic pilot. In a world that for the most part steers clear of the whole idea of holiness, art is one of the few places left where we can speak to each other of holy things.

Is it too much to say that Stop, Look, and Listen is also the most basic lesson that the Judeo-Christian tradition teaches us? Listen to history is the cry of the ancient prophets of Israel. Listen to social injustice, says Amos; to head-in-the-sand religiosity, says Jeremiah; to international treacheries and power-plays, says Isaiah; because it is precisely through them that God speaks his word of judgment and command.

And when Jesus comes along saying that the greatest command of all is to love God and to love our neighbor, he too is asking us to pay attention. If we are to love God, we must first stop, look, and listen for him in what is happening around us and inside us. If we are to love our neighbors, before doing anything else we must *see* our neighbors. With our imagination as well as our eyes, that is to say like artists, we must see not just their faces but the life behind and within their faces. Here it is love that is the frame we see them in.

In a letter to a friend Emily Dickinson wrote that "Consider the lilies of the field" was the only commandment she never broke. She could have done a lot worse. Consider the lilies. It is the *sine qua non* of art and religion both.

The Pains We Suffer Here ✳ February 21

Godric is traveling to Rome.

ALL ROADS LEAD TO Rome, they say, and ours leads us a crooked way. Great cities come and go. In Tours I catch a flux. In Lyons Aedwen twists her foot so I must load her on my back again. In Genoa a man found murdering a maid with child is cruelly punished. We watch them rope his arms and legs to four hot horses, then drive them to a rage with rods till each pulls hard a different way. But the man is young and stout and will not tear until the hangman risks their flying hooves to hack him with a sword about the joints, whereat he comes apart at last, and Aedwen swoons.

Except that there they have no end, the pains of Hell can be no sharper than the pains we suffer here, nor the Fiend himself more fiendish than a man. Oh Queen of Heaven, pray for us. Have pity on the pitiless for thy dear Son our Savior's sake.

Jobs ✳ February 22

JOBS ARE WHAT people do for a living, many of them for eight hours a day, five days a week, minus vacations, for most of their lives. It is tragic to think how few of them have their hearts in it. They work mainly for the purpose of making money enough to enjoy their moments of not working.

If not working is the chief pleasure they have, you wonder if they wouldn't do better just to devote themselves to that from the start. They would probably end up in bread-lines or begging, but even so the chances are they would be happier than pulling down a good salary as an insurance agent or a dental technician or a cab driver and hating every minute of it.

"What does man gain by all the toil at which he toils under the sun?" asks the Preacher (Ecclesiastes 1:3). If he's in it only for the money, the money is all he gains, and when he finally retires, he may well ask himself if it was worth giving most of his life for. If he's doing it for its own sake—if he enjoys doing it and the world needs it done—it may very possibly help to gain him his own soul.

Work ✳ February 23

I F YOU LOSE YOURSELF in your work, you find who you are.
   If you express the best you have in you in your work, it is more than just the best you have in you that you are expressing.

Jogging ✳ February 24

I T IS SUPPOSED TO be good for the heart, the lungs, the muscles, and physical well-being generally. It is also said to produce a kind of euphoria known as joggers' high.

The look of anguish and despair that contorts the faces of most of the people you see huffing and puffing away at it by the side of the road, however, is striking. If you didn't know directly from them that they are having the time of their lives, the chances are you wouldn't be likely to guess it.

Racism ✳ February 25

I N 1957 WHEN Governor Faubus of Arkansas refused to desegregate the schools in Little Rock, if President Eisenhower with all his enormous prestige had personally led a black child up the steps to where the authorities were blocking the school entrance, it might have been one of the great moments in history. It is heart-breaking to think of the opportunity missed.

Nothing in American history is more tragic surely than the relationship of the black and white races. Masters and slaves both were dehumanized. The Jim Crow laws carried the process on for decades beyond the Emancipation. The Ku Klux Klan and its like keep going forever. Politically, economically, socially, humanly the blacks continue to be the underdog.

Despite all the efforts of both races to rectify the situation and heal the wounds, despite all the progress that has been made, it is still as hard for any black to look at any white without a feeling of resentment as it is for any white to look at any black without a feeling of guilt.

Lent ✳ February 26

IN MANY CULTURES there is an ancient custom of giving a tenth of each year's income to some holy use. For Christians, to observe the forty days of Lent is to do the same thing with roughly a tenth of each year's days. After being baptized by John in the river Jordan, Jesus went off alone into the wilderness where he spent forty days asking himself the question what it meant to be Jesus. During Lent, Christians are supposed to ask one way or another what it means to be themselves.

If you had to bet everything you have on whether there is a God or whether there isn't, which side would get your money and why?

When you look at your face in the mirror, what do you see in it that you most like and what do you see in it that you most deplore?

If you had only one last message to leave to the handful of people who are most important to you, what would it be in twenty-five words or less?

Of all the things you have done in your life, which is the one you would most like to undo? Which is the one that makes you happiest to remember?

Is there any person in the world, or any cause, that, if circumstances called for it, you would be willing to die for?

If this were the last day of your life, what would you do with it?

To hear yourself try to answer questions like these is to begin to hear something not only of who you are but of both what you are becoming and what you are failing to become. It can be a pretty depressing business all in all, but if sackcloth and ashes are at the start of it, something like Easter may be at the end.

Ritual ✳ February 27

A WEDDING. A HANDSHAKE. A kiss. A coronation. A parade. A dance. A meal. A graduation. A Mass. A ritual is the performance of an intuition, the rehearsal of a dream, the playing of a game.

A sacrament is the breaking through of the sacred into the profane; a ritual is the ceremonial acting out of the profane in order to show forth its sacredness.

A sacrament is God offering his holiness to men; a ritual is men raising up the holiness of their humanity to God.

Christian ✳ February 28

SOME THINK OF A Christian as one who necessarily *believes* certain things. That Jesus was the son of God, say. Or that Mary was a virgin. Or that the Pope is infallible. Or that all other religions are all wrong.

Some think of a Christian as one who necessarily *does* certain things. Such as going to church. Getting baptized. Giving up liquor and tobacco. Reading the Bible. Doing a good deed a day.

Some think of a Christian as just a Nice Guy.

Jesus said, "I am the way, and the truth, and the life; no one comes to the Father, but by me" (John 14:6). He didn't say that any particular ethic, doctrine, or religion was the way, the truth, and the life. He said that he was. He didn't say that it was by believing or doing anything in particular that you could "come to the Father." He said that it was only by him—

by living, participating in, being caught up by, the way of life that he embodied, that was his way.

Thus it is possible to be on Christ's way and with his mark upon you without ever having heard of Christ, and for that reason to be on your way to God though maybe you don't even believe in God.

A Christian is one who is on the way, though not necessarily very far along it, and who has at least some dim and half-baked idea of whom to thank.

A Christian isn't necessarily any nicer than anybody else. Just better informed.

Judgment ✳ February 29

WE ARE ALL OF us judged every day. We are judged by the face that looks back at us from the bathroom mirror. We are judged by the faces of the people we love and by the faces and lives of our children and by our dreams. Each day finds us at the junction of many roads, and we are judged as much by the roads we have not taken as by the roads we have.

The New Testament proclaims that at some unforeseeable time in the future God will ring down the final curtain on history, and there will come a Day on which all our days and all the judgments upon us and all our judgments upon each other will themselves be judged. The judge will be Christ. In other words, the one who judges us most finally will be the one who loves us most fully.

Romantic love is blind to everything except what is lovable and lovely, but Christ's love sees us with terrible clarity and sees us whole. Christ's love so wishes our joy that it is ruthless against everything in us that diminishes our joy. The worst sentence Love can pass is that we behold the suffering which Love has endured for our sake, and that is also our acquittal. The justice and mercy of the judge are ultimately one.

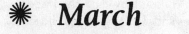 *March*

All the Doors ✳ March 1

A priest admonishes Godric:

THIS LIFE OF OURS is like a street that passes many doors,"
Ball said, "nor think you all the doors I mean are wood.
Every day's a door and every night. When a man throws wide
his arms to you in friendship, it's a door he opens same as
when a woman opens hers in wantonness. The street forks
out, and there's two doors to choose between. The meadow
that tempts you rest your bones and dream a while. The rack-
ribbed child that begs for scraps the dogs have left. The sea
that calls a man to travel far. They all are doors, some God's
and some the Fiend's. So choose with care which ones you
take, my son, and one day—who can say—you'll reach the
holy door itself."

"Which one is that, Father?" I asked for courtesy, for I was
hot to leave. I was on my knees before him and with his one
straight eye he held me there.

"Heaven's door, Godric," he said.

Bitter Need ✳ March 2

ALL THOSE YEARS ago Tom Ball blessed my ears to hear the
poor cry out for help, and I still hear them right enough.
I hear them when the mouse squeals in the owl's cruel claw.
I hear them when the famished wolf howls hunger at the
moon. I hear them when old Wear goes rattling past in weariness, and in the keening of the wind, and when the rain beats
hollow on my roof. In all such sounds I hear the poor folk's
bitter need and in the dimtongued silence too. But when melody wells up in thrushes' throats, and bees buzz honeysong,

and rock and river clap like hands in summer sun, then misery's drowned in minstrelsy, and Godric's glad in spite of all.

A Healing * March 3

Godric cleanses a leper perhaps:

I SEE THE SHAPE approaching still. Its clothes are patched with white and on its head a tall red hat all bent and faded pale from years of weather. *Frick-frack, frick-frack* its rattle goes, and as I climb the bank to let it pass, the very mist shrinks back to flee its touch. The mire is gullied deep, and as it nears my perch, it trips and topples to the ground. It tries to rise but flounders down again. It whimpers like a child that's being flogged. The rain is pelting hard, and flat on its belly in the muck it might well drown for all I know. So less from pity than from fear to have a murder on my soul, I go to help it to its feet. As I bend down, it turns to face me. Then I see it has no face.

I can't say if it was a man I kissed or maid or why I kissed at all. I've seen them make the sick eat broth by holding it so close the savor draws them on. Maybe misery has a savor too so if you're near enough, sick though you be with sin, your heart can't help but sup. In any case, I closed my eyes against that foul and ashen thing that once was human flesh like mine and kissed its pain. When it reached out to me, I fled till I was far enough away to puke my loathing in a ditch.

The tale they tell is of a leper cleansed. I do not know nor seek to know, for pride lies one way, rue the other. But from that time the word went forth that there was healing in my hands. *Something* was in my hands at least and rests there yet though they're all knotted now and stiff like claws. Folk come from miles to have me touch them. Could I but touch the churlishness within myself or kiss old Godric clean!

To Touch Godric ✳ March 4

To touch me and to feel my touch they come. To take at my hands whatever of Christ or comfort such hands have. Of their own, my hands have nothing more than any man's and less now at this tottering, lamewit age of mine when most of what I ever had is more than mostly spent. But it's as if my hands are gloves, and in them other hands than mine, and those the ones that folk appear with roods of straw to seek. It's holiness they hunger for, and if by some mad grace it's mine to give, if I've a holy hand inside my hand to touch them with, I'll touch them day and night. Sweet Christ, what other use are idle hermits for?

Tears for the Past ✳ March 5

Godric speaks of the coliseum in Rome:

Roaring like a lion through his yellowed teeth and making at us with his claws as if to tear our flesh, he took us to a roofless shell as vast as all of Bishop's Lynn, and there I guessed was where in Peter's day they cast poor Christian folk to savage beasts. I wept and Aedwen too except she had no tears but only that dry grief that shook her like the wind. She had not even strength enough by then to hide her face, so I hid mine instead, thus not to seem to goggle at her pain. When I peeped out again, our guide had gone and taken off the net of cheese we'd bought to sup upon.

Why did we weep? I asked myself. We wept for all that grandeur gone. We wept for martyrs cruelly slain. We wept for Christ, who suffered death upon a tree and suffers still to see our suffering. But more than anything, I think, we wept for us, and so it ever is with tears. Whatever be their outward cause, within the chancel of the heart it's we ourselves for whom they finally fall.

Re-living the Passion ✳ March 6

Godric is remembering:

I SAW THE SPOT Our Lady met thee carrying thy cross. She swooned and fell. I saw where thou didst wash the dusty feet of those who, when the soldiers came to haul thee off to death, took to their well-washed heels. With a candle in my hand I climbed the hill on which they nailed thee to a tree, thy tender flesh so rent and torn it was more full of wounds than ever was a dovehouse full of holes. In a round-shaped church of stone where knights kept vigil, I saw thy Holy Sepulchre itself, the very shelf they set thy body on. How dark those three days must have been that thou didst lie in death, nor any savior at God's throne to plead man's cause! I kissed a piece of that same stone the angel rolled away to set thee free, and at another church they'd built where thou didst rise to God, I kissed thy footprints in the rock and through an opening in the roof beheld the very channel in the sky that thou didst sail to Paradise.

"A Fool for Thee" ✳ March 7

OH LORD, THE coolness of the river's touch! The way it mirrored back the clouds as if I bathed in sky. I waded out to where the water reached my neck, my beard outspread, my garments floating free. I let my hands bob up like corks. At sixteen stone or more, I felt I had, myself, no weight at all. The soul, set free from flesh at last, must know such peace.

And oh, the heart, the heart! In Jordan to my chin, I knew not if I laughed or wept but only that the untold weight of sin upon my heart was gone. I ducked my head beneath, and in the dark I thought I heard that porpoise voice again that spoke to me the day I nearly drowned in Wash. "Take, eat me, Godric, to thy soul's delight. Hold fast to him who gave his life for thee and thine." When I came up again, I cried like one gone daft for joy.

"Be fools for Christ," said the Apostle Paul, and thus I was thy bearded Saxon fool and clown for sure. Nothing I ever knew before and nothing I have ever come to know from then till now can match the holy mirth and madness of that time. Many's the sin I've clipped to since. Many's the dark and savage night of doubt. Many's the prayer I haven't prayed, the friend I've hurt, the kindness left undone. But this I know. The Godric that waded out of Jordan soaked and dripping wet that day was not the Godric that went wading in.

O Thou that asketh much of him to whom thou givest much, have mercy. Remember me not for the ill I've done but for the good I've dreamed. Help me to be not just the old and foolish one thou seest now but once again a fool for thee. Help me to pray. Help me whatever way thou canst, dear Christ and Lord. Amen.

Vernacular ✳ March 8

Elric had studied with the monks. He wrote and read. He knew the Gospels back and forth. He had the psalms by heart. An oak grew near his cave with one great branch he'd climb to like a squirrel and perch there till he'd sung them through. He sang in Latin, but, for me, he put them into speech I understood.

"God keeps me as a shepherd keeps his flock. I want for nought," he said. "I bleat with hunger, and he pastures me in meadows green. I'm thirsty, and he leads me forth to water cool and deep and still. He hoists me to my feet when I am weak. Down goodly ways he guides me with his crook, for he himself is good. Yea, even when I lose my way in shadows dark as death, I will not fear, for he is ever close at hand with rod and staff to succor me."

The Missing Art of Bliss ✳ March 9

REJOICE!" SAYS THE Apostle Paul. "Rejoice ye always in the Lord. Again I say rejoice!" I think that Elric never did. He had no doubt that there were joys awaiting him in Paradise for all his grief on earth, but he'd lived so long in pain and penitence I feared that when his time for bliss came round at last, he'd find he'd lost the art.

Perched in his oak, he'd sing his psalms. "Make joyful music to the Lord with harp and horn and melody! Let the salt sea shout! Let all the waves toss high and clap their wild blue hands! Let shaggy mountains stomp their feet!" But he looked so sour even as he sang, it was as if the sound of all those merry revels hurt his ears.

Godric's Musing ✳ March 10

AN EASY THING it is to love a babe. A babe asks nothing, never chides. A babe is fair to see. A babe is hope for better things to come. All this and more. But babes grow into men at last. That's where it turns a bitter brew. "He hath no form or comeliness," Isaiah says. "No beauty that we should desire him. A man of sorrows we despise." Christ minds us to be good, to feed his sheep, take up our cross and follow him with Hell's hot fires if we fail. All this and more our Savior bids when he becomes a man, and to a man we say him nay. Thus when the Bishop tenders me with his own hands Christ's flesh and blood, I slobber them with tears.

Angels When They Sang ✳ March 11

IT ALSO FELL TO me to tend the lads who sang at mass lest, left alone, they'd tear Saint Giles to bits. They chirped and fought like sparrows in a trap. They'd steal up with their candles from behind and drop hot tallow on bald pates. At Pentecost they brought a cage of mice. They set them free. The women shrieked and held their skirts. One whiskered villain ran off with a morsel of the Host and scuttled up a drain. They puffed their cheeks with air and mocked at Little-fair behind his back or cupped their ears like Joan and hooted out, "How's that again?" I caught them once at unclean acts behind the crypt. And yet it was like angels when they sang!

Godric's View of Prayer ✳ March 12

WHAT'S PRAYER? IT'S shooting shafts into the dark. What mark they strike, if any, who's to say? It's reaching for a hand you cannot touch. The silence is so fathomless that prayers like plummets vanish in the sea. You beg. You whimper. You load God down with empty praise. You tell him sins that he already knows full well. You seek to change his changeless will. Yet Godric prays the way he breathes, for else his heart would wither in his breast. Prayer is the wind that fills his sail. Else waves would dash him on the rocks, or he would drift with witless tides. And sometimes, by God's grace, a prayer is heard.

A Vision ✳ March 13

ONE SUMMER DAY I lay upon the grass. I'd sinned, no matter how, and in sin's wake there came a kind of drowsy peace so deep I hadn't even will enough to loathe myself. I had no mind to pray. I scarcely had a mind at all, just eyes to see the greenwood overhead, just flesh to feel the sun.

A light breeze blew from Wear that tossed the trees, and as I lay there watching them, they formed a face of shadows and of leaves. It was a man's green, leafy face. He gazed at me from high above. And as the branches nodded in the air, he opened up his mouth to speak. No sound came from his lips, but by their shape I knew it was my name.

His was the holiest face I ever saw. My very name turned holy on his tongue. If he had bade me rise and follow to the end of time, I would have gone. If he had bade me die for him, I would have died. When I deserved it least, God gave me most. I think it was the Savior's face itself I saw.

Godric's Love of God ✳ March 14

WINTER CAME. OLD Wear froze hard. Snow fell on snow. The woods were still. William trapped small game, but food was scarce. The three of them dwelled in their house, I in my cell. We dug a path between, but it would often lie for days untrod. God was the cause, for he and I were like a couple newly wed. I ever spoke my love to him. I bared my heart for him to cleanse. I sought to please him any way I could, and since there were no riches I could give to him whose coffers hold the sun and moon, I'd give instead by taking from myself.

Elric taught me this. The fire that I didn't build for heat, the wool for warmth I went without, the food I didn't eat—

all these were like the trinkets that a man gives to a maid. More precious still, I gave him all the cheer I might have had with other mortals like myself. Sitting by a flaming hearth with bowls of broth and talk of times gone by, how we'd have laughed the winter wind to shame! And yet, instead, I gave it like a bright and fiery gem for God to pin upon his gown or deck some starless corner of the sky.

Denominations ✳ *March 15*

THERE ARE BAPTISTS, Methodists, Episcopalians. There are Presbyterians, Lutherans, Congregationalists. There are Disciples of Christ. There are Seventh-day Adventists and Jehovah's Witnesses. There are Moravians. There are Quakers. And that's only for starters. New denominations spring up. Old denominations split up and form new branches. The question is not, Are you a Baptist? but, What kind of a Baptist? It is not, Are you a member of the Presbyterian church? but Which Presbyterian church? A town with a population of less than five hundred may have churches of three or four denominations and none of them more than a quarter full on a good Sunday.

There are some genuine differences between them, of course. The methods of church government differ. They tend to worship in different forms all the way from chanting, incense, and saints' days to a service that is virtually indistinguishable from a New England town meeting with musical interludes. Some read the Bible more literally than others. If you examine the fine print, you may even come across some relatively minor theological differences among them, some stressing one aspect of the faith, some stressing others. But if you were to ask the average member of any congregation to explain those differences, you would be apt to be met with a long, unpregnant silence. By and large they all believe pretty much the same things and are confused about the same things and keep their fingers crossed during the same parts of the Nicene Creed.

However, it is not so much differences like these that keep the denominations apart as it is something more nearly approaching team spirit. Somebody from a long line of Congregationalists would no more consider crossing over to the Methodists than a Red Sox fan would consider rooting for the Mets. And even bricks and mortar have a lot to do with it. Your mother was married in this church building and so were you, and so was your oldest son. Your grandparents are buried in the cemetery just beyond the Sunday School wing. What on earth would ever persuade you to leave all that and join forces with the Lutherans in their building down the street? So what if neither of you can pay the minister more than a pittance and both of you have as hard a time getting more than thirty to fill the sanctuary built for two hundred as you do raising money to cover the annual heating bill.

All the duplication of effort and waste of human resources. All the confusion about what the Church is, both within the ranks and without. All the counterproductive competition. All the unnecessarily empty pews and unnecessary expense. Then add to that picture the Roman Catholic Church, still more divided from the Protestant denominations than they are from each other, and by the time you're through, you don't know whether to burst into laughter or into tears.

When Jesus took the bread and said, "This is my body which is broken for you" (1 Corinthians 11:24), it's hard to believe that even in his wildest dreams he foresaw the tragic and ludicrous brokenness of the Church as his body. There's no reason why everyone should be Christian in the same way and every reason to leave room for differences, but if all the competing factions of Christendom were to give as much of themselves to the high calling and holy hope that unites them as they do now to the relative inconsequentialities that divide them, the Church would look more like the Kingdom of God for a change and less like an ungodly mess.

Psychotherapy ✳ March 16

A FTER ADAM AND EVE ate the forbidden fruit, God came strolling through the cool of the day and asked them two questions: "Where are you?" and "What is this that you have done?" Psychotherapists, psychologists, psychiatrists, and the like have been asking the same ones ever since.

"Where are you?" lays bare the present. They are in hiding, that's where they are. What is it they want to hide? From whom do they want to hide it? What does it cost them to hide it? Why are they so unhappy with things as they are that they are trying to conceal it from the world by hiding, and from themselves by covering, their nakedness with aprons?

"What is this that you have done?" lays bare the past. What did they do to get this way? What did they hope would happen by doing it? What did they fear would happen? What did the serpent do? What was it that made them so ashamed?

God is described as cursing them then, but in view of his actions at the end of the story and right on through the end of the New Testament, it seems less a matter of vindictively inflicting them with the consequences than of honestly confronting them with the consequences. Because of who they are and what they have done, this is the result. There is no undoing it. There is no going back to the garden.

But then comes the end of the story where God with his own hands makes them garments of skins and clothes them. It is the most moving part of the story. They can't go back, but they can go forward clothed in a new way—clothed, that is, not in the sense of having their old defenses again behind which to hide who they are and what they have done but in the sense of having a new understanding of who they are and a new strength to draw on for what lies before them to do now.

Many therapists wouldn't touch biblical teachings with a ten-foot pole, but in their own way, and at their best, they are often following them.

One Step Forward ✳ March 17

SHE TAUGHT THEM holy matters as well. Her wood church was long as it was broad. It had a thatch on it and daubed with the gaudy doings of saints inside. It had a hewn stone for an altar and seven fine lamps on it lit day and night and a cross worked with faces and leaves twined together. Ita's voice when she sang was like a sheep caught under a gate nor could she keep a tune to save her soul from the fire but she had her little ones chirping mass to and fro so sweet as to wring tears from a limpet. All scrubbed up they was too in their snowy gowns like angels.

"May the shadow of Christ fall on thee. May the garment of Christ cover thee. May the breath of Christ breathe in thee," she told them each morning at sun-up. Winters they'd sit there with blue noses and frozen fingers and the way their breath come out of them in white puffs you could almost believe it was Christ's indeed.

True faith. A simple life. A helping hand. She said those was the three things prized most in Heaven. On earth it was a fair wife, a stout ox, a swift hound.

Beg not, refuse not, she said. One step forward each day was the way to the Land of the Blessed. Don't eat till your stomach cries out. Don't sleep till you can't stay awake. Don't open your mouth till it's the truth opens it.

Angels' Music ✳ March 18

NOBODY EVER TRIED harder at making God hear surely. He called on him till the veins on his neck swelled and his face went black. He kept at it till one eye got sucked deep into the socket and the other bulged out like a berry on a stem. He gaped his jaws at Heaven till his lips peeled back from his teeth and you could see down to where his lungs and liver was flapping like fish in a basket. Up out of the point of his head a jet of his heart's blood spurted black and smoking. That's how he told it.

"There came angels at last, Finn," he said. "They were spread out against the sky like a great wreath. The closest were close enough to touch nearly. The farthest were farther than the stars. I never saw so many stars. I could hear the stillness of them they were that still."

I see his pinched face go silvery watching. There's silver in the hollows of his cheeks. He has silver eyes. His shoulder-blades cast shadows dark as wings on his bony boy's back.

"Lofty and fair beyond telling was the angels' music," he said. "They heard me cry and they answered me. They weren't singing to me of the mercy of God, Finn. Their singing was itself the mercy of God. Do you think I could ever forget it even if I tried?"

Catechism ❋ March 19

H E STARTED PUTTING Brendan through his monkish paces. "Who is the Prince of Light then?" Erc asked.

"Him as is son to the King of the Stars, your honor," said Brendan.

"Which is the mightiest work of the Spirit of God?" Erc said.

"The begetting of the Prince of Light on the Queen of Glory," said Brendan.

Erc said, "Where might you find a house with fifty and a hundred windows and all of them looking out onto Heaven?"

"King David's book of psalms," Brendan said. His face was feverish pale. His lips was parted over his teeth.

Erc said, "There are three devils forever leading us into sin, boy. Would you be knowing their three names?"

"The tongue in our mouths is such a devil," Brendan said. "The eye in our heads another. The thoughts of our black hearts the third."

The Holy in the Commonplace ✸ March 20

IT HAPPENED ONE day when we was coming on to some holy feast or other. I was in the kitchen yard helping cut up a pig they'd slaughtered for it the day before. I'd been there for the slaughtering as well, catching the blood in a pail for black pudding when they shoved a knife in its throat and helping drag it over to the pile of straw where they got twists for singeing off the bristle. We poured water on the carcase and scraped it and singed it again and finally with a gambrel between the hind legs hoisted it up to a crossbeam. Then a monk with yellow braids sliced open its belly and groping around up to his elbows delivered it of a steaming tubful of pink slippery insides I carted off to the kitchen in my two arms. They left it hanging overnight to cool with a sack wrapped round its long snout to keep the cats from it and the next day after matins the yellow-braid monk and I set to cutting it up, Ita being at her quern across the yard from us. Hams, trotters, eyepieces, ears for making brawn with, brains, chops—we was laying it all out in the straw when Ita come over and drew me aside to where we kept a black stone on the wall for whetting. She told me with Jarlath's leave she wanted me to go with Brendan though she didn't so much as know my name then.

"It's a smirchy sort of business you're at with that pig, some would say," she said. "There's many a monkish boy either he'd beg out of it or turn green as a toad doing it. But it's neither of those with you, I see. You could be laying the holy table for mass the way you set those cuttings out. That's the deep truth of things too no matter or not if you know it."

Ita's eyes disappeared entirely when she smiled.

"Smirchy and holy is all one, my dear," she said. "I doubt Jarlath has taught you that. Monks think holiness is monkishness only. But somewheres you've learned the truth anyhow. You can squeeze into Heaven reeking of pig blood as well as clad in the whitest fair linen in the land."

Tongue for Holy Things ✳ March 21

FIRST HE LET Brendan baptize him all by himself in the deep bed of a stream with his whole kindred gawking from the banks. Then they all come wading in after him. They stood to their chests in the dark water. The children that was too small they took up in their arms. Me and Brendan sloshed among them soaking their heads one by one for an hour or more till at last the entire pack was done.

Then Brendan stood up in a grove of small-nutted branching green hazels and made them a grand speech. He told them how Christ was Prince of Light and King of the Stars and all such as that. He told them every nasty thing they ever did was washed clean away now so they wasn't to foul themselves ever doing the likes again. He told them the Holy Ghost was a gold-eyed milk-white dove would help them stay sweet as milk and true as gold. It was only Brendan with his big bottom and pointed red head talking. . . . Yet I had to own he cut a fine figure there by the river. Nor did any have a luckier tongue for holy things.

Like Flirting or Courting ✳ March 22

BRENDAN BAPTIZED NO others on that journey but there was more than a few he softened up against the day another of the new faith should come by. They was poor folk mostly. They'd be gathering white-stalked wild garlic or nuts as might be or grazing their bony cows on some common pasturage. He'd give them a bit to eat out of our plump sacks and tell them news of Christ like it was no older than a day. Nor did he tell it with gull eyes like Jarlath nor grinding it down to a fine dust like Erc. He'd make them laugh instead at how Christ gulled the elders out of stoning to death the woman caught in the act of darkness. He'd drop their jaws telling them how he hailed Lazarus out of his green grave and walked on water without making holes. He'd bring a mist to their eyes spinning out the holy words Christ said on the hill and telling them the way he shared his last loaf with his friends the night the bullies come for him in the garden.

It was like flirting or courting the way Brendan did it. He'd tease them along till they was hot for more and then skitter off saying he'd be back one day soon or another like him to tell them another tale or two if they'd mend their ways in the meantime. Once in a while he'd get me to join him singing psalms back and forth though it sounded more like cows calling to be milked than monks.

God's Grand Glory ✳ March 23

HIGGLEDY PIGGLEDY. WOMAN and man," she said, clapping her hands. "Is God either one of them, think you? Neither if you ask me. Or both. To my way of thinking God's more like the sun for the sun both brings forth like a mother and pierces deep like a father. Yet it's greater than either, look you, the way it draws all creatures under Heaven to its blessed light without raising so much as a thumb. Would Lough Dern itself was filled to the brim with beer so all the women and men in the land could drink to God's fiery grand glory!"

Cripples All of Us ✳ March 24

PUSHING DOWN HARD with his fists on the table-top he heaved himself up to where he was standing. For the first time we saw he wanted one leg. It was gone from the knee joint down. He was hopping sideways to reach for his stick in the corner when he lost his balance. He would have fallen in a heap if Brendan hadn't leapt forward and caught him.

"I'm as crippled as the dark world," Gildas said.

"If it comes to that, which one of us isn't, my dear?" Brendan said.

Gildas with but one leg. Brendan sure he'd misspent his whole life entirely. Me that had left my wife to follow him and buried our only boy. The truth of what Brendan said stopped all our mouths. We was cripples all of us. For a moment or two there was no sound but the bees.

"To lend each other a hand when we're falling," Brendan said. "Perhaps that's the only work that matters in the end."

The Annunciation ✳ March 25

Buechner describes works of art picturing the Annunciation:

AS THE ANCIENT prophecies foretold, it is a virgin who is to bear the holy child. "The Holy Ghost shall come upon thee," the angel announces, "and the power of the Highest shall overshadow thee." It is not old Joseph but God who is the father. Paul, Mark, Matthew, the earliest writers about Jesus, say nothing of a virgin birth, but by the time Luke wrote his gospel, it had come to seem that nothing less wonderful could account for the wonders he was gospeling. This extraordinary life could have had a beginning no less extraordinary. History creates heroes. Heredity is responsible for human greatness. Evil also evolves. Only holiness happens.

Mary pondered these things in her heart, and countless generations have pondered them with her. She is sitting on a Gothic throne with her hands crossed at her breast and the book she has been reading open on her lap. The dove of the Holy Ghost hovers in the archway above her, and Gabriel kneels close by with a lily in his hand this time, the emblem of purity, chastity, kingship.

Again Mary's head is bowed, and she looks up at him through her lashes. There is possibly the faintest trace of a skeptic's smile on her lips. "How shall this be, seeing that I know not a man?" she asks, and the angel's painted gaze turns her question back upon herself. The angel, the whole creation, even God himself, all hold their breath as they wait upon the answer of a girl.

"Be it unto me according to thy word," she finally says, and jewels blossom like morning-glories on the arch above them. Everything has turned to gold. A golden girl. A golden angel. They are on their feet now. Their knees are bent to a glittering rhythm. Gabriel's robe swings free about his ankles, and his scroll flies out from his waist like a sash. Mary's hands are raised, palms forward, and Gabriel reaches out to take one of them. They are caught up together in a stately, golden dance. Their faces are grave. From a golden cloud between them and above, the Leader of the Dance looks on.

The announcement has been made and heard. The world is with child.

In the Midst ✳ March 26

JESUS IS APT TO come, into the very midst of life at its most
real and inescapable. Not in a blaze of unearthly light, not
in the midst of a sermon, not in the throes of some kind of
religious daydream, but . . . at supper time, or walking along
a road. This is the element that all the stories about Christ's
return to life have in common: Mary waiting at the empty
tomb and suddenly turning around to see somebody standing
there—someone she thought at first was the gardener; all the
disciples except Thomas hiding out in a locked house, and
then his coming and standing in the midst; and later, when
Thomas was there, his coming again and standing in the
midst; Peter taking his boat back after a night at sea, and there
on the shore, near a little fire of coals, a familiar figure asking,
"Children, have you any fish?"; the two men at Emmaus who
knew him in the breaking of the bread. He never approached
from on high, but always in the midst, in the midst of people,
in the midst of real life and the questions that real life asks.

Lord's Prayer ✳ March 27

IN THE EPISCOPAL order of worship, the priest sometimes in-
troduces the Lord's Prayer with the words, "Now, as our
Savior Christ hath taught us, we are bold to say . . ." The word
bold is worth thinking about. We do well not to pray the
prayer lightly. It takes guts to pray it at all. We can pray it in
the unthinking and perfunctory way we usually do only by
disregarding what we are saying.

"Thy will be done" is what we are saying. That is the climax
of the first half of the prayer. We are asking God to be God.
We are asking God to do not what we want but what God
wants. We are asking God to make manifest the holiness that
is now mostly hidden, to set free in all its terrible splendor

the devastating power that is now mostly under restraint. "Thy kingdom come . . . on earth" is what we are saying. And if that were suddenly to happen, what then? What would stand and what would fall? Who would be welcomed in and who would be thrown the Hell out? Which if any of our most precious visions of what God is and of what human beings are would prove to be more or less on the mark and which would turn out to be phony as three-dollar bills? Boldness indeed. To speak those words is to invite the tiger out of the cage, to unleash a power that makes atomic power look like a warm breeze.

You need to be bold in another way to speak the second half. Give us. Forgive us. Don't test us. Deliver us. If it takes guts to face the omnipotence that is God's, it takes perhaps no less to face the impotence that is ours. We can do nothing without God. We can have nothing without God. Without God we are nothing.

It is only the words "Our Father" that make the prayer bearable. If God is indeed something like a father, then as something like children maybe we can risk approaching him anyway.

The Theologian and the Poet ✳ March 28

A T ITS HEART MOST theology, like most fiction, is essentially autobiography. Aquinas, Calvin, Barth, Tillich, working out their systems in their own ways and in their own language, are all telling us the stories of their lives, and if you press them far enough, even at their most cerebral and forbidding, you find an experience of flesh and blood, a human face smiling or frowning or weeping or covering its eyes before something that happened once. What happened once may be no more than a child falling sick, a thunderstorm, a dream, and yet it made for the face and inside the face a difference which no theology can ever entirely convey or entirely conceal. But for the theologian, it would seem, what happened once, the experience of flesh and blood that may lie at the root of the idea, never appears substantial enough to verify the idea, or at least by his nature the theologian chooses to set forth the idea in another language and to argue for its validity on another basis, and thus between the idea and the experience a great deal intervenes. But there is another class of men—at their best they are poets, at their worst artful dodgers—for whom the idea and the experience, the idea and the image, remain inseparable, and it is somewhere in this class that I belong. That is to say, I cannot talk about God or sin or grace, for example, without at the same time talking about those parts of my own experience where these ideas became compelling and real.

Possibility of Miracle ✳ March 29

LIKE MOST THEOLOGY, most fiction is of course also at its heart autobiography. In the case of this scene I, as the novelist, was being quite direct. In just such a place on just such a day I lay down in the grass with just such wild expectations. Part of what it means to believe in God, at least part of what it means for me, is to believe in the possibility of miracle, and because of a variety of circumstances I had a very strong feeling at that moment that the time was ripe for miracle, my life was ripe for miracle, and the very strength of the feeling itself seemed a kind of vanguard of miracle. Something was going to happen—something extraordinary that I could perhaps even see and hear—and I was so nearly sure of it that in retrospect I am surprised that by the power of auto-suggestion I was unable to make it happen. But the sunshine was too bright, the air too clear, some residual skepticism in myself too sharp to make it possible to imagine ghosts among the apple trees or voices among the yellow jackets, and nothing like what I expected happened at all.

This might easily have been the end of something for me—my faith exposed as superstition which in part I suppose it is, my most extravagant hope exposed as childish which in part I suppose it is—but it was not the end. Because something other than what I expected did happen. Those apple branches knocked against each other, went clack-clack. No more. No less. "The dry clack-clack of the world's tongue at the approach of the approach of splendor." And just this is the substance of what I want to talk about: the clack-clack of my life. The occasional, obscure glimmering through of grace. The muffled presence of the holy. The images, always broken, partial, ambiguous, of Christ. If a vision of Christ, then a vision such as those two stragglers had at Emmaus at suppertime: just the cracking of crust as the loaf came apart in his hands ragged and white before in those most poignant words of all Scripture, "He vanished from their sight"—whoever he was, whoever they were. Whoever we are.

Silence and Random Sounds ❋ March 30

OR SILENCE—SILENCE between people, strangers sitting beside each other on a train or at night or taking shelter under the same awning in a rainstorm. Two lives hidden behind faces, divided by fathoms of empty space, wrapped round in silence which one of them breaks then with maybe some word that in one way or another means Know me, Know me, clack-clack, and something that never was before comes into being as the other replies and something is made manifest—a lunar landing, a footprint on an alien star.

· Or out of silence prayer happens: waking at night when the silence in your room is no deeper than the silence in yourself because for a moment all thought is stilled and you do not know where you are or possibly even who you are or what you are, and then out of this noplace and nobody that is you, out of this silence that your flesh shells, the prayer comes—O Thou—out of silence, addressed to silence, then returning to silence like the holy syllable OM where it is the silence encircling the sound that is itself most holy.

Or the other way round. All at once or little by little, the disguise of words is dropped, the conversation dwindles like a mist thinning out, and for the first time the shape of another becomes at least partially visible, and eyes meet, or without apology for once hands touch, and the angel who troubles the waters troubles the in-between air and a healing becomes possible. For the miracle at least of the moment the deaf hear and the blind, the blind, see.

You get married, a child is born or not born, in the middle of the night there is a knocking at the door, on the way home through the park you see a man feeding pigeons, all the tests come in negative and the doctor gives you back your life again: incident follows incident helter-skelter leading apparently nowhere, but then once in a while there is the suggestion of purpose, meaning, direction, the suggestion of plot, the suggestion that, however clumsily, your life is trying to tell you something, take you somewhere.

Or random sounds: the clock's tick-tock, voices outside the window, footsteps on the stair, a bird singing, and then just for a moment a hint of melody.

The Holy Dream ✳ March 31

THE INVISIBLE MANIFESTS itself in the visible. I think of the alphabet, of letters literally—A, B, C, D, E, F, G, all twenty-six of them. I think of how poetry, history, the wisdom of the sages and the holiness of the saints, all of this invisible comes down to us dressed out in their visible, alphabetic drab.

I am thinking of incarnation, breath becoming speech through teeth and tongue, spirit becoming word, silence becoming prayer, the holy dream becoming the holy face. I am speaking of the humdrum events of our lives as an alphabet.

I am thinking of grace. I am thinking of the power beyond all power, the power that holds all things in manifestation, and I am thinking of this power as ultimately a Christ-making power, which is to say a power that makes Christs, which is to say a power that works through the drab and hubbub of our lives to make Christs of us before we're done or else, for our sakes, graciously to destroy us. In neither case, needless to say, is the process to be thought of as painless.

I am thinking of salvation. In the movie called *2001, A Space Odyssey,* a man goes hurtling through the universe to the outermost limits of the universe, the outermost limits of space and time. Through huge crevasses of racing light he passes finally beyond space and time altogether, and you sit there in the midnight of the movie theater watching him and wondering what fantastic secret he will discover there at the very secret heart of the fantastic itself, and then comes the movie's most interesting moment. Because when his space pod finally comes to rest, what the man steps out to discover is not some blinding cosmic revelation, some science-fiction marvel, but a room. He steps out into an almost everyday room of floor and ceiling and walls with a table in it and some chairs and a half-filled bookshelf and a vase of flowers and a bed. And in this room the man dies and is born again. At the heart of reality there is a room. At the heart of reality there is a heart beating life into all that lives and dies. Clack-clack.

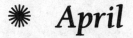 *April*

Where Your Feet Take You ✳ April 1

THE WAY I UNDERSTOOD it," she says, "you were supposed to devote these talks to religious matters. Incarnation and Grace and Salvation were some of the noble words you used."

I say that feet are very religious too. She says that's what you think. I say that if you want to know who you are, if you are more than academically interested in that particular mystery, you could do a lot worse than look to your feet for an answer. Introspection in the long run doesn't get you very far because every time you draw back to look at yourself, you are seeing everything except for the part that drew back, and when you draw back to look at the part that drew back to look at yourself, you see again everything except for what you are really looking for. And so on. Since the possibilities for drawing back seem to be infinite, you are, in your quest to see yourself whole, doomed always to see infinitely less than what there will always remain to see. Thus, when you wake up in the morning, called by God to be a self again, if you want to know who you are, watch your feet. Because where your feet take you, that is who you are.

Limitations ✳ April 2

WHAT BOTHERS ME is simply the everlasting sameness of my face. Those eyes, that nose, that mouth—the variations of expression they're capable of is really so restricted. The grimmest human tragedy can furrow the brow little more than the momentary pain of the dentist's drill. If an angel of God were to appear suddenly, the eyes that I beheld its glory with could light up little brighter than at the smell of coffee brewing in the morning. More than any other part of me, my face is the part where most of the time I live. It is so hard to disentangle ourselves that I can't be sure whether I am happy and therefore my face smiles or whether my face smiles and therefore I am happy—which is to say that my face and I are so much more involved with each other than my hands and I or my stomach and I that I am forced to conclude that to an alarming degree I *am* my face. Alarming because I am forced to conclude also that the limitations of my face are my limitations, that in more ways than merely spatial, my face is my farthest-flung frontier, the limit beyond which I cannot pass. My alarm as I look in the mirror, toothbrush in hand, is that I can do no more than my face can do, that I can be no better than the face that I have made out of my life and that my life has made out of me.

And yet: O purge me with hyssop and I shall be clean, wash me and I shall be whiter than snow. Out of the depths of my face I cry unto thee that of thy grace, thy mercy and miracle, thou wilt make me more than my face. If thy power is above all the power to make Christs, then reshape this face I wear and am. What hope is there for me? Thou art my only hope.

Living the Day Out ✳ April 3

FORGET YOURSELF IN the dream of daily life, Tolstoy says, and forget myself, yes. To forget myself in the very process of being myself, I ask no better. Perhaps there is no gift more precious than the gift of spontaneity, the ability of certain men and animals to act straight and fresh and self-forgettingly out of the living center of who they are without the paralyzing intervention of self-awareness. But the dream of daily life, no. I have had enough for awhile of dreams. Certainly it is often dreamlike enough as you move from morning to evening with little sense of how you got from one to the other, as you move from conversation to conversation, living your life like the food you eat in dreams which neither tastes nor nourishes.

But I don't want to dream this day out. I want to live this day out. I want to live this day out as though it were the first day of my life because that is of course what it is.

Who knows whether there is life on any other planet anywhere else in the universe, but there is life on this planet. And what is life like? Think of not knowing what life is and then finding out: a book suddenly learning how to read; a rock jutting out into the sea suddenly knowing the thump and splatter of the waves, the taste of salt. You are alive. It needn't have been so. It wasn't so once, and it will not be so forever. But it is so now. And what is it like: to be alive in this maybe one place of all places anywhere where life is? Live a day of it and see. Take any day and be alive in it. Nobody claims that it will be entirely painless, but no matter. It is your birthday, and there are many presents to open. The world is to open.

It rattles softly at the window like the fingers of a child as I sit on the edge of the tub to tie my shoes. It comes down the glass in crooked paths to stir my heart absurdly as it always has, and dear God in Heaven, the sound of it on the roof, on the taut black silk of the umbrella, on the catalpa leaves, dimpling the glassy surface of the peepering pond. It is the rain, and it tastes of silver; it is the rain, and it smells of christening. The rain is falling on the morning of my first day, and everything is wet with it: wet earth, wet fur, the smell of the grass when it is wet, the smell of the wet pavements of the city and the sound of tires on the wet streets, the wet hair and face of a woman doing errands in the rain. Wherever my feet take me now, it will be to something wet, something new, that I have never seen before.

Be Alive ✹ April 4

YOU ARE SEEING everything for the last time, and everything you see is gilded with goodbyes. The child's hand like a starfish on the pillow, your hand on the doorknob. Caught between screen and window, a wasp unfolds one wing. With a sick smile, guilt-ridden, the old dachshund lurches off the forbidden couch when you come through the door, his nose dry with sleep, and makes for the pillow by the hot-air register. It is the room where for years Christmases have happened, snow falling so thick by the window that sometimes it has started to snow in the room, brightness falling on tables, books, chairs, the gaudy tree in the corner, a family sitting there snowmen, snowbound, snowblind to the crazy passing of what they think will never pass. And today now everything will pass because it is the last day. For the last time you are seeing this rain fall and in your mind that snow, this child asleep, this cat. For the last time you are hearing this house come alive because you who are part of its life have come alive. All the unkept promises if they are ever to be kept have to be kept today. All the unspoken words if you do not speak them today will never be spoken. The people, the ones you love and the ones who bore you to death, all the life you have in you to live with them, if you do not live it with them today will never be lived.

It is the first day because it has never been before and the last day because it will never be again. Be alive if you can all through this day today of your life. What's to be done? What's to be done?

Follow your feet. Put on the coffee. Start the orange juice, the bacon, the toast. Then go wake up your children and your wife. Think about the work of your hands, the book that of all conceivable things you have chosen to add to the world's pain. Live in the needs of the day.

Congenital Believer ✳ *April 5*

I HAVE ALWAYS loved fairy tales and to this day read E. Nesbit and the Oz books, Andrew Lang and the Narnia books and Tolkien with more intensity than I read almost anything else.

And I believe in magic or want to. I want flying saucers to be true, and I want life to exist on Mars, and I dream of a heaven where old friends meet and old enemies embrace one another and weep. And just at dawn in an eighteenth-century castle built of rose-colored stone in Dumfriesshire, I have reason to think I saw a ghost. All of which is to say I am a congenital believer, a helpless hungerer after the marvelous as solace and adventure and escape. I am also a fabricator, and I am willing to believe that the whole business of God in my life may be something I have fabricated out of my need for solace and adventure if not for escape because religion has never seemed escape to me. Escape would be for me to get out of religion—with all its demands and promises—rather than to get into religion. Maybe it is all just a dream. Maybe none of it is true except in some wispy sense true for me. . . . But I did get mixed up with it, and I am mixed up with it and by it still, and as I stand here in the kitchen waiting for the water to boil, waiting for the time to wake up the children, I must speak of this. Such faith as I have, where did it come from and why?

Artful Dodging ✳ April 6

I HEAR THE CREAKING of a chair being tipped back on its hind legs. "Sir, this is all fairly effective in a literary sort of way, I suppose, but since you have already put most of it in a novel, I'm afraid it's a little stale."

My interlocutor is a student who under various names and in various transparent disguises has attended all the religion classes I have ever taught and listened to all my sermons and read every word I've ever written, published and unpublished, including diaries and letters. He is on the thin side, dark, brighter than I am and knows it. He is without either guile or mercy. "You know, you were just getting down to the one thing people might be interested in," he says, "because it is always interesting to hear why a man believes what he believes. But then instead of giving it to them straight, you started paraphrasing from a work of your own fiction. I've heard you do the same sort of thing in sermons. Just as you are about to reach what ought to be the real nub of the matter, you lapse off into something that in the words of one of your early reviewers is either poetry or Williams' Aqua Velva. I would hesitate to use the phrase "artful dodger" if you hadn't already used it artfully yourself. Why don't you really tell them this time? Give it to them straight?"

God. Jesus. The ministry, of all things. Why I believe. He cannot possibly want me to give it straight any more than I want myself to give it straight, get it straight once and for all. For my own sake. I tell him this, and he brushes his hand over his mouth to conceal the glimmer of a smile.

"A question then," he says. "Have you ever had what you yourself consider a genuine, self-authenticating religious experience?"

There are these things I have already mentioned—the monastery visit, the great laughter sermon, the apple tree branches. They all really happened, I tell him, and I don't see why just because I've used them already in a novel I shouldn't use them again now. And the dream of writing the name on the bar. I really dreamed it. God knows I know what he means about artful dodging, but what can be straighter than telling the actual experiences themselves? What more can he want?

"I just told you," he says, "what I want."

Not the least of my problems is that I can hardly even imagine what kind of an experience a genuine, self-authenticating religious experience would be. Without somehow destroying me in the process, how could God reveal himself in a way that would leave no room for doubt? If there were no room for doubt, there would be no room for me.

Driving home from church one morning full of Christ, I thought, giddy in the head almost and if not speaking in tongues at least singing in tongues some kind of witless, wordless psalm, I turned on the radio for the twelve o'clock news and heard how a four year old had died that morning somewhere. The child had kept his parents awake all night with his crying and carrying on, and the parents to punish him filled the tub with scalding water and put him in. These parents filled the scalding water with their child to punish him and, scalding and scalded, he died crying out in tongues as I heard it reported on the radio on my way back from of all places church and prayed to almighty God to kick to pieces such a world or to kick to pieces Himself and His Son and His Holy Ghost world without end standing there by the side of that screaming tub and doing nothing while with his scrawny little buttocks bare, the hopeless little four-year-old whistle, the child was lowered in his mother's arms. I am acquainted with the reasons that theologians give and that I have given myself for why God does not, in the name of human freedom must not, by the very nature of things as he has himself established that nature cannot and will not, interfere in these sordid matters, but I prayed nonetheless for his interference.

"You were going to explain why you believe," the interlocutor says, not unkindly.

I believe without the miracles I have prayed for then; that is what I am explaining. I believe because certain uncertain things have happened, dim half-miracles, sermons and silences and what not. Perhaps it is my believing itself that is the miracle I believe by. Perhaps it is the miracle of my own life: that I, who might so easily not have been, am; who might so easily at any moment, even now, give the whole thing up, nonetheless by God's grace do not give it up and am not given up by it. There is maybe no such thing, old friend and adversary, as a genuine, self-authenticating experience of anything, let alone God. Maybe at the latter day my redeemer shall stand upon the earth and mine eyes shall behold him and not as a stranger, but in the meantime I behold him on the earth as a name which when I write it wakes me up weeping, as a joke too rich to tell on certain silent faces, occasionally even my own face; as a hand which I am able sometimes to believe that only the thin glove of night I wear keeps me from touching.

Trying to Tell Us Something ✳ *April 8*

THE ALPHABET OF grace is full of sibilants—sounds that can't be shouted but only whispered: the sounds of bumblebees and wind and lovers in the dark, of whitecaps hissing up flat over the glittering sand and cars on wet roads, of crowds hushed in vast and vaulted places, the sound of your own breathing. I believe that in sibilants life is trying to tell us something. The trees, ghosts, dreams, faces, the waking up and eating and working of life, are trying to tell us something, to take us somewhere. If this is above all a Christ-making universe, then the place where we are being taken is the place where the silk purse is finally made out of the sow's ear, and the word that life is trying to speak to us is that little by little, squealing and snuffling all the way, a pig either starts turning into at least the first primal, porcine version of a hero, or else is put out of his piggish misery. At the heart of reality—who would have guessed it?—there is a room for dying and being born again.

How do I happen to believe in God? I will give one more answer which can be stated briefly. Writing novels, I got into the habit of looking for plots. After awhile, I began to suspect that my own life had a plot. And after awhile more, I began to suspect that life itself has a plot.

Creation Is Underway ✳ *April 9*

L IFE WILL BE BAD for the children someday, needless to say, bad for us all before we're done, but I wake them up anyway into this rainy morning because it is not good for man to be alone and I need them more than they or I know to be whoever I am. I suppose that if the occasion presented itself, I would even die for them—not heroically like the dinner-jacketed millionaires on the *Titanic* helping their ladies into the last lifeboats, but just piggishly as usual, because I couldn't help myself.

I am Adam, and it is my birthday, and the world is mine to name, and *Katherine,* I say, and the whole creation stops breathing or starts breathing as I reach out to touch the sleeping hand. All flesh is grass and like the flower of the field fades, and yet the morning stars sing together and all the sons of God shout for joy as she raises her head and opens one eye the color of wet slate. Two is not twice one, G. K. Chesterton wrote. Two is a thousand times one. For all I know maybe it was not even good for God to be alone.

Creation is underway. Breakfast is underway. Steam from the tea kettle is fogging up the windows. The cat mews to be let in out of the wet. Getting her bathrobe hooked on the knob of a drawer as she tears by, my wife throws up her hands: "Is it going to be *this* kind of a day?" With my ear to the radio, I try to catch what the weather will be. Somebody is crying while somebody else says it is her own fault that she is crying. We break fast together, break bread together fast, with the clock on the wall over my wife's head tick-tocking our time away, time away. Soon it will be time to leave for school. Soon enough it will be time to leave.

Under a Delusion   ✹   April 10

I F THE WORLD IS sane, then Jesus is mad as a hatter and the Last Supper is the Mad Tea Party. The world says, Mind your own business, and Jesus says, There is no such thing as your own business. The world says, Follow the wisest course and be a success, and Jesus says, Follow me and be crucified. The world says, Drive carefully—the life you save may be your own—and Jesus says, Whoever would save his life will lose it, and whoever loses his life for my sake will find it. The world says, Law and order, and Jesus says, Love. The world says, Get and Jesus says, Give. In terms of the world's sanity, Jesus is crazy as a coot, and anybody who thinks he can follow him without being a little crazy too is laboring less under a cross than under a delusion.

Eyes of Faith   ✹   April 11

W E ARE FOOLS FOR Christ's sake," Paul says, faith says— the faith that ultimately the foolishness of God is wiser than the wisdom of men, the lunacy of Jesus saner than the grim sanity of the world. Through the eyes of faith too, the Last Supper, though on one level a tragic farewell and failure . . . is also, at its deepest level, the foreshadowing of great hope and the bodying forth of deep mystery. Frail, fallible, foolish as he knows the disciples to be, Jesus feeds them with himself. The bread is his flesh, the wine his blood, and they are all of them including Judas to eat and drink him down. They are to take his life into themselves and come alive with it, to be his hands and feet in a world where he no longer has hands and feet, to feed his lambs. "Do this in remembrance of me," Paul quotes him as saying. In eating the bread and drinking the wine, they are to remember him, Jesus tells them, and to remember him not merely in the sense of letting their minds drift back to him in the dim past but in the sense of recalling him to the immediate present. They are to remember him the way when we remember someone we love who has died, he is alive again within us to the point where we can all but hear him speak and our hearts kindle to the reality of his presence.

Only by Dying ✸ *April 12*

I F DEATH WAS TO be truly defeated, it was only by dying himself that Jesus believed he could defeat it. If he was to reach the hearts of men, it was only by suffering his own heart to be broken on their behalf that he believed he could reach them. To heal the sick and restore sight to the blind; to preach good news to the poor and liberty to the captives; to wear himself out with his endless teaching and traveling the whole length and breadth of the land—it had not worked because it was not enough. There had to be more. "He set his face to go to Jerusalem," the Gospel says, and it was a journey from which he seems to have known that he would both never return and return always even unto the end of time and beyond.

"Not What I Will" ✸ *April 13*

W HAT YOU ARE GOING to do," Jesus says, "do quickly."
What Judas is going to do, he does in a garden, but though he goes about it as quickly as he can, there is a little time to wait before he gets there. It is night, and they are all tired. Jesus tells them, "My soul is very sorrowful, even to death," and then asks the disciples to stay and watch for him while he goes off to pray. One thinks of the stirring and noble way others have met their deaths—the equanimity of Socrates as he raised the hemlock to his lips, the exaltation of Joan as they bound her to the stake, Nathan Hale's "I only regret that

I have but one life to lose for my country." Jesus sounds like none of them. Maybe it is because it is to the ones who are most fully alive that death comes most unbearably. His prayer is, "Abba, Father, all things are possible for thee; remove this cup from me; yet not what I will but what thou wilt," this tormented muddle of a prayer which Luke says made him sweat until it "became like great drops of blood falling down upon the ground." He went back to find some solace in the company of his friends then, but he found them all asleep when he got there. "The spirit indeed is willing, but the flesh is weak," he said, and you feel that it was to himself that he was saying it as well as to them.

Betrayal ✺ April 14

THE SOLDIERS ARE there with their swords and lanterns. The high priest's slave is whimpering over his wounded ear. There can be no doubt in Jesus' mind what the kiss of Judas means, but it is Judas that he is blessing, and Judas that he is prepared to go out and die for now. Judas is only the first in a procession of betrayers two thousand years long. If Jesus were to exclude him from his love and forgiveness, to one degree or another he would have to exclude mankind.

Maybe this is all in the mind of Jesus as he stands there with his eyes closed, or possibly there is nothing in his mind at all. As he feels his friend's lips graze his cheek, for an instant maybe he feels nothing else. It is another of his last times. On this last evening of his life he has eaten his last meal, and this is the last time that he will ever feel the touch of another human being except in torment. It is not the Lamb of God and his butcher who meet here, but two old friends embracing in a garden because they both of them know that they will never see one another again.

"My God, My God" ✳ April 15

"MY GOD, MY GOD, why hast thou forsaken me?" As Christ speaks those words, he too is in the wilderness. He speaks them when all is lost. He speaks them when there is nothing even he can hear except for the croak of his own voice and when as far as even he can see there is no God to hear him. And in a way his words are a love song, the greatest love song of them all. In a way his words are the words we all of us must speak before we know what it means to love God as we are commanded to love him.

"My God, *my* God." Though God is not there for him to see or hear, he calls on him still because he can do no other. Not even the cross, not even death, not even life, can destroy his love for God. Not even God can destroy his love for God because the love he loves God with is God's love empowering him to love in return with all his heart even when his heart is all but broken.

Good Friday ✳ April 16

"GOD SO LOVED THE world," John writes, "that he gave his only son, that whoever believes in him should not perish but have eternal life." That is to say that God so loved the world that he gave his only son even to this obscene horror; so loved the world that in some ultimately indescribable way and at some ultimately immeasurable cost he gave the world himself. Out of this terrible death, John says, came eternal life not just in the sense of resurrection to life after death but in the sense of life so precious even this side of death that to live it is to stand with one foot already in eternity. To participate in the sacrificial life and death of Jesus Christ is to live already in his kingdom. This is the essence of the Christian message, the heart of the Good News, and it is why the cross has become the chief Christian symbol. A cross of all things—a guillotine, a gallows—but the cross at the same time as the crossroads of eternity and time, as the place where such a mighty heart was broken that the healing power of God himself could flow through it into a sick and broken world. It was for this reason that of all the possible words they could have used to describe the day of his death, the word they settled on was "good." *Good* Friday.

Remnant ✳ April 17

THROUGHOUT ALL THESE centuries there were always the prophets thundering out at king and people to remember their ancient mission to be the kingdom of priests that God had called them to be, but each time the prophetic cry went largely unheeded, and each time Israel went down to another defeat with only a remnant of the pious left to be, as Isaiah put it, a green branch growing out of a hewn stump. Remnant led to remnant until finally, in terms of New Testament faith, the remnant became just Jesus and his twelve disciples. When the last of the disciples abandoned him, the remnant became just Jesus himself.

The kingdom of priests was reduced at last to this One, who was both priest and sacrifice, and so it is Israel itself that hangs there on the cross, the suffering one who was "bruised for our iniquities and upon whom was the chastisement that made us whole." Jesus is all Jews and in a sense also the only Jew as he hovers there in the purple sky. It is out of his passion that the Church will be born as the new Israel, a kingdom of priests at last. It is through his intercession that at the end of history the holy city, New Jerusalem, will come down out of heaven like a bride adorned for her husband.

The Risen Christ ✳ April 18

*A*S YOU DID IT *to one of the least of these my brethren, you did it to me.* Just as Jesus appeared at his birth as a helpless child that the world was free to care for or destroy, so now he appears in his resurrection as the pauper, the prisoner, the stranger: appears in every form of human need that the world is free to serve or to ignore. The risen Christ is Christ risen in his glory and enthroned in all this glorious canvas, stained glass, mosaic as Redeemer and Judge. But he is also Christ risen in the shabby hearts of those who, although they have never touched the mark of the nails, have been themselves so touched by him that they believe anyway. However faded and threadbare, what they have seen of him is at least enough to get their bearings by.

No Metaphor ✳ April 19

*F*OR PAUL THE Resurrection was no metaphor; it was the power of God. And when he spoke of Jesus as raised from the dead, he meant Jesus alive and at large in the world not as some shimmering ideal of human goodness or the achieving power of hopeful thought but as the very power of life itself. If the life that was in Jesus died on the cross; if the love that was in him came to an end when his heart stopped beating; if the truth that he spoke was no more if no less timeless than the great truths of any time; if all that he had in him to give to the world was a little glimmer of light to make bearable the inexorable approach of endless night—then all was despair.

The Resurrection ✳ April 20

*W*E CAN SAY THAT the story of the Resurrection means simply that the teachings of Jesus are immortal like the plays of Shakespeare or the music of Beethoven and that their wisdom and truth will live on forever. Or we can say that the Resurrection means that the spirit of Jesus is undying, that he himself lives on among us, the way that Socrates does, for instance, in the good that he left behind him, in the lives of all who follow his great example. Or we can say that the language in which the Gospels describe the Resurrection of Jesus is the language of poetry and that, as such, it is not to be taken literally but as pointing to a truth more profound than the literal. Very often, I think, this is the way that the Bible is written, and I would point to some of the stories about the birth of Jesus, for instance, as examples; but in the case of the Resurrection, this simply does not apply because there really is no story about the Resurrection in the New Testament. Except in the most fragmentary way, it is not described at all. There is no poetry about it. Instead, it is simply proclaimed as a fact. *Christ is risen!* In fact, the very existence of the New Testament itself proclaims it. Unless something very real indeed took place on that strange, confused morning, there would be no New Testament, no Church, no Christianity.

Yet we try to reduce it to poetry anyway: the coming of spring with the return of life to the dead earth, the rebirth of hope in the despairing soul. We try to suggest that these are the miracles that the Resurrection is all about, but they are not. In their way they are all miracles, but they are not this miracle, this central one to which the whole Christian faith points.

Unlike the chief priests and the Pharisees, who tried with soldiers and a great stone to make themselves as secure as they could against the terrible possibility of Christ's really rising again from the dead, we are considerably more subtle. We tend in our age to say, "Of course, it was bound to happen. Nothing could stop it." But when we are pressed to say what it was that actually did happen, what we are apt to come out with is something pretty meager: this "miracle" of truth that never dies, the "miracle" of a life so beautiful that two thousand years have left the memory of it undimmed, the "miracle" of doubt turning into faith, fear into hope. If I believed that this or something like this was all that the Resurrection meant, then I would turn in my certificate of ordination and take up some other profession. Or at least I hope that I would have the courage to.

His Living Presence ✳ April 21

THE EARLIEST REFERENCE to the Resurrection is Saint Paul's, and he makes no mention of an empty tomb at all. But the fact of the matter is that in a way it hardly matters how the body of Jesus came to be missing because in the last analysis what convinced the people that he had risen from the dead was not the absence of his corpse but his living presence. And so it has been ever since.

All Is Well ✳ April 22

ANXIETY AND FEAR are what we know best in this fantastic century of ours. Wars and rumors of wars. From civilization itself to what seemed the most unalterable values of the past, everything is threatened or already in ruins. We have heard so much tragic news that when the news is good we cannot hear it.

But the proclamation of Easter Day is that all is well. And as a Christian, I say this not with the easy optimism of one who has never known a time when all was not well but as one who has faced the Cross in all its obscenity as well as in all its glory, who has known one way or another what it is like to live separated from God. In the end, his will, not ours, is done. Love is the victor. Death is not the end. The end is life.

His life and our lives through him, in him. Existence has greater depths of beauty, mystery, and benediction than the wildest visionary has ever dared to dream. Christ our Lord has risen.

Easter Thoughts ✳ April 23

WE WILL SPEND Easter eve afloat at our prayers, I tell them. We'll have mass on the rocks at daybreak. They sleep like rocks themselves. I sit in the bows and watch the moon glint white in the flat pool.

At first sunlight we tuck up our cloaks and wade ashore through the shallow surf. The shepherd's loaf serves as Thy white body, his wine for Thy dark blood. A choir of wings flutters over us. I feel a fluttering behind my eyes as well. Perhaps it's the wine. We've been fasting three full days.

"O jubilate! O jubilo!" cry the five of us to the wind. Our beards blow free.

Clown Crosan picks stones off the beach. He juggles them grave-faced.

"They blocked him in his grave with stones like these. They might as well have used eggs," says he.

He follows their curved path through the air with his eyes.

"Whoopsa! Now you don't see him, now you do!" he cries. "Fresh as dawn rose he. There's no such ugly thing at all as death for them as have their sunrise life from him."

He lets the stones fall to his feet in a heap.

"Huzzah for clown Christ!" cries he. He tosses his hat in the air. "Huzzah for our precious lovely zany!"

We all throw our hats in the air save hatless Colman.

"O kittiwake Christ!" cries Colman. "Peck Heaven open wide, dear heart, to all that yearn for Thee!"

Real Tears ✳ April 24

WHEN THEY BROUGHT Jesus to the place where his dead friend lay, Jesus wept. It is very easy to sentimentalize the scene and very tempting because to sentimentalize something is to look only at the emotion in it and at the emotion it stirs in us rather than at the reality of it, which we are always tempted not to look at because reality, truth, silence are all what we are not much good at and avoid when we can. To sentimentalize something is to savor rather than to suffer the sadness of it, is to sigh over the prettiness of it rather than to tremble at the beauty of it, which may make fearsome demands of us or pose fearsome threats. Not just as preachers but as Christians in general we are particularly given to sentimentalizing our faith as much of Christian art and Christian preaching bear witness—the sermon as tearjerker, the Gospel an urn of long-stemmed roses and baby's breath to brighten up the front of the church, Jesus as Gregory Peck.

But here standing beside the dead body of his dead friend he is not Gregory Peck. He has no form or comeliness about him that we should desire him, and as one from whom men hide their faces we turn from him. To see a man weep is not a comely sight, especially this man whom we want to be stronger and braver than a man, and the impulse is to turn from him as we turn from anybody who weeps because the sight of real tears, painful and disfiguring, forces us to look to their source where we do not choose to look because where his tears come from, our tears also come from.

To Be Himself ✳ April 25

BUT LET HIM TAKE heart. He is called not to be an actor, a magician, in the pulpit. He is called to be himself. He is called to tell the truth as he has experienced it. He is called to be human, to be human, and that is calling enough for any man. If he does not make real to them the human experience of what it is to cry into the storm and receive no answer, to be sick at heart and find no healing, then he becomes the only one there who seems not to have had that experience because most surely under their bonnets and shawls and jackets, under their afros and ponytails, all the others there have had it whether they talk of it or not. As much as anything else, it is their experience of the absence of God that has brought them there in search of his presence, and if the preacher does not speak of that and to that, then he becomes like the captain of a ship who is the only one aboard who either does not know that the waves are twenty feet high and the decks awash or will not face up to it so that anything else he tries to say by way of hope and comfort and empowering becomes suspect on the basis of that one crucial ignorance or disingenuousness or cowardice or reluctance to speak in love any truths but the ones that people love to hear.

Words Without Knowledge ✳ April 26

I T IS OUT OF the whirlwind that Job first hears God say "Who is this that darkens counsel by words without knowledge?" (Job 42:3). It is out of the absence of God that God makes himself present, and it is not just the whirlwind that stands for his absence, not just the storm and chaos of the world that knock into a cocked hat all man's attempts to find God in the world, but God is absent also from all Job's words about God, and from the words of his comforters, because they are words without knowledge that obscure the issue of God by trying to define him as present in ways and places where he is not present, to define him as moral order, as the best answer man can give to the problem of his life. God is not an answer man can give, God says. God himself does not give answers. He gives himself, and into the midst of the whirlwind of his absence gives himself.

God Makes Himself Scarce ✳ *April 27*

WHEN JESUS WEPT over the dead body of his friend Lazarus, many things seem to have been at work in him, and there seem to have been many levels to his grief. He wept because his friend was dead and he had loved him. Beneath that he wept because, as Mary and Martha both tactlessly reminded him, if he had only been present, Lazarus needn't have died, and he was not present. Beneath that, he wept perhaps because if only God had been present, then too Lazarus needn't have died, and God was not present either, at least not in the way and to the degree that he was needed. Then, beneath even that, it is as if his grief goes so deep that it is for the whole world that Jesus is weeping and the tragedy of the human condition, which is to live in a world where again and again God is not present, at least not in the way and to the degree that man needs him. Jesus sheds his tears at the visible absence of God in the world where the good and bad alike go down to defeat and death. He sheds his tears at the audible silence of God at those moments especially when a word from him would mean the difference between life and death, or at the deafness of men which prevents their hearing him, the blindness of men which prevents even Jesus himself as a man from seeing him to the extent that at the moment of all moments when he needs him most he cries out his Eloi Eloi, which is a cry so dark that of the four evangelists, only two of them have the stomach to record it as the last word he spoke while he still had a human mouth to speak with. Jesus wept, we all weep, because even when man is good, even when he is Jesus, God makes himself scarce for reasons that no theodicy has ever fathomed.

WHAT IS THE kingdom of God? Jesus does not speak of a reorganization of society as a political possibility or of the doctrine of salvation as a doctrine. He speaks of what it is like to find a diamond ring that you thought you'd lost forever. He speaks of what it is like to win the Irish Sweepstakes. He suggests rather than spells out. He evokes rather than explains. He catches by surprise. He doesn't let the homiletic seams show. He is sometimes cryptic, sometimes obscure, sometimes irreverent, always provocative. He tells stories. He speaks in parables, and though we have approached these parables reverentially all these many years and have heard them expounded as grave and reverent vehicles of holy truth, I suspect that many if not all of them were originally not grave at all but were antic, comic, often more than just a little shocking. I suspect that Jesus spoke many of his parables as a kind of sad and holy joke and that that may be part of why he seemed reluctant to explain them because if you have to explain a joke, you might as well save your breath. I don't mean jokes for the joke's sake, of course. I don't mean the kind of godly jest the preacher starts his sermon with to warm people up and show them that despite his Geneva tabs or cassock he can laugh with the rest of them and is as human as everybody else. I mean the kind of joke Jesus told when he said it is harder for a rich person to enter Paradise than for a Mercedes to get through a revolving door, harder for a rich person to enter Paradise than for Nelson Rockefeller to get through the night deposit slot of the First National City Bank. And then added that though for man it is impossible, for God all things are possible because God is the master of the impossible, and he is a master of the impossible because in terms of what man thinks possible he is in the end a wild and impossible god. It seems to me that more often than not the parables can be read as high and holy jokes about God and about man and about the Gospel itself as the highest and holiest joke of them all.

Those Who Hear ✳ April 29

A ND FINALLY THE Gospel itself as comedy—the coming to-gether of Mutt and Jeff, the Captain and the Kids, the Wizard of Oz and the Scarecrow: the coming together of God in his unending greatness and glory and man in his unending littleness, prepared for the worst but rarely for the best, prepared for the possible but rarely for the impossible. The good news breaks into a world where the news has been so bad for so long that when it is good nobody hears it much except for a few. And who are the few that hear it? They are the ones who labor and are heavy-laden like everybody else but who, unlike everybody else, know that they labor and are heavy-laden. They are the last people you might expect to hear it, themselves the bad jokes and stooges and scarecrows of the world, the tax collectors and whores and misfits. They are the poor people, the broken people, the ones who in terms of the world's wisdom are children and madmen and fools. They have cut themselves shaving. Rich or poor, successes or failures as the world counts it, they are the ones who are willing to believe in miracles because they know it will take a miracle to fill the empty place inside them where grace and peace belong with grace and peace. Old Sarah with her China teeth knows it will take a miracle to fill the empty place inside her where she waits for a baby that will never come, so when the angel appears and tells her a baby is coming she laughs and Abraham laughs with her because, having used up all their tears, they have nothing but laughter left. Because although what the angel says may be too good to be true, who knows? Maybe the truth of it is that it's too good not to be true.

Preaching the Gospel ✳ *April 30*

SWITCHING ON THE lectern light and clearing his throat, the preacher speaks both the word of tragedy and the word of comedy because they are both of them of the truth and because Jesus speaks them both, blessed be he. The preacher tells the truth by speaking of the visible absence of God because if he doesn't see and own up to the absence of God in the world, then he is the only one there who doesn't see it, and who then is going to take him seriously when he tries to make real what he claims also to see as the invisible presence of God in the world? Sin and grace, absence and presence, tragedy and comedy, they divide the world between them and where they meet head on, the Gospel happens. Let the preacher preach the Gospel of their preposterous meeting as the high, unbidden, hilarious thing it is.

 *May*

Tobias ✳ May 1

TOBIAS WAS A YOUNG man when he ran into the angel Raphael, and not knowing that he was an angel at all, let alone one of seven great ones who stand and enter before the glory of the Lord, Tobias hired him at a drachma a day to be his traveling companion. Accompanied by Tobias's dog, they had a series of adventures that were nothing less than extraordinary.

Tobias almost lost his foot to a great fish. He discovered a cure for his father's blindness. He picked up a large sum of money that his father had left with a friend. And after first curing a young woman named Sarah of a demon who had caused her first seven husbands to perish on their wedding nights, he not only married her himself but lived to tell the tale.

But the best part of the story is the short, no-nonsense prayer with which he married her. "And now I take not this my sister for lust, but in truth," he said. "Command that I and she may find mercy and grow old together. Amen" (Tobit 8:8–9).

Never has the knot been more securely or simply or eloquently tied, and it's small wonder that it lasted them through a long and happy marriage that did not come to an end until Tobias died in peace at the age of one hundred and seventeen.

Memory ✳ May 2

THERE ARE TWO WAYS of remembering. One is to make an excursion from the living present back into the dead past. The old sock remembers how things used to be when you and I were young, Maggie. The faraway look in his eyes is partly the beer and partly that he's really far away.

The other way is to summon the dead past back into the living present. The young widow remembers her husband, and he is there beside her.

When Jesus said, "Do this in remembrance of me" (1 Corinthians 11:24) he was not prescribing a periodic slug of nostalgia.

Our Search ✺ May 3

WE DO OUR TWENTY minutes of meditation a day in the hope that, properly stilled, our minds will stop just reflecting back to us the confusion and multiplicity of our world but will turn to a silvery mist like Alice's looking glass that we can step through into a world where the beauty that sleeps in us will come awake at last. We send scientific expeditions to Loch Ness because if the dark and monstrous side of fairy tales can be proved to exist, who can be sure that the blessed side doesn't exist, too? I suspect that the whole obsession of our time with the monstrous in general—with the occult and the demonic, with exorcism and black magic and the great white shark—is at its heart only the shadow side of our longing for the beatific, and we are like the knight in Ingmar Bergman's film *The Seventh Seal,* who tells the young witch about to be burned at the stake that he wants to meet the devil her master, and when she asks him why, he says, "I want to ask him about God. He, if anyone, must know."

Shakespeare's Truth ✺ May 4

A BRITISH FILM that came out of World War II has a scene in it showing a couple of air-raid wardens sitting out on the roof of a building in London during the blitz. It is night and enemy planes are overhead. Bombs are falling and much of the city is in flames. There are the sounds of antiaircraft guns and sirens. Then, during a lull, one of the men turns to the other and recites a speech of Caliban's out of *The Tempest*:

> *Be not afear'd: this isle is full of noises,*
> *Sounds and sweet airs, that give delight and hurt not:*
> *Sometimes a thousand twangling instruments*
> *Will hum about mine ears, and sometimes voices,*
> *That, if I then had wak'd after long sleep,*
> *Will make me sleep again: and then, in dreaming,*
> *The clouds methought would open and show riches*
> *Ready to drop upon me; that, when I wak'd,*
> *I cried to dream again.*

[3.2.144–55]

◆ ◆ ◆

At the close of his career, after the period of the great tragedies, Shakespeare turned to something much closer to true fairy tales. He wrote *Cymbeline*, where innocence is vindicated and old enemies reconciled, and *The Winter's Tale*, where the dead queen turns out not to be dead at all, the lost child, Perdita, restored to those who love her. And he wrote *The Tempest* itself, where the same great storm of the world that drowned the Franciscan nuns aboard the *Deutschland* and lashed old Lear to madness and stung Job in his despair is stilled by Prospero's magic; and justice is done, and lovers reunited, and the kingdom restored to its rightful king so that in a way it is the beautiful dream of Caliban that turns out to be real and the storm of the world with all its cloud-capped towers and gorgeous palaces and solemn temples that turns out to be the insubstantial pageant that fades into thin air and leaves not a rack behind.

The Gospel World ✳ May 5

LIKE THE FAIRY-TALE world, the world of the Gospel is a world of darkness, and many of the great scenes take place at night. The child is born at night. He had his first meal in the dark at his mother's breast, and he had his last meal in the dark too, the blinds drawn and everybody straining to catch the first sound of heavy footsteps on the stair, the first glint of steel in the shadowy doorway. In the garden he could hardly see the face that leaned forward to kiss him, and from the sixth hour to the ninth hour the sun went out like a match so he died in the same darkness that he was born in and rose in it, too, or almost dark, the sun just barely up as it was just barely up again when only a few feet offshore, as they were hauling their empty nets in over the gunnels, they saw him once more standing there barefoot in the sand near the flickering garnets of a charcoal fire.

In the world of the fairy tale, the wicked sisters are dressed as if for a Palm Beach wedding, and in the world of the Gospel it is the killjoys, the phonies, the nitpickers, the holier-than-thous, the loveless and cheerless and irrelevant who more often than not wear the fancy clothes and go riding around in sleek little European jobs marked Pharisee, Corps Diplomatique, Legislature, Clergy. It is the ravening wolves who wear sheep's clothing. And the good ones, the potentially good anyway, the ones who stand a chance of being saved by God because they know they don't stand a chance of being saved by anybody else? They go around looking like the town whore, the village drunk, the crook from the IRS, because that is who they are. When Jesus is asked who is the greatest in the Kingdom of Heaven, he reaches into the crowd and pulls out a child with a cheek full of bubble gum and eyes full of whatever a child's eyes are full of and says unless you can become like that, don't bother to ask.

The Child in Us ✳ May 6

WE WEREN'T BORN yesterday. We are from Missouri. But we are also from somewhere else. We are from Oz, from Looking-Glass Land, from Narnia, and from Middle Earth. If with part of ourselves we are men and women of the world and share the sad unbeliefs of the world, with a deeper part still, the part where our best dreams come from, it is as if we were indeed born yesterday, or almost yesterday, because we are also all of us children still. No matter how forgotten and neglected, there is a child in all of us who is not just willing to believe in the possibility that maybe fairy tales are true after all but who is to some degree in touch with that truth. You pull the shade on the snow falling, white on white, and the child comes to life for a moment. There is a fragrance in the air, a certain passage of a song, an old photograph falling out from the pages of a book, the sound of somebody's voice in the hall that makes your heart leap and fills your eyes with tears. Who can say when or how it will be that something easters up out of the dimness to remind us of a time before we were born and after we will die? The child in us lives in a world where nothing is too familiar or unpromising to open up into the world where a path unwinds before our feet into a deep wood, and when that happens, neither the world we live in nor the world that lives in us can ever entirely be home again any more than it was home for Dorothy in the end either because in the Oz books that follow *The Wizard,* she keeps coming back again and again to Oz because Oz, not Kansas, is where her heart is, and the wizard turns out to be not a humbug but the greatest of all wizards after all.

Steward of the Wildest Mystery ✳ *May 7*

SCIENTISTS SPEAK OF intelligent life among the stars, of how at the speed of light there is no time, of consciousness as more than just an epiphenomenon of the physical brain. Doctors speak seriously about life after death, and not just the mystics anymore but the housewife, the stockbroker, the high-school senior speak about an inner world where reality becomes transparent to a reality realer still. The joke of it is that often it is the preacher who as steward of the wildest mystery of them all is the one who hangs back, prudent, cautious, hopelessly mature and wise to the last when no less than Saint Paul tells him to be a fool for Christ's sake, no less than Christ tells him to be a child for his own and the kingdom's sake.

Let the preacher tell the truth. . . . And finally let him preach this overwhelming of tragedy by comedy, of darkness by light, of the ordinary by the extraordinary, as the tale that is too good not to be true because to dismiss it as untrue is to dismiss along with it that "catch of the breath, that beat and lifting of the heart near to or even accompanied by tears," which I believe is the deepest intuition of truth that we have.

Pentecostal Fire ✳ May 8

The following seven meditations (through May 14) are from the novel The Final Beast. *The protagonist is Theodore Nicolet, a minister.*

NICOLET HAD GONE to sleep thinking of Pentecost, and it returned to him now, just coming awake in the shade— a moment not unlike this, he imagined. There were all the accustomed sounds of morning—the traffic, the pneumatic drill at work on the parking lot by the bank, footsteps and voices—and then just the first unaccustomed intensification or distortion of it so that the man unloading vegetables from his pick-up stopped with a crate of tomatoes in his arms and shook his head vigorously sideways as though he had water in his ear. The hum of blood in the head of someone about to faint: the sound began to drift and spread like a cloud swelling in the slow wind. A horn honked and kept up a steady blast that began to reverberate like a bell, a noise within a noise. Nicolet drew his feet together and leaned forward with his chin in his hands, his shirt tail coming out in back. The fire began unspectacularly: whispering flames from hair and fingertips. Then it spread to the shoulders, a conflagration swept high by the hastening wind, and upturned faces burst into flame with everyone getting out of cars at once and yelling, and only then did the big man raise his voice: "Men of Judea, and all who dwell in Jerusalem, let this be known to you . . ." Nicolet watched a butterfly open and close its wings on a cannon ball. "The birthday of the church took place in the midst of terrible fire." That might be a way to begin. He got up with his jacket hooked over his shoulder on one finger and walked away.

So Corny, the Prayers ✳ May 9

S HE'S TRIED TO teach me how to pray, and I'm lousy at it. She's prayed for me. I thought I'd die when she started except she's so matter-of-fact—like the president of a woman's club. But it would kill you, Nick. They're so corny, the prayers. She admits it. She always says them to Jesus, and she says it's important to call him that—not Christ or Lord or anything—because Jesus is the part of his name that embarrasses people to death when they use it alone, just Jesus. She says that underneath that embarrassment is the part of us that's revolted by him. It's so damned queer. So you say Jesus to get that part out in the open where he can get at it."

◆　◆　◆

"I've got to tell you about it because you're the first person I've seen since I got here. It's been so queer, Nick. I don't believe anything much, God knows, but sometimes I thought I could feel something happening. Once in the rain. She lays her hands on your head, and the prayer is really just her talking about you to him. She could be talking to anybody, nothing fancy. Once she even laughed because he already seemed to be doing what she was asking him to do, not a creepy laugh, but the way if a child does something especially clever. She said it was amazing what God could do on his own sometimes. What she asked him to do for me was to walk back through my memory, as though it was a long hall. She asked him to open all the closed doors, and to bless whatever he found inside. Is it just mumbo-jumbo, Nick?"

What All of Us Want ✳ ,May 10

SHE DOESN'T KNOW God forgives her. That's the only power you have—to tell her that. Not just that he forgives her the poor little adultery. But the faces she can't bear to look at now. The man's. Her husband's. Her own, half the time. Tell her he forgives her for being lonely and bored, for not being full of joy with a houseful of children. That's what sin really is. You know—not being full of joy. Tell her that sin is forgiven because whether she knows it or not, that's what she wants more than anything else—what all of us want. What on earth do you think you were ordained for?"

God Pardon and Deliver You ✳ May 11

THEN HE SLOWLY walked the great distance to where she sat and stood beside her, looking down at her profile bright against the dark panes as she gazed away from him at nothing. With his palms flat.against her temples, he tipped her face to him, and she raised her own hands and pressed them against his so that each seemed to be preventing the other's escape while robed in shadow he heard himself pronounce like a stranger, "The almighty and merciful God pardon and deliver you, forgive you every face you cannot look upon with joy," and what he saw was Raggedy Ann with a mouth stitched shut in a ragged smile and the shoebutton eyes shining bright for maybe no more than a child to maul and mother her to life.

Clack-Clack ✳ May 12

"PLEASE," HE WHISPERED. Still flat on his back, he stretched out his fists as far as they would reach "Please . . ." then opened them, palms up, and held them there as he watched for something, for the air to cleave, fold back like a tent flap, to let a splendor through. You prayed to the Christ in the people you knew, the living and the dead: what should you do, who should you be? And sometimes they told you. But to pray now this other prayer, not knowing what you were asking, only "Please, please . . ." Somewhere a screen door slammed, and all the leaves were still except for one that fluttered like a bird's wing.

"Please come," he said, then "Jesus," swallowing, half blind with the sun in his eyes as he raised his head to look. The air would part like a curtain, and the splendor would not break or bend anything but only fill the empty places between the trees, the trees and the house, between his hands which he brought together now. "Fear not," he thought. He was not afraid. Nothing was happening except that everything that he could see—the shabby barn, weeds, orchard—had too much the look of nothing happening, a tense, self-conscious innocence—that one startled leaf. He listened for "Feed my sheep . . . feed my lambs . . ."

◆ ◆ ◆

Two apple branches struck against each other with the limber clack of wood on wood. That was all—a tick-tock rattle of branches—but then a fierce lurch of excitement at what was only daybreak, only the smell of summer coming, only starting back again for home, but oh Jesus, he thought, with a great lump in his throat and a crazy grin, it was an agony of gladness and beauty falling wild and soft like rain.

120

Just clack-clack, but praise him, he thought. Praise him. Maybe all his journeying, he thought, had been only to bring him here to hear two branches hit each other twice like that, to see nothing cross the threshold but to see the threshold, to hear the dry clack-clack of the world's tongue at the approach of the approach perhaps of splendor.

Calypso or Something ✳ May 13

IF THE LIFE OF faith was a dance, Denbigh, and this was the only music—all you could hear anyway—" with a few more double raps he began to suggest a kind of erratic rhythm "—do you think a man could dance it, Denbigh?"

"It sounds like calypso or something. I suppose you could dance to it," Denbigh said. "I'm not sure what you're talking about."

"I'm not sure what I'm talking about either." He tossed the rung toward the barn which it struck and fell. "But whatever this is we move around through . . ." He raked his hand slowly back and forth through the air. "Reality . . . the air we breathe . . . this emptiness . . . If you could get hold of it by the corner somewhere, just slip your fingernail underneath and peel it back enough to find what's there behind it, I think you'd be—"

Roy had appeared on the back porch and cupping his mouth with one hand, called to them through the still morning haze. "Breakfast," he called. "Breakfast." His shoulders hunched, he leaned forward on the railing.

"I think the dance that must go on back there," Nicolet began, "way down deep at the heart of space, where being comes from . . . There's dancing there, Denbigh. My kids have dreamed it. Emptiness is dancing there. The angels are dancing. And their feet scatter new worlds like dust." He raised one arm to show his father that he had heard him, but he did not turn. Some magic in his voice had lulled Denbigh, the frown had gone. He sat there listening as though he could hear the angels himself, the lenses of his glasses afire with the splendor of their wings. "If we saw any more of that dance than we do, it would kill us sure," Nicolet said. "The glory of it. Clack-clack is all a man can bear."

Healing Grace ✳ May 14

Madge Cusper is an alcoholic parishioner of Nicolet's.

SHE WAS DRESSED AS if for a garden party in powder blue with powder blue gloves, a string of white summer beads tight about her thick neck. She turned away from him toward the window, her lion-face softening. "Will you help a lady in distress, kind sir? A lady like me. . . . "

Did you pray when you made your calls? Always the silent prayer, entering anywhere—"Peace be in this house"—and when you were asked to, of course: a grace at meals, a prayer for the bereaved, the dying. But how about when you were not asked? It was not for a prayer that Madge Cusper was pleading but for comfort, advice, reproof, all of which he had given her often before. She could not bring herself to look at him now, asking for what she knew was of no use to either of them. She was purring again, gazing out beneath the green and amber panes as out of a cave.

He stood behind her chair with his two hands on her head, seeing himself in the convex mirror as some kind of hairdresser. The carroty hair was surprisingly thin, her scalp hot and hard through it. Her skull beneath his hands. She sat stiff.

"Lie down with a plastered old lion, thou blessed lamb of God," he prayed. "Place thy hands on my hands and use my guttering love to love her through, a channel to her of thy healing grace, that she may kindle to thy dancing at the heart. . . . "

Hate ✳ May 15

HATE IS AS all-absorbing as love, as irrational, and in its own way as satisfying. As lovers thrive on the presence of the beloved, haters revel in encounters with the one they hate. They confirm him in all his darkest suspicions. They add fuel to all his most burning animosities. The anticipation of them makes the hating heart pound. The memory of them can be as sweet as young love.

The major difference between hating and loving is perhaps that whereas to love somebody is to be fulfilled and enriched by the experience, to hate somebody is to be diminished and drained by it. Lovers, by losing themselves in their loving, find themselves, become themselves. Haters simply lose themselves. Theirs is the ultimately *consuming* passion.

Charismatic ✳ May 16

MOST OF THE TIME when we say people are charismatic, we mean simply that they have presence. Bill Cosby, Charles Manson, the Princess of Wales, Dr. Ruth Westheimer all have it in varying degrees and forms. So did Benito Mussolini and Mae West. You don't have to be famous to have it either. You come across it in children and nobodies. Even if you don't see such people enter a room, you can feel them enter. They shimmer the air like a hot asphalt road. Without so much as raising a finger, they make you sit up and take notice.

On the other hand, if you took Mother Teresa, or Francis of Assisi, or Mahatma Gandhi, or the man who risked his neck smuggling Jews out of Nazi Germany, and dressed them up to look like everybody else, nobody would probably notice them any more than they would the woman who can make your day just by dropping by to borrow your steam iron, or the high school commencement speaker who without any eloquence or special intelligence can bring tears to your eyes, or the people who can quiet an hysterical child or stop somebody's cracking headache just by touching them with their hands. These are the true charismatics, from the Greek word *charis* meaning 'grace'. According to Saint Paul, out of sheer graciousness God gives certain men and women extraordinary gifts or *charismata* such as the ability to heal, to teach, to perform acts of mercy, to work miracles.

These people are not apt to have presence, and you don't feel any special vibrations when they enter a room. But they are all in their own ways miracle-workers, and even if you don't believe in the God who made them that way, you believe in them.

Questions ✳ May 17

ON HER DEATHBED, Gertrude Stein is said to have asked, "What is the answer?" Then, after a long silence, "What is the question?" Don't start looking in the Bible for the answers it gives. Start by listening for the questions it asks.

We are much involved, all of us, with questions about things that matter a good deal today but will be forgotten by this time tomorrow—the immediate wheres and whens and hows that face us daily at home and at work—but at the same time we tend to lose track of the questions about things that matter always, life-and-death questions about meaning, purpose, and value. To lose track of such deep questions as these is to risk losing track of who we really are in our own depths and where we are really going. There is perhaps no stronger reason for reading the Bible than that somewhere among all those India-paper pages there awaits each reader whoever he is the one question which, though for years he may have been pretending not to hear it, is the central question of his own life. Here are a few of them:

- What is a man profited if he shall gain the whole world and lose his own soul? (Matthew 16:26)
- Am I my brother's keeper? (Genesis 4:9)
- If God is for us, who can be against us? (Romans 8:31)
- What is truth? (John 18:38)
- How can a man be born when he is old? (John 3:4)
- What does a man gain by all the toil at which he toils under the sun? (Ecclesiastes 1:3)
- Whither shall I go from thy Spirit? (Psalm 139:7)
- Who is my neighbor? (Luke 10:29)
- What shall I do to inherit eternal life? (Luke 10:25)

When you hear the question that is your question, then you have already begun to hear much. Whether you can accept the Bible's answer or not, you have reached the point where at least you can begin to hear it too.

No Telling What You Might Hear ✻ May 18

WHEN A MINISTER reads out of the Bible, I am sure that at least nine times out of ten the people who happen to be listening at all hear not what is really being read but only what they expect to hear read. And I think that what most people expect to hear read from the Bible is an edifying story, an uplifting thought, a moral lesson—something elevating, obvious, and boring. So that is exactly what very often they do hear. Only that is too bad because if you really listen—and maybe you have to forget that it is the Bible being read and a minister who is reading it—there is no telling what you might hear.

The Gods Are Dying ✳ May 19

THE GODS ARE DYING. The gods of this world are sick unto death. If someone does not believe this, the next time he happens to wake up in the great silence of the night or of the day, just listen. And after a while, at the heart of the silence, he will hear the sound that gives it away: the soft, crazy thud of the feet of the gods as they stagger across the earth; the huge white hands fluttering like moths; the little moans of bewilderment and anguish. And we all shudder at the sound because to witness the death of gods is a fearsome thing.

Which gods? The gods that we worship. The gods that our enemies worship. Their sacred names? There is Science, for one: he who was to redeem the world from poverty and disease, on whose mighty shoulders mankind was to be borne onward and upward toward the high stars. There is Communism, that holy one so terrible in his predilection for blood sacrifice but so magnificent in his promise of the messianic age: from each according to his ability, to each according to his need. Or Democracy, that gentler god with his gospel of freedom for all peoples, including those people who after centuries of exploitation and neglect at the hands of the older democracies can be set free now only to flounder in danger of falling prey to new exploiters. And we must not leave out from this role of the dying what often passes for the god of the church: the god who sanctifies our foreign policy and our business methods, our political views and our racial prejudices. The god who, bless him, asks so little and promises so much: peace of mind, the end of our inferiority complexes. Go to church and feel better. The family that prays together stays together. Not everybody can afford a psychiatrist or two weeks of solid rest in the country, but anybody can afford this god. He comes cheap.

These are the gods in whom the world has puts its ultimate trust. Some of them are our particular gods, and there are plenty of others, each can name for himself. And where are they now? They are dying, dying, and their twilight thickens into night. Where is the security that they promised? Where is the peace? The terrible truth is that the gods of this world are no more worthy of our ultimate trust than are the men who created them. Conditional trust, not ultimate trust.

Sound of God's Voice ✳ May 20

I BELIEVE THAT we know much more about God than we admit that we know, than perhaps we altogether know that we know. God speaks to us, I would say, much more often than we realize or than we choose to realize. Before the sun sets every evening, he speaks to each of us in an intensely personal and unmistakable way. His message is not written out in starlight, which in the long run would make no difference; rather it is written out for each of us in the humdrum, helter-skelter events of each day; it is a message that in the long run might just make all the difference.

Who knows what he will say to me today or to you today or into the midst of what kind of unlikely moment he will choose to say it. Not knowing is what makes today a holy mystery as every day is a holy mystery. But I believe that there are some things that by and large God is always saying to each of us. Each of us, for instance, carries around inside himself, I believe, a certain emptiness—a sense that something is missing, a restlessness, the deep feeling that somehow all is not right inside his skin. Psychologists sometimes call it anxiety, theologians sometimes call it estrangement, but whatever you call it, I doubt that there are many who do not recognize the experience itself, especially no one of our age, which has been variously termed the age of anxiety, the lost generation, the beat generation, the lonely crowd. Part of the inner world of everyone is this sense of emptiness, unease, incompleteness, and I believe that this in itself is a word from God, that this is the sound that God's voice makes in a world that has explained him away. In such a world, I suspect that maybe God speaks to us most clearly through his silence, his absence, so that we know him best through our missing him.

But he also speaks to us about ourselves, about what he wants us to do and what he wants us to become; and this is the area where I believe that we know so much more about him than we admit even to ourselves, where people hear God speak even if they do not believe in him. A face comes toward us down the street. Do we raise our eyes or do we keep them lowered, passing by in silence? Somebody says something about somebody else, and what he says happens to be not only cruel but also funny, and everybody laughs. Do we laugh too, or do we speak the truth? When a friend has hurt us, do we take pleasure in hating him, because hate has its pleasures as well as love, or do we try to build back some flimsy little bridge? Sometimes when we are alone, thoughts come swarming into our heads like bees—some of them destructive, ugly, self-defeating thoughts, some of them creative and glad. Which thoughts do we choose to think then, as much as we have the choice? Will we be brave today or a coward today? Not in some big way probably but in some little foolish way, yet brave still. Will we be honest today or a liar? Just some little pint-sized honesty, but honest still. Will we be a friend or cold as ice today?

All the absurd little meetings, decisions, inner skirmishes that go to make up our days. It all adds up to very little, and yet it all adds up to very much. Our days are full of nonsense, and yet not, because it is precisely into the nonsense of our days that God speaks to us words of great significance—not words that are written in the stars but words that are written into the raw stuff and nonsense of our days, which are not nonsense just because God speaks into the midst of them. And the words that he says, to each of us differently, are *be brave . . . be merciful . . . feed my lambs . . . press on toward the goal.*

Threadbare Language ✳ May 21

"I SHALL GO TO my grave," a friend of mine once wrote me, "feeling that Christian thought is a dead language—one that feeds many living ones to be sure, one that still sets these vibrating with echoes and undertones, but which I would no more use overtly than I would speak Latin." I suppose he is right, more right than wrong anyway. If the language that clothes Christianity is not dead, it is at least, for many, dying; and what is really surprising, I suppose, is that it has lasted as long as it has.

Take any English word, even the most commonplace, and try repeating it twenty times in a row—*umbrella,* let us say, *umbrella, umbrella, umbrella*—and by the time we have finished, *umbrella* will not be a word any more. It will be a noise only, an absurdity, stripped of all meaning. And when we take even the greatest and most meaningful words that the Christian faith has and repeat them over and over again for some two thousand years, much the same thing happens. There was a time when such words as *faith, sin, redemption,* and *atonement* had great depth of meaning, great reality; but through centuries of handling and mishandling they have tended to become such empty banalities that just the mention of them is apt to turn people's minds off like a switch, and wise and good men like this friend of mine whom I have quoted wonder seriously why anyone at all in tune with his times should continue using them. And sometimes I wonder myself.

But I keep on using them. I keep plugging away at the same old words. I keep on speaking the language of the Christian faith because, although the words themselves may well be mostly dead, the longer I use them, the more convinced I become that the realities that the words point to are very real and un-dead, and because I do not happen to know any other language that for me points to these realities so well. Certain branches of psychology point to them, certain kinds of poetry and music, some of the scriptures of Buddhism and other religions. But for me, threadbare and exhausted as the Christian language often is, it remains the richest one even so. And when I ask myself, as I often do, what it is that I really hope to accomplish as a teacher of "religion," I sometimes think that I would gladly settle for just the very limited business of clarifying to some slight degree the meaning of four or five of these great, worn-out Christian words, trying to suggest something of the nature of the experiences that I believe they are describing.

Life-Giving Power ✳ May 22

M OST OF THE TIME we tend to think of life as a neutral kind of thing, I suppose. We are born into it one fine day, given life, and in itself life is neither good nor bad except as we make it so by the way that we live it. We may make a full life for ourselves or an empty life, but no matter what we make of it, the common view is that life itself, whatever life is, does not care one way or another any more than the ocean cares whether we swim in it or drown in it. In honesty one has to admit that a great deal of the evidence supports such a view. But rightly or wrongly, the Christian faith flatly contradicts it. To say that God is spirit is to say that life does care, that the life-giving power that life itself comes from is not indifferent as to whether we sink or swim. It wants us to swim. It is to say that whether you call this life-giving power the Spirit of God or Reality or the Life Force or anything else, its most basic characteristic is that it wishes us well and is at work toward that end.

Heaven knows terrible things happen to people in this world. The good die young, and the wicked prosper, and in any one town, anywhere, there is grief enough to freeze the blood. But from deep within whatever the hidden spring is that life wells up from, there wells up into our lives, even at their darkest and maybe especially then, a power to heal, to breathe new life into us. And in this regard, I think, every man is a mystic because every man at one time or another experiences in the thick of his joy or his pain the power out of the depths of his life to bless him. I do not believe that it matters greatly what name you call this power—the Spirit of God is only one of its names—but what I think does matter, vastly, is that we open ourselves to receive it; that we address it and let ourselves be addressed by it; that we move in the direction that it seeks to move us, the direction of fuller communion with itself and with one another. Indeed, I believe that for our sakes this Spirit beneath our spirits will make Christs of us before we are done, or, for our sakes, it will destroy us.

He Who Seeks, Finds ❋ *May 23*

IN LUKE. JESUS tells a strange story. At midnight an unexpected guest arrives. He is hungry, but you have nothing to feed him. So you go to the house of a friend to borrow some food. "Don't bother me," the friend says. "The door's locked. The children are all asleep. I can't give you anything now. Go home." But you keep on pestering him. You are so persistent that he finally gets up and gives you what you want. Then Jesus adds, "For every one who asks, receives; and he who seeks, finds; and to him who knocks, it will be opened." And his point seems to be that the secret of prayer is persistence. Keep at it, keep speaking into the darkness, and even if nothing comes, speak again and then again. And finally the answer is given.

It may not be the kind of answer that we want—the kind of stopgap peace, the kind of easy security, the kind of end to loneliness that we are apt to pray for. Christ never promises peace in the sense of no more struggle and suffering. Instead, he helps us to struggle and suffer as he did, in love, for one another. Christ does not give us security in the sense of something in this world, some cause, some principle, some value, which is forever. Instead, he tells us that there is nothing in this world that is forever, all flesh is grass. He does not promise us unlonely lives. His own life speaks loud of how, in a world where there is little love, love is always lonely. Instead of all these, the answer that he gives, I think, is himself. If we go to him for anything else, he may send us away empty or he may not. But if we go to him for himself, I believe that we go away always with this deepest of all our hungers filled.

A Child or a Saint ✳ May 24

IN CHRIST'S PARABLE, a third man finally did come along, of course. He looked, really looked, and saw not just a man, a man, a man, but saw what was actually sprawled out there in the dust with most of the life whaled out of him. He bound up his wounds, set him on his own beast, took care of him, and his reward was to go down in fame as the *Good* Samaritan, which seems to be a marvelously inept title somehow, because just as I prefer to think of the priest and the Levite as less than really bad, more just half blind, in the same way I prefer to think of the Samaritan as more than merely good. I prefer to think that the difference between the Samaritan and the other two was not just that he was more morally sensitive than they were but that he had, as they had not, the eye of a poet or a child or a saint—an eye that was able to look at the man in the ditch and see in all its extraordinary unexpectedness the truth itself, which was that at the deepest level of their being, he and that other one there were not entirely separate selves at all. Not really at all.

Your life and my life flow into each other as wave flows into wave, and unless there is peace and joy and freedom for you, there can be no real peace or joy or freedom for me. To see reality—not as we expect it to be but as it is—is to see that unless we live for each other and in and through each other, we do not really live very satisfactorily: that there can really be life only where there really is, in just this sense, love. This is not just the way things ought to be. Most of the time it is not the way we want things to be. It is the way things are. And not for one instant do I believe that it is by accident that it is the way things are. That would be quite an accident.

Do This ❊ May 25

IT IS NOT UNUSUAL when a person dies for the people who knew him best and loved him most to try to remember the last time that they ever saw him or the last time, like Christmas for instance, or somebody's birthday, or a picnic on the beach, when they all came together, perhaps ate together, when they all *were* together in the special way that people who love each other are at some special moment like that. And then, as time goes by and Christmas comes round again, or that birthday, or another picnic on that same beach, the person who has since died is apt to be very much on the minds of the people who are there. They may never actually mention his name for fear of seeming sentimental or of upset-· ting the others or perhaps just from fear of upsetting themselves, but that does not greatly matter. Because the air rings loud, of course, with the name that they do not mention, and in a unique sense he is with them there, the absent one. He is there at least as a memory, at least as a lump in the throat, but maybe as much more than that. He may be there as a presence, a benediction, a terrible reproach, or possibly as all of these at once.

It is with something like this, I think, that you have to start if you try to understand why it is that in all of its long history and in most of its many branches, the Christian faith has made so much of the Last Supper. To begin with it was, of course, the *last* supper. They never all ate together again. In a sense they never even saw him again, at least not really, because within a few hours of their eating, all Hell broke loose, to put it quite literally. It was night time, and there were soldiers, and there was the fear of their own deaths as well as of his, and they were scared stiff, and so it seems unlikely that from that time forward they saw anything very clearly except their own terror or heard anything very clearly except the pounding of their own hearts. So that supper was virtually if not in fact the last time that they saw him, and they had good reason to know that it was even at the time.

Certainly he knew it, and he did not have to be omniscient to know it either. Anybody with eyes in his head could see that the Romans and the Jews alike were out to get him. He had attacked the Jews' most ancient and sacred tradition, which was their Law, and he was a threat also to what the Romans held most sacred, which was, ironically, peace in the Empire, the *pax Romana*. He had every reason to know that his death was upon him, and although it would seem that he could have avoided it easily enough—all that he had to do, presumably, was to get out of the city and lay low for a while—he chose to stay and die because he was convinced that this was the will of God. He felt that his death was necessary if the world was to be saved from the very evil that was destroying him.

He spoke of his death this way, and as he spoke, he performed a symbolic act, taking up the loaf of bread, breaking it in his hands, and saying, "This is my body which is broken for you"—in other words, "I die willingly, for your sake, just as I break this bread now for your sake." And then the cup of wine, which he spoke of as the blood that he would shed for them. Afterward, he invited the disciples to eat and drink this food, and with this the symbol is expanded somewhat and shifted; that is, he invites them to share in his life, to take his life into themselves, to live out in their own lives both the suffering and also the joy of it. And for all these centuries the Church has been re-enacting this last supper as a symbol of these things, a symbol of his giving his life away for the sake of the world, and a symbol of his followers' participating in this life, this giving.

Sunset ✳ May 26

LATE ONE WINTER afternoon as I was walking to a class that I had to teach, I noticed the beginnings of what promised to be one of the great local sunsets. There was just the right kind of clouds and the sky was starting to burn and the bare trees were black as soot against it. When I got to the classroom, the lights were all on, of course, and the students were chattering, and I was just about to start things off when I thought of the sunset going on out there in the winter dusk, and on impulse, without warning, I snapped off the classroom lights. I am not sure that I ever had a happier impulse. The room faced west so as soon as it went dark, everything disappeared except what we could see through the windows, and there it was—the entire sky on fire by then, like the end of the world or the beginning of the world. You might think that somebody would have said something. Teachers do not usually plunge their students into that kind of darkness, and you might have expected a wisecrack or two or at least the creaking of chairs as people turned around to see if the old bird had finally lost his mind. But the astonishing thing was that the silence was as complete as you can get it in a room full of people, and we all sat there unmoving for as long as it took the extraordinary spectacle to fade slowly away.

For over twenty minutes nobody spoke a word. Nobody *did* anything. We just sat there in the near-dark and watched one day of our lives come to an end, and it is no immodesty to say that it was a great class because my only contribution was to snap off the lights and then hold my tongue. And I am not being sentimental about sunsets when I say that it was a great class because in a way the sunset was the least of it. What was great was the unbusy-ness of it. It was taking un-labeled, unallotted time just to look with maybe more than our eyes at what was wonderfully there to be looked at without any obligation to think any constructive thoughts about it or turn it to any useful purpose later, without any weapon at hand in the dark to kill the time it took. It was the sense too that we were not just ourselves individually looking out at the winter sky but that we were in some way also each other looking out at it. We were bound together there simply by the fact of our being human, by our splendid insignificance in face of what was going on out there through the window, and by our curious significance in face of what was going on in there in that classroom. The way this world works, people are very apt to use the words they speak not so much as a way of revealing but, rather, as a way of concealing who they really are and what they really think, and that is why more than a few moments of silence with people we do not know well are apt to make us so tense and uneasy. Stripped of our verbal camouflage, we feel unarmed against the world and vulnerable, so we start babbling about anything just to keep the silence at bay. But if we can bear to let it be, silence, of course, can be communion at a very deep level indeed, and that half hour of silence was precisely that, and perhaps that was the greatest part of it all.

A Point of No Return ✳ May 27

THE WORLD IS FULL of people who seem to have listened to the wrong voice and are now engaged in life-work in which they find no pleasure or purpose and who run the risk of suddenly realizing someday that they have spent the only years that they are ever going to get in this world doing something which could not matter less to themselves or to anyone else. This does not mean, of course, people who are doing work that from the outside looks unglamorous and humdrum, because obviously such work as that may be a crucial form of service and deeply creative. But it means people who are doing work that seems simply irrelevant not only to the great human needs and issues of our time but also to their own need to grow and develop as humans.

In John Marquand's novel *Point of No Return*, for instance, after years of apple-polishing and bucking for promotion and dedicating all his energies to a single goal, Charlie Gray finally gets to be vice-president of the fancy little New York bank where he works; and then the terrible moment comes when he realizes that it is really not what he wanted after all, when the prize that he has spent his life trying to win suddenly turns to ashes in his hands. His promotion assures him and his family of all the security and standing that he has always sought, but Marquand leaves you with the feeling that maybe the best way Charlie Gray could have supported his family would have been by giving his life to the kind of work where he could have expressed himself and fulfilled himself in such a way as to become in himself, as a person, the kind of support they really needed.

There is also the moment in the Gospels where Jesus is portrayed as going into the wilderness for forty days and nights and being tempted there by the devil. And one of the ways that the devil tempts him is to wait until Jesus is very hungry from fasting and then to suggest that he simply turn the stones into bread and eat. Jesus answers, "Man shall not live by bread alone," and this just happens to be, among other things, true, and very close to the same truth that Charlie Gray comes to when he realizes too late that he was not made to live on status and salary alone but that something crucially important was missing from his life even though he was not sure what it was any more than, perhaps, Marquand himself was sure what it was.

There is nothing moralistic or sentimental about this truth. It means for us simply that we must be careful with our lives, for Christ's sake, because it would seem that they are the only lives we are going to have in this puzzling and perilous world, and so they are very precious and what we do with them matters enormously. Everybody knows that. We need no one to tell it to us. Yet in another way perhaps we do always need to be told, because there is always the temptation to believe that we have all the time in the world, whereas the truth of it is that we do not. We have only a life, and the choice of how we are going to live it must be our own choice, not one that we let the world make for us. Because surely Marquand was right that for each of us there comes a point of no return, a point beyond which we no longer have life enough left to go back and start all over again.

No Man Is an Island ✳ May 28

"NO MAN IS AN Island," Dr. Donne wrote, "intire of it selfe; every man is a peece of the Continent, a part of the maine; if a Clod be washed away by the Sea, Europe is the lesse, as well as if a Promontorie were, as well as if a Mannor of thy friends or of thine owne were; any mans death diminishes me, because I am involved in Mankinde; And therefore never send to know for whom the bell tolls; It tolls for thee."

Or to use another metaphor, humanity is like an enormous spider web, so that if you touch it anywhere, you set the whole thing trembling. Sometime during the extraordinary week that followed the assassination of John F. Kennedy in Dallas, the newspapers carried the story that when that crusty old warhorse, Andrei Gromyko, signed the memorial volume at the United States embassy in Moscow, there were tears in his eyes; and I do not think that you have to be either naïve or sentimental to believe that they were real tears. Surely it was not that the Soviet Foreign Minister had any love for the young American President, but that he recognized that in some sense every man was diminished by that man's death. In some sense I believe that the death of Kennedy was a kind of death for his enemies no less than for his countrymen. Just as John Donne believed that any man's death, when we are confronted by it, reminds us of our common destiny as human beings: to be born, to live, to struggle a while, and finally to die. We are all of us in it together.

Nor does it need anything as cataclysmic as the death of a President to remind us of this. As we move around this world and as we act with kindness, perhaps, or with indifference, or with hostility, toward the people we meet, we too are setting the great spider web a-tremble. The life that I touch for good or ill will touch another life, and that in turn another, until who knows where the trembling stops or in what far place and time my touch will be felt. Our lives are linked together. No man is an island.

The Heart of It ✳ May 29

THE REALITY OF the bride and groom, which is also their joy, is of course that they love each other; but whereas sentimentality tends to stop right there and have a good cry, candor has to move on with eyes at least dry enough to see through. They love each other indeed, and in a grim world their love is a delight to behold, but love as a response of the heart to loveliness, love as primarily an emotion, is only part of what a Christian wedding celebrates, and beyond it are levels that sentimentality cannot see. Because the promises that are given are not just promises to love the other when the other is lovely and lovable, but to love the other for better or for worse, for richer or for poorer, in sickness and in health, and that means to love the other even at half-past three in the morning when the baby is crying and to love each other with a terrible cold in the head and when the bills have to be paid. The love that is affirmed at a wedding is not just a condition of the heart but an act of the will, and the promise that love makes is to will the other's good even at the expense sometimes of its own good—and that is quite a promise.

Whether the bride and groom are to live happily ever after or never to be so happy again depends entirely on how faithfully, by God's grace, they are able to keep that promise, just as the happiness of us all depends on how faithfully we also are able to keep such promises, and not just to a husband or a wife, because even selfless love when it is limited to that can become finally just another kind of self-centeredness with two selves in the center instead of one and all the more impregnable for that reason.

Dostoevski describes Alexei Karamazov falling asleep and dreaming about the wedding at Cana, and for him too it is a dream of indescribable joy, but when he wakes from it he does a curious thing. He throws himself down on the earth and embraces it. He kisses the earth and among tears that are in no way sentimental because they are turned not inward but outward he forgives the earth and begs its forgiveness and vows to love it forever. And that is the heart of it, after all, and matrimony is called holy because this brave and fateful promise of a man and a woman to love and honor and serve each other through thick and thin looks beyond itself to more fateful promises still and speaks mightily of what human life at its most human and its most alive and most holy must always be.

In Search ✴ May 30

FOR ADAM AND EVE, time started with their expulsion from the garden. For me, it started with the opening of a door. For all the sons and daughters of Eve, it starts at whatever moment it is at which the unthinking and timeless innocence of childhood ends, which may be either a dramatic moment, as it was for me, or a moment or series of moments so subtle and undramatic that we scarcely recognize them. But one way or another the journey through time starts for us all, and for all of us, too, that journey is in at least one sense the same journey because what it is primarily, I think, is a journey *in search*. Each must say for himself what he searches for, and there will be as many answers as there are searchers, but perhaps there are certain general answers that will do for us all. We search for a self to be. We search for other selves to love. We search for work to do. And since even when to one degree or another we find these things, we find also that there is still something crucial missing which we have not found, we search for that unfound thing too, even though we do not know its name or where it is to be found or even if it is to be found at all.

Boredom ✳ May 31

A S *ACEDIA*, BOREDOM is one of the Seven Deadly Sins. It deserves the honor.

You can be bored by virtually anything if you put your mind to it, or choose not to. You can yawn your way through *Don Giovanni* or a trip to the Grand Canyon or an afternoon with your dearest friend or a sunset. There are doubtless those who nodded off at the coronation of Napoleon or the trial of Joan of Arc or when Shakespeare appeared at the Globe in *Hamlet* or Lincoln delivered himself of a few remarks at Gettysburg. The odds are that the Sermon on the Mount had more than a few of the congregation twitchy and glassy-eyed.

To be bored is to turn down cold whatever life happens to be offering you at the moment. It is to cast a jaundiced eye at life in general including most of all your own life. You feel nothing is worth getting excited about because you are yourself not worth getting excited about.

To be bored is a way of making the least of things you often have a sneaking suspicion you need the most.

To be bored to death is a form of suicide.

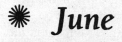 *June*

Risky and Holy ✳ June 1

THAT SPRING, ON the first of June, 1958, I was ordained in the chapel of the Madison Avenue Presbyterian Church, where some four and a half years earlier I had heard George Buttrick give the sermons that had started me on my way. I sat by myself in the front pew feeling awkward and unreal. Dr. Muilenburg preached on Elijah's handing his mantle over to Elisha. Dr. John Knox preached on two texts from Matthew. In one of them, Jesus commanded his disciples to go out into the world and proclaim the Gospel, Dr. Knox said, but in the other he told them that it would be better to have a millstone fastened around their necks and be drowned in the depths of the sea than to cause anyone who believed in him to sin. As I knelt there in the chancel with the hands of all the assembled ministers and elders heavy on my skull, I had no doubts, if I had ever had any before, that it was a risky as well as a holy trade that I had chosen.

Such a Gift ✳ June 2

WAR IS HELL, BUT sometimes in the midst of that Hell men do things that Heaven itself must be proud of. A hand grenade is hurled into a group of men. One of the men throws himself on top of it, making his body a living shield. In the burst of wild fire he dies, and the others live. Heroism is only a word, often a phony one. This is an action for which there is no good word because we can hardly even imagine it, let alone give it its proper name. Very literally, one man takes death into his bowels, takes fire into his own sweet flesh, so that the other men can take life, some of them men he hardly knows.

Who knows why a man does such a thing or what thoughts pass through his mind just before he does it. Maybe no thoughts at all. Maybe if he stopped to think, he would never do it. Maybe he just acts spontaneously out of his passion the way, when you are a child and somebody attacks your brother, you attack the attacker with no fear for yourself but just because it is your brother and somebody is attacking him. Or if you are a cynic, you might say that a man must be temporarily insane to do such a thing because no man in his right mind would ever willingly give his life away, hardly even for somebody he loved, let alone for people he barely knows. Or that he must have acted out of a crazy thirst for glory, believing that not even death was too high a price to pay for a hero's honors. Or if you are an idealist, you might insist that although the human spirit is full of darkness, every once in a while it is capable of the Godlike act. Maybe in some complex way, something of all of these is involved. It is impossible for us to imagine the motive.

But I think that it is not so hard to imagine how the men whose lives are saved might react to the one who died to save them—not so hard, I suppose, for the obvious reason that most of us are more experienced at receiving sacrifices than at making them. In their minds' eyes, those saved men must always see the dead one where he lay in the ruins of his own mortality, and I suspect that at least part of what they feel must be a revulsion so strong that they come to believe that if they could somehow have stopped him from doing what he did, they would have stopped him. We say "life at any price," but I have the feeling that to have somebody else pay such a price for us would be almost more than we would choose to bear. I have the feeling that given the choice, we would not have let him do it, not for his sake but for our own sakes.

Because we have our pride, after all. We make our own way in the world, we fight our own battles, we are not looking for any handouts, we do not want something for nothing. It threatens our self-esteem, our self-reliance. And because to accept such a gift from another would be to bind us closer to him than we like to be bound to anybody. And maybe most of all because if another man dies so that I can live, it imposes a terrible burden on my life. From that point on, I cannot live any longer just for myself. I have got to live also somehow for him, as though in some sense he lives through me now as, in another sense, I live through him. If what he would have done with his life is going to be done, then I have got to do it. My debt to him is so great that the only way I can approach paying it is by living a life as brave and beautiful as his death. So maybe I would have prevented his dying if I could, but since it is too late for that, I can only live my life for what it truly is: not a life that is mine by natural right, to live any way I choose, but a life that is mine only because he gave it to me, and I have got to live it in a way that he also would have chosen.

To Put It Quite Simply ✳ *June 3*

The following seven meditations (through June 9) are drawn from The Book of Bebb, *comprising four novels having as their central character Leo Bebb, who presided over a religious diploma mill in Florida as well as the Church of Holy Love, Inc. The following passage is the final paragraph of the first of the novels,* Lion Country. *The words are those of Antonio Parr, the first person narrator, who is discussing the terminal illness of his twin sister Miriam. The allusion at the end of the paragraph is to an old radio serial called "Mr. Keen, Tracer of Lost Persons."*

WHEN MIRIAM'S BONES were breaking, for instance, if I could have pushed a button that would have stopped not her pain but the pain of her pain in me, I would not have pushed the button because, to put it quite simply, my pain was because I loved her, and to have wished my pain away would have been somehow to wish my love away as well. And at my best and bravest I do not want to escape the future either, even though I know that it contains what will someday be my own great and final pain. Because a distaste for dying is twin to a taste for living, and again I don't think you can tamper with one without somehow doing mischief to the other. But this is at my best and bravest. The rest of the time I am a fool and a coward just like most of the other lost persons that in the end it will take no less than Mr. Keen himself to trace.

Beauty in It ✳ June 4

HE SAID, "FOLKS, Jesus was a prisoner too. I don't mean Jesus was a prisoner in a prison though the Jews, they booked him there for a few days at the end. But I don't mean that kind of prisoner. And I don't mean Jesus was a prisoner inside his own skin like you and I, because Jesus was Rose of Sharon, brothers, he was Lily of the Valley. He was the royal Bengal tiger and the lamb without blemish both. There was no sin in him, nothing he had to jail up inside. He had the seat of honor in Heaven, and it was through him the earth was made. Only then he come down. He come down from Heaven. From *Heaven!* You ever stop to think what that means? You ever stop to think what it means to come down out of Heaven into this two-bit world?

"Up there in Heaven Scripture says the streets are of pure gold like unto clear glass and the twelve gates are twelve pearls and there is no Temple where people go to worship the Almighty because up there the Almighty is worshiped all over the place and day and night the angels sing praises at his throne. That's the place Jesus left to come here.

"He come down out of the heavenly place to this place. Down, down he come, and what did he find when he got here? He found a place where there's not enough food to stretch round. He found a place where every single night there's little children go to bed crying because that day it wasn't their turn to eat. He found a place where people are scared stiff of each other most of the time and hide from each other and sometimes come out of their hiding places to do hateful things to each other.

"You take your nine-year-old girl found beat-up and raped in the park. You take your old woman shipped off to some cheap-jack nursing home to die of lonesomeness. Jesus found a place where even nature's gone bad. Where babies are born with little shriveled-up arms and young men with their whole life ahead of them get cancers, and there's droughts and floods, and peaches are piled up along the road going rotten to keep the price up when there's people don't have the price of a peach.

"Friends, Jesus come down to a place where every last man, woman, and child is living on death row. You'd think the least thing we could do was draw close and comfort each other, but no. Except for a few loved ones, we close the doors of our hearts and bolt them tight on each other."

Bebb's voice grew quieter toward the end. He held on to the sides of his new pulpit with his shoulders hunched up. He said, "This world Jesus come down to, it's got good things in it too, praise God. It's got love in it and kindness in it and people doing brave and honest things, not just hateful things. It's got beauty in it. It's got the silver light of the moon by night and the golden beams of the sun by day. It's got the sound of the rain on the roof and the smell of the rain on the fresh-turned earth. It's got human forms and faces that are so beautiful they break your heart for yearning after them. But coming down from where he come down from, all the good things of the world must have just made Jesus homesick for the place he come down from. Brothers and sisters, the whole planet was a prison for Jesus. He got born here like the rest of us and did the work here he come to do, and he died here. But it was never like it was home to him.

"Same as creatures from some other part of the universe, Jesus was a stranger in this place, and that's another meaning to Saint Paul's words when he says, 'I am a prisoner for Christ.' Saint Paul means this whole planet's my prison because I don't belong to this planet. I'm down here just for your sake same as Jesus was. That's all. I belong to someplace else far, far away. Sometimes I get homesick for it something wicked."

Like a Great Feast ✳ *June 5*

HE SAID, "THE KINGDOM of Heaven is like a great feast. That's the way of it. The Kingdom of Heaven is a love feast where nobody's a stranger. Like right here. There's strangers everywheres else you can think of. There's strangers was born twin brothers out of the same womb. There's strangers was raised together in the same town and worked side by side all their life through. There's strangers got married and been climbing in and out of the same fourposter thirty-five, forty years, and they're strangers still. And Jesus, it's like most of the time he is a stranger too. But here in this place there's no strangers, and Jesus, he isn't a stranger either. The Kingdom of Heaven's like this."

He said, "We all got secrets. I got them same as everybody else—things we feel bad about and wish hadn't ever happened. Hurtful things. Long ago things. We're all scared and lonesome, but most of the time we keep it hid. It's like every one of us has lost his way so bad we don't even know which way is home any more only we're ashamed to ask. You know what would happen if we would own up we're lost and ask?

Why, what would happen is we'd find out home is each other. We'd find out home is Jesus that loves us lost or found or any whichway."

Stay Put ✳ June 6

H E SAID, "WHY, IF you couldn't stand the sight of each other, that's one thing. If you treated each other like dirt and went around saying cruel and spiteful things and cheating on each other every chance you got, that's one thing. Sometimes maybe a divorce is made in Heaven same as a marriage even though it don't say so in Scripture. But you've been through thick and thin together, and it's made you the best friends either one of you's ever like to find again. Even if you split up and get married off each one to somebody different, you'll be forever phoning each other long distance and trading the kids back and forth. Antonio, he'll be coming round every time there's a birthday or somebody's took sick. They'll all of them say isn't it something how those two get on so friendly even so.

"If there's one thing makes me want to puke, it's a friendly divorce," Bebb said. "If it's got to be, give me a divorce that's hateful. When you're friends, stay put. So what if it's not all moonlight and roses? What is? Stay put because if you don't, you'll spend the rest of your life looking to find each other in the face of strangers."

Hidden Treasure ✳ June 7

B EBB SAYS, "THE KINGDOM of Heaven, it's like unto treasure hid in a field the which when a man hath found it, he hideth it and for joy thereof"—Bebb comes down so hard on *joy* it makes the machine rattle—"he goeth and selleth all he hath or ever hopes to hath and buyeth that field. Well, it's like you're poking around a junk shop, and inside a old humpback trunk with the lid half stove in you come across a pack of letters somebody's great granddad tied up with a string from a chum back home name of Abe Lincoln that's worth a clear five thousand bucks each if they're worth a dime. Now you tell me what a man would give to lay his hands on that trunk. Why he'd give his bottom dollar. He'd give his right arm for a treasure like that, and for the Kingdom of Heaven—Listen," Bebb says, "he'd give ten years, twenty years, off his life. You know why? Why because the Kingdom of Heaven, that's what it is. It's life. Not the kind of half-baked, moth-eaten life we most of us live most of the time but the real honest-to-God thing. Life with a capital L. It's the treasure a man spends all his born days looking for, no matter if he knows it or not. The Kingdom of Heaven, it's the treasure that up till a man finds it, every other treasure that comes his way doesn't amount to spit."

Bebb says, "The Kingdom comes by looking for it. The Kingdom comes sometimes by not looking for it too hard. There's times the Kingdom comes by it looking for you."

Like a Thief ✳ June 8

H E SAYS, "ANTONIO, he comes like a thief in the night, like a bridegroom to the bride he's got waiting for him with flowers in her hair. You should see how they turn pale when he comes, some of them. The cheaters of widows and orphans, for one, and the lawyers they pay to make it legal. The flag-waving politicians with their hand in the till. The folks that run the sex movies and the smut stores that poison the air of the world like a open sewer. The whole miserable pack of them. He doesn't do a thing in the world to hurt them because just standing there seeing him go by is hurtful enough, all that glory galloping by they missed by being spiteful and mean. Their hearts just break against the sight of him the way waves break against a rock."

Bebb said, "But it's the others that's the real sight to see, the ones that aren't any better than they ought to be but not all that much worse either. That means all of us pretty near. He comes riding up so fast on them there's no time to put on their Sunday suit and go wait for him in the front parlor with the Scriptures laying open on the table. The midwest farmgirl that run away from home and don't have any other way to make ends meet, she's sitting all painted up on a bar stool trying to look like she knows the difference between a martini cocktail and a root beer float. The middle-age drummer that hasn't made a sale all day is stretched out on his bed in a cheap motel staring at the ceiling with the TV on. The big-time executive is bawling out his secretary for coming back from her dinner ten minutes late, and the old waitress with varicose veins is taking the weight off her feet a few minutes in the help's toilet. Of that day and hour knoweth no man, Antonio. Therefore be ye also ready, for in such an hour as ye think not the Son of Man cometh."

◆　◆　◆

Bebb said, "You ever looked at somebody's face sitting in the window watching for his folks to come home? Say it's gotten dark and the roads are slippery and there's been some bad accidents come over the radio. One by one he watches the headlights of cars come winding up the hill. He's got his heart in his mouth hoping this time for sure it's going to be the one to slow down and pull into the yard, but one after the other they all just keep on driving past till his face goes grey waiting for what looks like it's never going to come. Antonio, that's the face we all of us got when we're not doing anything special with our face. You look at somebody the next time he's just sitting around staring into space when he doesn't know anybody's watching.

"Then finally when he's about given up hope and maybe dozed off a minute or two, he hears the back door open. He hears footsteps in the kitchen. He hears the voice out of all the voices of the world he's waiting for call out his name. Then you watch his face. Antonio, all over the world there'll be faces like that when the rider comes."

Time's Wingéd Chariot ✳ June 9

THE WEIGHT OF this sad time we must obey," says dull, dutiful Edgar at the end of Act Five, "Speak what we feel, not what we ought to say," and by and large I have tried to do that in this account of my life and times, my own search, I suppose, for whatever it is we search for in Poinsett, South Carolina, and Sutton, Connecticut, for whatever it is that is always missing. I am not sure I have ever seen it even from afar, God knows, and I know I don't have forever to see it in either. Already, if I make the mistake of listening, I can hear a dim humming in the tracks, Time's wingéd chariot hurrying near, as Andrew Marvell said to his coy mistress. But to be honest I must say that on occasion I can also hear something else too—not the thundering of distant hoofs, maybe, or *Hi-yo, Silver. Away!* echoing across the lonely sage, but the faint chunk-chunk of my own moccasin heart, of the Tonto afoot in the dusk of me somewhere who, not because he ought to but because he can't help himself, whispers *Kemo Sabe* every once in a while to what may or may not be only a silvery trick of the failing light.

Darkness ✳ June 10

THE OLD TESTAMENT begins with darkness, and the last of the Gospels ends with it.

"Darkness was upon the face of the deep," Genesis says. Darkness was where it all started. Before darkness, there had never been anything other than darkness, void and without form.

At the end of John, the disciples go out fishing on the Sea of Tiberias. It is night. They have no luck. Their nets are empty. Then they spot somebody standing on the beach. At first they don't see who it is in the darkness. It is Jesus.

The darkness of Genesis is broken by God in great majesty speaking the word of creation. "Let there be light!" That's all it took.

The darkness of John is broken by the flicker of a charcoal fire on the sand. Jesus has made it. He cooks some fish on it for his old friends' breakfast. On the horizon there are the first pale traces of the sun getting ready to rise.

All the genius and glory of God are somehow represented by these two scenes, not to mention what Saint Paul calls God's foolishness.

The original creation of light itself is almost too extraordinary to take in. The little cook-out on the beach is almost too ordinary to take seriously. Yet if Scripture is to be believed, enormous stakes were involved in them both and still are. Only a saint or a visionary can begin to understand God setting the very sun on fire in the heavens, and therefore God takes another tack. By sheltering a spark with a pair of cupped hands and blowing on it, the Light of the World gets enough of a fire going to make breakfast. It's not apt to be your interest in cosmology or even in theology that draws you to it so much as it's the empty feeling in your stomach. You don't have to understand anything very complicated. All you're asked is to take a step or two forward through the darkness and start digging in.

To Find What We Have Lost ✳ June 11

WHAT I MEAN IS that if we come to a church right, we come to it more fully and nakedly ourselves, come with more of our humanness showing, than we are apt to come to most places. We come like Moses with muck on our shoes—foot-sore and travel-stained with the dust of our lives upon us, our failures, our deceits, our hypocrisies, because if, unlike Moses, we have never taken anybody's life, we have again and again withheld from other people, including often even those who are nearest to us, the love that might have made their lives worth living, not to mention our own. Like Moses we come here as we are, and like him we come as strangers and exiles in our way because wherever it is that we truly belong, whatever it is that is truly home for us, we know in our hearts that we have somehow lost it and gotten lost. Something is missing from our lives that we cannot even name—something we know best from the empty place inside us all where it belongs. We come here to find what we have lost. We come here to acknowledge that in terms of the best we could be we are lost and that we are helpless to save ourselves. We come here to confess our sins.

At the Heart of Things ✳ June 12

THERE ARE TIMES for all of us when life seems without purpose or meaning, when we wake to a sense of chaos like a great cat with its paws on our chests sucking our breath. What can we do? Where can we turn? Well, you can thank your lucky stars, say many among us, that the world is full of specialists who are working on all these problems; and you can turn to them, men and women who have put behind them all the ancient myths and dreams and superstitions and have dedicated themselves to finding solutions to these problems in the only place where solutions or anything else can be found—which is here in the midst of the vast complexities of the cosmos itself, which is all there is or ever was or ever will be.

The existence of the Church bears witness to the belief that there is only one thing you can say to such a view and that is that it is wrong. There is only one answer you can give to this terrible sanity, and that is that it is ultimately insane. The ancient myths and dreams of a power beyond power and a love beyond love that hold the cosmos itself, hold all things, in existence reflect a reality which we can deny only to our great impoverishment; and the dream of a holiness and mystery at the heart of things that humankind with all its ingenuity and wisdom can neither explain away nor live fully without goes on being dreamed. Moments continue to go up in flames like the bush in Midian to illumine, if only for a moment, a path that stretches before us like no other path. And such moments call out in a voice which, if we only had courage and heart enough, we would follow to the end of time.

The King Does Come ✳ *June 13*

WHEN JESUS OF Nazareth rode into Jerusalem on Palm Sunday and his followers cried out, "Blessed is the King who comes in the name of the Lord," the Pharisees went to Jesus and told him to put an end to their blasphemies, and Jesus said to them, "I tell you, if these were silent, the very stones would cry out."

This church. The church on the other side of town, the other side of the world. All churches everywhere. The day will come when they will lie in ruins, every last one of them. The day will come when all the voices that were ever raised in them, including our own, will be permanently stilled. But when that day comes, I believe that the tumbled stones will cry aloud of the great, deep hope that down through the centuries has been the one reason for having churches at all and is the one reason we have for coming to this one now: the hope that into the world the King does come. And in the name of the Lord. And is always coming, blessed be he. And will come afire with glory, at the end of time.

In the meantime, King Jesus, we offer all churches to you as you offer them to us. Make thyself known in them. Make thy will done in them. Make our stone hearts cry out thy kingship. Make us holy and human at last that we may do the work of thy love.

The Bible Without Tears ✳ June 14

What follows are some practical suggestions on how to read the Bible without tears. Or maybe with them.

1 DON'T START AT the beginning and try to plow your way straight through to the end. At least not without help. If you do, you're almost sure to bog down somewhere around the twenty-fifth chapter of Exodus. Concentrate on the high points at first. There is much to reward you in the valleys too, but at the outset keep to the upper elevations. There are quite a few.

There is the vivid, eyewitness account of the reign of King David, for instance (2 Samuel plus the first two chapters of 1 Kings), especially the remarkable chapters that deal with his last years when the crimes and blunders of his youth have begun to catch up with him. Or the Joseph stories (Genesis 39–50). Or the Book of Job. Or the Sermon on the Mount (Matthew 5–7). Or the seventh chapter of Paul's letter to the Romans, which states as lucidly as it has ever been stated the basic moral dilemma of man and then leads into the eighth chapter, which contains the classic expression of Christianity's basic hope.

2. The air in such upper altitudes is apt to be clearer and brighter than elsewhere, but if you nevertheless find yourself getting lost along the way, try a good Bible commentary which

gives the date and historical background of each book, explains the special circumstances which it was written to meet, and verse by verse tries to illumine the meaning of the difficult sections. Even when the meaning seems perfectly clear, a commentary can greatly enrich your understanding. The Book of Jonah, for instance—only two or three pages long and the one genuine comedy in the Old Testament—takes on added significance when you discover its importance in advancing the idea that God's love is extended not just to the children of Israel but to all mankind.

3. If you have even as much as a nodding acquaintance with a foreign language, try reading the Bible in that. Then you stand a chance of hearing what the Bible is actually saying instead of what you assume it must be saying because it is the Bible. Some of it you may hear in such a new way that it is as if you had never heard it before. "Blessed are the meek" is the way the English version goes, whereas in French it comes out, *"Heureux sont les débonnaires"* (Happy are the debonair). The *debonair* of all things! Doors fly open. Bells ring out.

4. If you don't know a foreign language, try some English version that you've never tried before—the New English Bible, Goodspeed's translation, J. B. Phillips's New Testament, or any other you can lay your hands on. The more far-out the better. Nothing could be farther out than the Bible itself. The trouble with the King James or Authorized Version is that it is too full of Familiar Quotations. The trouble with Familiar Quotations is that they are so familiar you don't hear them. When Jesus was crucified, the Romans nailed over his head a sign saying "King of the Jews" so nobody would miss the joke. To get something closer to the true flavor, try translating the sign instead: "Head Jew."

5. It may sound like fortune-telling, but don't let that worry you. Let the Bible fall open in your lap and start there. If you don't find something that speaks to you, let it fall open

to something else. Read it as though it were as exotic as the *I Ching* or the Tarot deck. Because it is.

6. If somebody claims that you have to take the Bible literally, word for word, or not at all, ask him if you have to take John the Baptist literally when he calls Jesus the Lamb of God.

If somebody claims that no rational person can take a book seriously which assumes that the world was created in six days and man in an afternoon, ask him if he can take Shakespeare seriously whose scientific knowledge would have sent a third-grader into peals of laughter.

7. Finally this. If you look *at* a window, you see fly-specks, dust, the crack where Junior's Frisbie hit it. If you look *through* a window, you see the world beyond.

Something like this is the difference between those who see the Bible as a Holy Bore and those who see it as the Word of God which speaks out of the depths of an almost unimaginable past into the depths of ourselves.

Trinity ✳ *June 15*

THE MUCH-MALIGNED doctrine of the Trinity is an assertion that, appearances to the contrary notwithstanding, there is only one God.

Father, Son, and Holy Spirit mean that the mystery beyond us, the mystery among us, and the mystery within us are all the same mystery. Thus the Trinity is a way of saying something about us and the way we experience God.

The Trinity is also a way of saying something about God and the way he is within himself, i.e., God does not need the Creation in order to have something to love because within himself love happens. In other words, the love God is is love not as a noun but as a verb. This verb is reflexive as well as transitive.

If the idea of God as both Three and One seems far-fetched and obfuscating, look in the mirror someday.

There is (*a*) the interior life known only to yourself and those you choose to communicate it to (the Father). There is (*b*) the visible face which in some measure reflects that inner life (the Son). And there is (*c*) the invisible power you have in order to communicate that interior life in such a way that others do not merely know *about* it, but know it in the sense of its becoming part of who they are (the Holy Spirit). Yet what you are looking at in the mirror is clearly and indivisibly the one and only You.

Where We Started ✳ June 16

THE STORY OF CHRIST is where we all started from, though we've come so far since then that there are times when you'd hardly know it to listen to us and when we hardly know it ourselves. The story of Christ is what once, somehow and somewhere, we came to Christ through. Maybe it happened little by little—a face coming slowly into focus that we'd been looking at for a long time without really seeing it, a voice gradually making itself heard among many other voices and in such a way that we couldn't help listening after a while, couldn't help trying somehow, in some unsatisfactory way, to answer. Or maybe there was more drama to it than that—a sudden catch of the breath at the sound of his name on somebody's lips at a moment we weren't expecting it, a sudden welling up of tears out of a place where we didn't think any tears were. Each of us has a tale to tell if we would only tell it. But however it happened, it comes to seem a long time ago and a long way away, and so many things have happened since—so many books read, so many sermons heard or preached, so much life lived—that to be reminded at this stage of the game of the story of Jesus, where we all started, is like being suddenly called by your childhood name when you have all but forgotten your childhood name and maybe your childhood too.

We Have It in Us ✳ June 17

Y ET THEY MEET AS well as diverge, our stories and Christ's, and even when they diverge, it is *his* they diverge from, so that by his absence as well as by his presence in our lives we know who he is and who we are and who we are not.

We have it in us to be Christs to each other and maybe in some unimaginable way to God too—that's what we have to tell finally. We have it in us to work miracles of love and healing as well as to have them worked upon us. We have it in us to bless with him and forgive with him and heal with him and once in a while maybe even to grieve with some measure of his grief at another's pain and to rejoice with some measure of his rejoicing at another's joy almost as if it were our own. And who knows but that in the end, by God's mercy, the two stories will converge for good and all, and though we would never have had the courage or the faith or the wit to die for him any more than we have ever managed to live for him very well either, his story will come true in us at last. And in the meantime, this side of Paradise, it is our business (not like so many peddlers of God's word but as men and women of sincerity) to speak with our hearts (which is what sincerity means) and to bear witness to, and live out of, and live toward, and live by, the true word of his holy story as it seeks to stammer itself forth through the holy stories of us all.

To Give Yourself ✳ June 18

B Y ALL THE LAWS both of logic and simple arithmetic, to give yourself away in love to another would seem to mean that you end up with less of yourself left than you had to begin with. But the miracle is that just the reverse is true, logic and arithmetic go hang. To give yourself away in love to somebody else—as a man and a woman give themselves away to each other at a wedding—is to become for the first time yourself fully. To live not just for yourself alone anymore but for another self to whom you swear to be true—plight your troth to, your truth to—is in a new way to come fully alive. Things needn't have been that way as far as we know, but that is the way things are, that is the way life is, and if you and I are inclined to have any doubts about it, we can always put it to the test. The test, needless to say, is our lives themselves.

Nobody with any sense claims that marriage is going to be clear sailing all the way, least of all the author of the marriage service. "For better for worse, for richer for poorer, in sickness and in health"—there will be good times and bad times both. There will be times when the vows exchanged here—wild and implausible as in countless ways they are—seem all but impossible to keep. But by holding fast to each other in trust, in patience, in hope, and by holding fast also to him who has promised to be present whenever two or three are gathered together in his name as he was present that day in Cana of Galilee, the impossible becomes possible. The water becomes wine. And by grace we become, little by little, human in spite of ourselves, become whole, become truly loving and lovely at last.

The Final Secret ❋ June 19

THE FINAL SECRET, I think, is this: that the words "You shall love the Lord your God" become in the end less a command than a promise. And the promise is that, yes, on the weary feet of faith and the fragile wings of hope, we will come to love him at last as from the first he has loved us—loved us even in the wilderness, especially in the wilderness, because he has been in the wilderness with us. He has been in the wilderness for us. He has been acquainted with our grief.

And, loving him, we will come at last to love each other too so that, in the end, the name taped on every door will be the name of the one we love.

"And these words which I command you this day shall be upon your heart; and you shall teach them diligently to your children, and you shall talk of them when you sit in your house, and when you walk by the way, and when you rise."

And rise we shall, out of the wilderness, every last one of us, even as out of the wilderness Christ rose before us. That is the promise, and the greatest of all promises.

The Word * June 20

THE BIBLE IS usually very universal and makes you want to *see* something—some image to imagine it by. "The light shines in the darkness," John says, and maybe you see an agonizing burst of light with the darkness folding back like petals, like hands. But the imagery of John is based rather on sound than on sight. It is a Word you hear breaking through the unimaginable silence—a creating word, a word that calls forth, a word that stirs life and is life because it is God's word, John says, and has God in it as your words have you in them, have in them your breath and spirit and tell of who you are. Light and dark, the visual, occur in space, but sound, this Word spoken, occurs in time and starts time going. "Let there *be*" the Word comes, and then there *is*, Creation *is*. Something *is* where before there was nothing and the morning stars sing together and all the Sons of God shout for joy because sequence has begun, time has begun, a story has begun.

Something Dimly Seen * June 21

I REMEMBER A spring or so ago walking with a friend through a stand of maple trees at sugaring time. The sap buckets were hung from the trees, and if you were quiet, you could hear the sap dripping into them: all through the woods, if you kept still, you could hear the hushed drip-dropping of the sap into a thousand buckets or more hung out in the early spring woods with the sun coming down in long shafts through the trees. The sap of a maple is like rainwater, very soft, and almost without taste except for the faintest tinge of sweetness to it, and when my friend said he'd never tried it, I offered to give him a taste. I had to unhook the bucket from the tap to hold it for him, and when he bent his head to drink from it, I tipped the bucket down to his lips, and just as he was about to take a sip, he looked up at me and said, "I have a feeling you ought to be saying some words."

Well, my friend is no more or less religious than the next person, and we'd been chattering on about nothing in particular as we walked along until just at that moment as I tipped the bucket to his lips, he said what he said, and said it partly as a joke. He had a feeling I should be saying some words, he said, as I tipped the bucket to his lips so he could taste for the first time the taste of the lifeblood of a tree. And of course for a moment those unsaid words fell through the air of those woods like the shafts of sun, and it was no joke because the whole place became another place or became more deeply the place it truly was; and he and I became different, something happened for a second to the air around us and between us. It was not much and lasted only for a moment before it was gone. But it happened—this glimpse of something dimly seen, dimly heard, this sense of something deeply hidden.

No Miracle Happens ✳ June 22

IN DOSTOEVSKI'S NOVEL *The Brothers Karamazov* there is an extraordinary scene where the old monk Father Zossima dies. They lay him out in his coffin in the chapel, and all of the monks wait around to see a miracle—for the body to give off the fragrance of a rose, maybe, or his dead face to flicker with a holy light. But no miracle happens, and not only does no miracle happen, but as time goes by something else happens instead. After a while the body shows signs of decomposition, and gradually—though at first the monks try not to notice it— the chapel is filled with the stink of death. No miracle happens, but decay and death happen, the stench of dust returning to dust; and the one who loved the old man most—Alyosha, the youngest of the brothers—stands ready to give the whole thing up as a bad joke, to give up all hope of miracle, to give up his life, to give up if not God himself then the dusty world that hides God from our sight. Then he has this dream.

He is keeping vigil at the old man's coffin while one of the monks reads the story of the Wedding at Cana over it, and when he falls asleep, the dream comes. It is a dream about Cana. There are the guests, there are the young couple sitting, the wise governor of the feast, and suddenly there is old Zossima too—a little thin old man with tiny wrinkles on his face, and of all the things he could be doing, what he is doing in that dream is laughing, laughing at that great feast like a child. And when Alyosha wakes up, he does something that he himself does not fully understand. He tears out of the chapel and rushes down into the monastery yard. He hears inside himself the words, "Water the earth with the tears of your joy and love those tears" and suddenly he gets down on all fours and kisses the earth with his lips; and when he gets up, he's no longer a teary wreck of a boy but a "champion," Dostoevski writes—some kind of crazy champion and hero.

Our Own Story ✸ *June 23*

THE WORDS INSCRIBED on the Statue of Liberty where it stands on Bedloe's Island in New York harbor are familiar to all of us:

Give me your tired, your poor,
Your huddled masses yearning to be free,

The wretched refuse of your teeming shore.
Send these, the homeless, tempest-tossed, to me;
I lift my torch beside the golden door.

It is not great poetry, perhaps, and many a cynical word could be spoken about how the golden door that the goddess of liberty lights with her torch turned out for many to be the door to a wretchedness greater than any they had left behind on the teeming shores of their homelands. But nevertheless I think the old words have power in them still, if we let them, to move us, to touch us close to where we live. And the reason they have such power, I believe, is that one way or another they are words about us. Whether we're rich or poor, whether our forebears came to this country on the Mayflower or a New England slave ship or a nineteenth-century clipper or in a twentieth-century jet, those huddled masses are part of who all of us are, both as individuals and as a people. They are our fathers and mothers. They are our common past. Yet it goes farther and deeper than that. They are our past, and yet they are also ourselves. In countless ways, both hidden and not so hidden, it is you and I who are the homeless and tempest-tossed, waiting on our own Ellis Islands for the great promise to be kept of a new world, a new life, which we haven't yet found. We are the ones who yearn to breathe free. We stand not merely like them but in a sense with them beside the golden door. To read the story of our immigrant forebears as it is summarized on the base of the old statue is to read our own story, and maybe it is only when we see that it is our own story that we can really understand either it or ourselves.

Saying Grace ✳ *June 24*

THERE IS A restaurant in a city somewhere, a sort of quick-lunch place with no tablecloths on the tables, just the ketchup and mustard jars on the bare wood. It seems to be raining outside. An elderly man with a raincoat and umbrella has turned at the door. Another man glances up as he sits there smoking a cigar over a newspaper and the remains of his coffee. Two teenagers sit at a table, one of them with a cigarette in his mouth. They are all looking at the same thing, which is an old woman and a small boy who are sharing a table with the teenagers. Their heads are bowed. They are saying grace. The people watching them watch with dazed fascination. The small boy's ears stick out from his head like the handles of a jug. The old woman's eyes are closed, her hair untidy under a hat that has seen better days. The people are watching something that you feel they may have been part of once but are part of no longer. Through the plate-glass window and the rain, the city looks dim, monotonous, industrial. The old woman and the boy are saying grace there, and for a moment the silence in the place is fathomless. The watchers are watching something that they've all but forgotten and will probably forget again as soon as the moment passes. They could be watching creatures from another planet. The old woman and the boy in their old-fashioned clothes, praying their old-fashioned prayer, are leftovers from a day that has long since ceased to be.

It is not fashionable to praise Norman Rockwell overmuch, that old master of nostalgia and American corn, but we have to praise him at least for this most haunting and maybe most enduring of all his *Saturday Evening Post* covers which touches on something that I think touches us all. It was some thirty years ago that he painted it, but the likeness remains fresh and true to this day, and of course it is a likeness of us and of a world not unlike the one the Seventy-fourth Psalm describes.

A Game We Play ✳ June 25

THERE IS A game we play sometimes. If we could somehow meet one of the great ones of history, which one would we choose? Would it be Shakespeare, maybe, because nobody knew better than he the Hamlet of us and the Ophelia of us, nobody knew better than he this mid-summer night's dream of a darkly enchanted world. Or maybe it would be Abraham Lincoln, with feet no less of clay than our own feet, but whose face, in those last great photographs, seems somehow to have not only all of human suffering in it but traces of goodness and compassion that seem almost more than human. Or maybe it would be Saint Joan, the Maid of Orleans, whose very weakness was her strength, her innocence her armor, lighting up the dark skies of the fifteenth century like a star. But the great ones of the world, if you and I were to meet them, would have nothing to give us but their greatness, nothing to ask of us but our admiration; and we would go to such a meeting full of awe to be sure but knowing more or less what to expect. In the saints and heroes of the past, we would find someone greater than we are, more human, more complete, but cut from the same cloth as we are after all, someone who was as often lost, as full of doubt, as full of hope, waiting no less than you and I wait for we're not sure what to deliver us at last.

We Catch Glimmers ✳ June 26

RELIGION AS A word points to that area of human experience where in one way or another man comes upon mystery as a summons to pilgrimage; where he senses meanings no less overwhelming because they can be only hinted at in myth and ritual; where he glimpses a destination that he can never know fully until he reaches it.

We are all of us more mystics than we believe or choose to believe—life is complicated enough as it is, after all. We have seen more than we let on, even to ourselves. Through some moment of beauty or pain, some sudden turning of our lives, we catch glimmers at least of what the saints are blinded by;

only then, unlike the saints, we tend to go on as though nothing has happened. To go on as though something has happened, even though we are not sure what it was or just where we are supposed to go with it, is to enter the dimension of life that religion is a word for.

Some, of course, go to the typewriter. First the lump in the throat, the stranger's face unfurling like a flower, and then the clatter of the keys, the ting-a-ling of the right-hand margin. One thinks of Pascal sewing into his jacket, where after his death a servant found it, his "since about half past ten in the evening until about half past midnight. Fire. Certitude. Certitude. Feeling. Joy. Peace," stammering it out like a child because he had to. Fire, fire, and then the scratch of pen on paper. There are always some who have to set it down in black and white.

Shakespeare at His Greatest ✳ June 27

THERE IS VERY little religion in Shakespeare, but when he is greatest, he is most religious. It is curious that the plays that fit this best are, like The Lord of the Rings, in their own way fairy tales. There is The Tempest, that masque of his old age where all comes right in the end, where like Rembrandt in his last self-portraits Shakespeare smiles up out of his wrinkles and speaks into the night a golden word too absurd to be anything perhaps but true, the laughter of things beyond the tears of things.

And there is King Lear, its Cinderella opening with the wicked sisters and the good one. But then the fairy tale is turned on its head, and although everything comes right in the end, everything also does not come right—religion books are usually tidier. Blinded, old Gloucester sees the truth about his sons but too late to save the day. Cordelia is

vindicated in her innocence only to be destroyed more gro-
tesquely because more pointlessly than her sisters in their
lustful cunning. And Lear himself emerges from his madness
to become truly a king at last, but dies then babbling that his
dead darling lives and fumbling with a button at his throat.

Power of Words ✳ June 28

IF LITERATURE IS a metaphor for the writer's experience, a
mirror in which that experience is at least partially reflected, it is at the same time a mirror in which the reader can
also see his or her experience reflected in a new and potentially transforming way. This is what it is like to search for
God in a world where cruelty and pain hide God, Dostoevski
says—"How like a winter hath my absence been from thee";
how like seeing a poor woman in a dream with a starving
child at her breast; how like Father Zossima kneeling down
at the feet of Dmitri Karamazov because he sees that great
suffering is in store for him and because he knows, as John
Donne did, that suffering is holy. And you and I, his readers,
come away from our reading with no more proof of the existence or nonexistence of God than we had before, with no
particular moral or message to frame on the wall, but em-
powered by a new sense of the depths of love and pity and
hope that is transmitted to us through Dostoevski's powerful
words.

Words written fifty years ago, a hundred years ago, a thousand years ago, can have as much of this power today as ever
they had it then to come alive for us and in us and to make
us more alive within ourselves. That, I suppose, is the final
mystery as well as the final power of words: that not even
across great distances of time and space do they ever lose their
capacity for becoming incarnate. And when these words tell
of virtue and nobility, when they move us closer to that truth

and gentleness of spirit by which we become fully human, the reading of them is sacramental; and a library is as holy a place as any temple is holy because through the words which are treasured in it the Word itself becomes flesh again and again and dwells among us and within us, full of grace and truth.

Final Answers ✳ June 29

N OT LONG AGO I listened to an astrophysicist talk fascinatingly about the extraordinary strides science has made in understanding such things as the origin of the universe, the nature of matter, the relationship of space to time, and he spoke with such conviction and authority that I found myself asking him finally if he could conceive of a time, maybe a hundred years hence, when all his answers to these great questions might look as primitive and inadequate as the theories of, say, medical science a hundred years ago look to us now. His reply was unabashed. He said that as far as he was concerned, these answers that modern science has reached are final answers, and all we need now is time and money enough to continue research into their ramifications and implications. Nobody could be less qualified than I am to pass judgment on the findings of science at any level, but because I know that, like all answers, these scientific answers are expressed in words and in numbers, which I take to be only another form of words, I simply cannot believe them to be final. It is as impossible for me to believe that the words even of scientific genius can say all there is to say about the origin of the universe as it is impossible for me to believe that the words even of Sophocles or Shakespeare can say all there is to say about human tragedy or the words even of Jesus Christ can say all there is to say about God and about our lives under God. Part, at least, of what I believe the New Testament means by calling Jesus himself the Word of God is that in the final analysis not even the most authentic and inspired words he ever spoke could exhaust the mystery he came to reveal, and that when he proclaimed not "What I say is the truth" but, instead, "I am the truth," he meant, among other things, that the truth cannot be fully caught in any expression of the truth in words but only in the great eloquence and complexity and simplicity of his own life.

Unthinkable ✳ June 30

DYING AND DISSOLUTION continue to strike fear in me. Death itself does not. Ten years ago if somebody had offered me a vigorous, healthy life that would never end, I would have said yes. Today I think I would say no. I love my life as much as I ever did and will cling on to it for as long as I can, but life without death has become as unthinkable to me as day without night or waking without sleep.

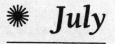 *July*

By Letting Go ✳ July 1

WE FIND BY LOSING. We hold fast by letting go. We become something new by ceasing to be something old. This seems to be close to the heart of that mystery. I know no more now than I ever did about the far side of death as the last letting-go of all, but I begin to know that I do not need to know and that I do not need to be afraid of not knowing. God knows. That is all that matters.

Out of Nothing he creates Something. Out of the End he creates the Beginning. Out of selfness we grow, by his grace, toward selflessness, and out of that final selflessness, which is the loss of self altogether, "eye hath not seen nor ear heard, neither have entered into the heart of man" what new marvels he will bring to pass next. All's lost. All's found. And if such words sound childish, so be it. Out of each old self that dies some precious essence is preserved for the new self that is born; and within the child-self that is part of us all, there is perhaps nothing more precious than the fathomless capacity to trust.

Principles ✳ July 2

PRINCIPLES ARE WHAT people have instead of God.

To be a Christian means among other things to be willing if necessary to sacrifice even your highest principles for God's or your neighbor's sake the way a Christian pacifist must be willing to pick up a baseball bat if there's no other way to stop a man from savagely beating a child.

Jesus didn't forgive his executioners on principle but because in some unimaginable way he was able to love them.

"Principle" is an even duller word than "Religion."

Avarice ✳ July 3

A VARICE, GREED, concupiscence, and so forth are all based on the mathematical truism that the more you get, the more you have. The remark of Jesus that it is more blessed to give than to receive (Acts 20:35) is based on the human truth that the more you give away in love, the more you are. It is not just for the sake of other people that Jesus tells us to give rather than get, but for our own sakes too.

Patriotism ✳ July 4

A LL "ISMS" RUN OUT IN the end, and good riddance to most of them. Patriotism for example.

If patriots are people who stand by their country right or wrong, Germans who stood by Adolf Hitler and the Third Reich should be adequate proof that we've had enough of them.

If patriots are people who believe not only that anything they consider unpatriotic is wrong but that anything they consider wrong is unpatriotic, the late Senator Joseph McCarthy and his backers should be enough to make us avoid them like the plague. .

If patriots are people who believe things like "Better Dead Than Red," they should be shown films of Hiroshima and Nagasaki on August 6 and 9, 1945, respectively, and then be taken off to the funny farm.

The only patriots worth their salt are the ones who love their country enough to see that in a nuclear age it is not going to survive unless the world survives. True patriots are no longer champions of Democracy, Communism, or anything like that but champions of the Human Race. It is not the Homeland that they feel called on to defend at any cost but the planet Earth as Home. If in the interests of making sure we don't blow ourselves off the map once and for all, we end up relinquishing a measure of national sovereignty to some international body, so much the worse for national sovereignty.

There is only one Sovereignty that matters ultimately, and it is of another sort altogether.

Crux of the Matter ✻ July 5

The following eight meditations (through July 12) are drawn from a 200th anniversary sermon at the Congregational church in Rupert, Vermont:

SINCE 1786 PEOPLE have been coming here the way you and I came here today. Men who fought in the American Revolution and the widows of men who never got back from it. Civil War veterans. Two centuries worth of farmers, dairymen, mill workers, an occasional traveler. Old men and old women with most of their lives behind them, and young men and young women with most of their lives ahead of them. People who made a go of it and are remembered still, and people who somehow never left their mark in any way the world noticed and aren't remembered anymore by anybody. Despite the enormous differences between them, all these men and women entered this building just the way you and I entered it a few minutes ago because of one thing they had in common.

What they had in common was that, like us, they believed (or sometimes believed and sometimes didn't believe; or wanted to believe; or liked to think they believed) that the universe, that everything there is, didn't come about by chance but was created by God. Like us they believed, on their best days anyway, that all appearances to the contrary notwithstanding, this God was a God like Jesus, which is to say a God of love. That, I think, is the crux of the matter. In 1786 and 1886 and 1986 and all the years between, that is at the heart of what has made this place a church. That is what all the whooping has been about. In the beginning it was not some vast cosmic explosion that made the heavens and the earth. It was a loving God who did. That is our faith and the faith of all the ones who came before us.

Music So Lovely ✳ July 6

I DON'T SUPPOSE there is any passage in either the Old Testament or the New that sums up the faith this church was founded on more eloquently and movingly than the 23rd Psalm. "The Lord is my shepherd. I shall not want." How many times would you guess those words have been spoken here over the years, especially at dark moments when people needed all the faith they could muster? How many times have we spoken them ourselves, at our own dark moments? But for all their power to bring comfort, do the words hold water? This faith in God that they affirm, is it borne out by our own experience of life on this planet? That is a hard and painful question to raise, but let us honor the occasion by raising it anyway. Does this ancient and beautiful psalm set forth a faith that in the secrecy of our hearts we can still honestly subscribe to? And what exactly is that faith it sets forth? The music of the psalm is so lovely that it's hard sometimes to hear through it to what the psalm is saying.

Like a Shepherd ✳ July 7

GOD'S IN HIS HEAVEN, all's right with the world," Robert Browning wrote, and the psalm is certainly not saying that any more than you or I can say it either. Whoever wrote it had walked through the valley of the shadow the way one way or another you and I have walked there too. He says so himself. He believed that God was in his Heaven despite the fact that he knew as well as we do that all was far from right with the world. And he believed that God was like a shepherd.

When I think of shepherds, I think of one man in particular I know who used to keep sheep here in Rupert a few years back. Some of them he gave names to, and some of them he didn't, but he knew them equally well either way. If one of them got lost, he didn't have a moment's peace till he found it again. If one of them got sick or hurt, he would move Heaven and earth to get it well again. He would feed them out of a bottle when they were new-born lambs if for some reason the mother wasn't around or wouldn't "own" them, as he put it. He always called them in at the end of the day so the wild dogs wouldn't get them. I've seen him wade through snow up to his knees with a bale of hay in each hand to feed them on bitter cold winter evenings, shaking it out and putting it in the manger. I've stood with him in their shed with a forty watt bulb hanging down from the low ceiling to light up their timid, greedy, foolish, half holy faces as they pushed and butted each other to get at it because if God is like a shepherd, there are more than just a few ways, needless to say, that people like you and me are like sheep. Being timid, greedy, foolish, and half holy is only part of it.

Like sheep we get hungry, and hungry for more than just food. We get thirsty for more than just drink. Our *souls* get hungry and thirsty; in fact it is often that sense of inner emptiness that makes us know we have souls in the first place. There is nothing that the world has to give us, there is nothing that we have to give to each other even, that ever quite fills them. But once in a while that inner emptiness is filled even so. That is part of what the psalm means by saying that God is like a shepherd, I think. It means that, like a shepherd, he feeds us. He feeds that part of us which is hungriest and most in need of feeding.

I Shall Not Want ✸ July 8

I SHALL NOT WANT," the psalm says. Is that true? There are lots of things we go on wanting, go on lacking, whether we believe in God or not. They are not just material things like a new roof or a better paying job, but things like good health, things like happiness for our children, things like being understood and appreciated, like relief from pain, like some measure of inner peace not just for ourselves but for the people we love and for whom we pray. Believers and unbelievers alike we go on wanting plenty our whole lives through. We long for what never seems to come. We pray for what never seems to be clearly given. But when the psalm says "I shall not want," maybe it is speaking the utter truth anyhow. Maybe it means that if we keep our eyes open, if we keep our hearts and lives open, we will at least never be in want of the one thing we want more than anything else. Maybe it means that whatever else is withheld, the shepherd never withholds himself, and he is what we want more than anything else.

The Paths of Trust ✸ July 9

N OT AT EVERY moment of our lives, Heaven knows, but at certain rare moments of greenness and stillness, we are shepherded by the knowledge that though all is far from right with any world you and I know anything about, all is right deep down. All will be right at last. I suspect that is at least part of what "He leadeth me in the paths of righteousness" is all about. It means righteousness not just in the sense of *doing* right but in the sense of *being* right—being right with God, trusting the deep-down rightness of the life God has created for us and in us, and riding that trust the way a red-tailed hawk rides the currents of the air in this valley where we live. I suspect that the paths of righteousness he leads us in are more than anything else the paths of trust like that and the kind of life that grows out of that trust. I think that is the shelter he calls us to with a bale in either hand when the wind blows bitter and the shadows are dark.

Saints and Sinners Alike ✳ July 10

"YEA, THOUGH I walk through the valley of the shadow of death, I will fear no evil." The psalm does not pretend that evil and death do not exist. Terrible things happen, and they happen to good people as well as to bad people. Even the paths of righteousness lead through the valley of the shadow. Death lies ahead for all of us, saints and sinners alike, and for all the ones we love. The psalmist doesn't try to explain evil. He doesn't try to minimize evil. He simply says he will not fear evil. For all the power that evil has, it doesn't have the power to make him afraid.

Extraordinary Event ✳ July 11

IN THE YEAR 1831, it seems, this church was repaired and several new additions were made. One of them was a new steeple with a bell in it, and once it was set in place and painted, apparently, an extraordinary event took place. "When the steeple was added," Howard Mudgett writes in his history, "one agile Lyman Woodard stood on his head in the belfry with his feet toward Heaven."

That's the one and only thing I've been able to find out about Lyman Woodard, whoever he was, but it is enough. I love him for doing what he did. It was a crazy thing to do. It was a risky thing to do. It ran counter to all standards of New England practicality and prudence. It stood the whole idea that you're supposed to be nothing but solemn in church on its head just like Lyman himself standing upside down on his. And it was also a magical and magnificent and Mozartian thing to do.

If the Lord is indeed our shepherd, then everything goes topsy-turvy. Losing becomes finding and crying becomes laughing. The last become first and the weak become strong. Instead of life being done in by death in the end as we always supposed, death is done in finally by life in the end. If the Lord is our host at the great feast, then the sky is the limit.

Our Richest Treasure ✳ *July 12*

THERE IS PLENTY of work to be done down here, God knows. To struggle each day to walk the paths of righteousness is no pushover, and struggle we must because just as we are fed like sheep in green pastures, we must also feed his sheep, which are each other. Jesus, our shepherd, tells us that. We must help bear each other's burdens. We must pray for each other. We must nourish each other, weep with each other, rejoice with each other. Sometimes we must just learn to let each other alone. In short, we must love each other. We must never forget that. But let us never forget Lyman Woodard either silhouetted up there against the blue Rupert sky. Let us join him in the belfry with our feet toward Heaven like his because Heaven is where we are heading. That is our faith and what better image of faith could there be? It is a little crazy. It is a little risky. It sets many a level head wagging. And it is also our richest treasure and the source of our deepest joy and highest hope. Through Jesus Christ our Lord.

Pride ✳ July 13

PRIDE IS SELF-LOVE, and in one sense a Christian is enjoined to be proud; i.e., another way of saying Love your neighbor as yourself is to say Love yourself as your neighbor. That doesn't mean your pulse is supposed to quicken every time you look in the mirror any more than it's supposed to quicken every time your neighbor passes the window. It means simply that the ability to work for your own good despite all the less than admirable things you know about yourself is closely related to the ability to work for your neighbor's good despite all the less than admirable things you know about him. It also means that just as in this sense love of self and love of neighbor go hand in hand, so do dislike of self and dislike of neighbor. For example (a) the more I dislike my neighbor, the more I'm apt to dislike myself for disliking him and him for making me dislike myself and so on, and (b) I am continually tempted to take out on my neighbor the dislike I feel for myself, just the way if I crack my head on a low door I'm very apt to kick the first cat, child, or chair unlucky enough to catch my bloodshot eye.

Self-love or pride is a sin when, instead of leading you to share with others the self you love, it leads you to keep your self in perpetual safe-deposit. You not only don't accrue any interest that way but become less and less interesting every day.

Worship ✳ July 14

PHRASES LIKE WORSHIP Service or Service of Worship are tautologies. To worship God *means* to serve him. Basically there are two ways to do it. One way is to do things for him that he needs to have done—run errands for him, carry messages for him, fight on his side, feed his lambs, and so on. The other way is to do things for him that you need to do—sing songs for him, create beautiful things for him, give things up for him, tell him what's on your mind and in your heart, in general rejoice in him and make a fool of yourself for him the way lovers have always made fools of themselves for the one they love.

A Quaker Meeting, a Pontifical High Mass, the Family Service at First Presbyterian, a Holy Roller Happening—unless there is an element of joy and foolishness in the proceedings, the time would be better spent doing something useful.

Below a Time ✸ July 15

WHAT CHILD, WHILE summer is happening, bothers to think much that summer will end? What child, when snow is on the ground, stops to remember that not long ago the ground was snowless? It is by its content rather than its duration that a child knows time, by its quality rather than its quantity—happy times and sad times, the time the rabbit bit your finger, the time you had your first taste of bananas and cream, the time you were crying yourself to sleep when somebody came and lay down beside you in the dark for comfort. Childhood's time is Adam and Eve's time before they left the garden for good and from that time on divided everything into before and after. It is the time before God told them that the day would come when they would surely die with the result that from that point on they made clocks and calendars for counting their time out like money and never again lived through a day of their lives without being haunted somewhere in the depths of them by the knowledge that each day brought them closer to the end of their lives.

THE ANCIENT DRUIDS are said to have taken a special interest in in-between things like mistletoe, which is neither quite a plant nor quite a tree, and mist, which is neither quite rain nor quite air, and dreams which are neither quite waking nor quite sleep. They believed that in such things as those they were able to glimpse the mystery of two worlds at once.

Adolescents can have the same glimpse by looking in the full-length mirror on back of the bathroom door. The opaque glance and the pimples. The fancy new nakedness they're all dressed up in with no place to go. The eyes full of secrets they have a strong hunch everybody is on to. The shadowed brow. Being not quite a child and not quite a grown-up either is hard work, and they look it. Living in two worlds at once is no picnic.

One of the worlds, of course, is innocence, self-forgetfulness, openness, playing for fun. The other is experience, self-consciousness, guardedness, playing for keeps. Some of us go on straddling them both for years.

The rich young ruler of the Gospels comes to mind (Matthew 19:16–22). It is with all the recklessness of a child that he asks Jesus what he must do to be perfect. And when Jesus tells him to give everything to the poor, it is with all the prudence of a senior vice-president of Morgan Guaranty that he walks sadly away.

We become fully and undividedly human, I suppose, when we discover that the ultimate prudence is a kind of holy recklessness, and our passion for having finds peace in our passion for giving, and playing for keeps is itself the greatest fun. Once this has happened and our adolescence is behind us at last, the delight of the child and the sagacity of the Supreme Court Justice are largely indistinguishable.

Quality of Time ✳ July 17

THE GREEK WORD *chronos* means "time" in a quantitative sense, chronological time, time that you can divide into minutes and years, time as duration. It is the sense that we mean when we say, "What time is it?" or "How much time do I have?" or "Time like an ever-flowing stream," in one of the hymns that we sing. But in Greek there is also the word *kairos*, which means "time" in a qualitative sense—not the kind that a clock measures but time that cannot be measured at all, time that is characterized by what happens in it. *Kairos* time is the kind that you mean when you say that "the time is ripe" to do something, "It's time to tell the truth," a truth-telling kind of time. Or "I had a good time"—the time had something about it that made me glad. The ancient poet who wrote the Book of Ecclesiastes was using time in a *kairos* sense when he wrote of a time to weep and a time to laugh, a time to keep silence and a time to speak.

Vocation ✳ July 18

IT COMES FROM the Latin *vocare*, to call, and means the work a man is called to by God.

There are all different kinds of voices calling you to all different kinds of work, and the problem is to find out which is the voice of God rather than of Society, say, or the Super-ego, or Self-Interest.

By and large a good rule for finding out is this. The kind of work God usually calls you to is the kind of work (*a*) that you need most to do and (*b*) that the world most needs to have done. If you really get a kick out of your work, you've presumably met requirement (*a*), but if your work is writing TV deodorant commercials, the chances are you've missed requirement (*b*). On the other hand, if your work is being a doctor in a leper colony, you have probably met requirement (*b*), but if most of the time you're bored and depressed by it, the chances are you have not only bypassed (*a*) but probably aren't helping your patients much either.

Neither the hair shirt nor the soft berth will do. The place God calls you to is the place where your deep gladness and the world's deep hunger meet.

Algebraic Preaching ✳ July 19

X + Y = Z. IF YOU know the value of one of the letters, you know something. If you know the value of two, you can probably figure out the whole thing. If you don't know the value of any, you don't know much.

Preachers tend to forget this. "Accept Jesus Christ as your personal Lord and Savior and be saved from your sins," or something like that, has meaning and power and relevance only if the congregation has some notion of what, humanly speaking, sin is, or being saved is, or who Jesus is, or what accepting him involves. If preachers make no attempt to flesh out these words in terms of everyday human experience (maybe even their own) but simply repeat with variations the same old formulas week after week, then the congregation might just as well spend Sunday morning at home with the funnies.

The blood atonement. The communion of saints. The Holy Ghost. If people's understanding of theological phrases goes little deeper than their dictionary or catechetical definitions, then to believe in them has just about as much effect on their lives as to believe that Columbus discovered America in 1492 or that $E = mc^2$.

Coming home from church one snowy day, Emerson wrote, "The snow was real but the preacher spectral." In other words nothing he heard from the pulpit suggested that the preacher was a human being more or less like everybody else with the same dark secrets and high hopes, the same doubts and passions, the same weaknesses and strengths. Undoubtedly he preached on matters like sin and salvation but without ever alluding to the wretched, lost moments or the glad, liberating moments of his own life or anybody else's.

There is perhaps no better proof for the existence of God than the way year after year he survives the way his professional friends promote him. If there are people who remain unconvinced, let them tune in their TVs to almost any of the big-time pulpit-pounders almost any Sunday morning of the year.

Jonathan ✳ *July 20*

WHEN KING SAUL found his oldest son, Jonathan, siding with David, whom he considered his arch-enemy, he cursed him out by saying that he had made David a friend "to your own shame, and to the shame of your mother's nakedness" (1 Samuel 20:30). They are strong words, and some have interpreted them as meaning that Saul suspected a sexual relationship between the two young men.

This view can be further buttressed by such verses as "The soul of Jonathan was knit to the soul of David, and Jonathan loved him as his own soul" (1 Samuel 18:1) and the words David spoke when he learned of Jonathan's death, "Your love to me was wonderful, passing the love of women" (2 Samuel 1:26). When David and Jonathan said good-bye to each other for almost the last time, they "kissed one another and wept" (1 Samuel 20:41), we're told, and there are undoubtedly those who would point to that too as evidence.

There seem to be at least three things to say in response to all this.

The first is that both emotions and the language used to express them ran a good deal higher in the ancient Near East than they do in Little Rock, Arkansas, or Boston, Massachusetts, or even Los Angeles, California, and for that and other reasons the theory that such passages as have been cited necessarily indicate a homosexual relationship is almost certainly false.

The second is that it's sad, putting it rather mildly, that we live at a time when in many quarters two men can't embrace or weep together or speak of loving one another without arousing the suspicion that they must also go to bed together.

Third, in the unlikely event that there was a sexual dimension to the friendship between Jonathan and David, it is significant that the only one to see it as shameful was King Saul, who was a manic depressive with homicidal tendencies and an eventual suicide.

Everywhere else in the Book of Samuel it seems to be assumed that what was important about the relationship was not what may or may not have been its physical side but the affection, respect, and faithfulness that kept it alive through thick and thin until finally Jonathan was killed in battle and David rent his garments and wept over him.

(1 SAMUEL 19–2 SAMUEL 1, PASSIM)

"Creative" Writing ✳ July 21

The next four meditations are from a talk on the occasion of the presentation of the Whiting Writers' awards.

SOMETIME IN THE early 1950s, for two years running, I taught creative writing at the summer session of the Washington Square branch of N.Y.U. . . . I was uneasy about teaching creative writing for a number of reasons, one of which was that I've never been sure that it is something that can really be taught—for better or worse, I don't think anybody ever taught it to me anyway—and another that I had absolutely no idea how to teach it right if it was. But my main uneasiness came from somewhere else. Suppose, I thought, that by some fluke I did teach it at least right enough so that maybe a couple of people, say, learned how to write with some real measure of effectiveness and power. The question then became for me what were they going to write effectively and powerfully about? Suppose they chose to write effective and powerful racist tracts or sadistic pornography or novels about warped and unpleasant people doing warped and unpleasant things? Or, speaking less sensationally, suppose they used the skills I had somehow managed to teach them to write books simply for the sake of making a name for themselves, or making money, or making a stir. It seemed to me and still does that to teach people how to write well without knowing what they are going to write about is like teaching people how to shoot well without knowing what or whom they are going to shoot at.

Word and Deed ✻ July 22

I THINK OF PAINTING and music as *subcutaneous* arts. They get under your skin. They may get deeper than that eventually, but it takes a while, and they get there to some extent tinged by if not diluted by the conditions under which you saw them or heard them. Writing on the other hand strikes me as *intravenous*. As you sit there only a few inches from the printed page, the words you read go directly into the bloodstream and go into it at full strength. More than the painting you see or the music you hear, the words you read become in the very act of reading them part of who you are, especially if they are the words of exceptionally promising writers. If there is poison in the words, you are poisoned; if there is nourishment, you are nourished; if there is beauty, you are made a little more beautiful. In Hebrew, the word *dabar* means both word and also deed. A word doesn't merely say something, it does something. It brings something into being. It makes something happen. What do writers want their books to make happen?

"Open a Vein" ✳ July 23

I WISH THAT I had told my writing students to give some thought to what they wanted their books to make happen inside the people who read them, and I also wish that I had told them what Red Smith said about writing although I suppose it is possible that he hadn't gotten around to saying it yet . . . . What Red Smith said was more or less this: "Writing is really quite simple; all you have to do is sit down at your typewriter and open a vein"—another haematological image. From the writer's vein into the reader's vein: for better or worse a transfusion.

I couldn't agree with Red Smith more. For my money anyway, the only books worth reading are books written in blood. . . .

Write about what you really care about is what he is saying. Write about what truly matters to you—not just things to catch the eye of the world but things to touch the quick of the world the way they have touched you to the quick, which is why you are writing about them. Write not just with wit and eloquence and style and relevance but with passion. Then the things that your books make happen will be things worth happening—things that make the people who read them a little more passionate themselves for their pains, by which I mean a little more alive, a little wiser, a little more beautiful, a little more open and understanding, in short a little more human. I believe that those are the best things that books can make happen to people, and we could all make a list of the particular books that have made them happen to us.

Books Like These ✳ July 24

THE WRITERS WHO get my personal award are the ones who show exceptional promise of looking at their lives in this world as candidly and searchingly and feelingly as they know how and then of telling the rest of us what they have found there most worth finding. We need the eyes of writers like that to see through. We need the blood of writers like that in our veins.

◆　◆　◆

J. D. Salinger's *The Catcher in the Rye* was one of the first books I read that did it to me, that started me on the long and God knows far from finished journey on the way to becoming a human being—started making *that* happen. What I chiefly learned from it was that even the slobs and phonies and morons that Holden Caulfield runs into on his travels are, like Seymour Glass's Fat Lady, "Christ Himself, buddy," as Zooey explains it to his sister Franny in the book that bears her name. Even the worst among us are precious. Even the most precious among us bear crosses. That was a word that went straight into my bloodstream and has been there ever since. Along similar lines I think also of Robertson Davies' Deptford trilogy, Ford Madox Ford's *The Good Soldier*, Rose Macaulay's *The Towers of Trebizond*, George Garrett's *Death of the Fox*, some of the early novels of John Updike like *The Poorhouse Fair* and *The Centaur*, John Irving's *A Prayer for Owen Meany*. I think of stories like Flannery O'Connor's "The Artificial Nigger" and Raymond Carver's "Feathers" and works of non-fiction, to use that odd term (like calling poetry non-prose) such as Annie Dillard's *Holy the Firm* and Geoffrey Wolff's *The*

Duke of Deception and Robert Capon's *The Supper of the Lamb* or plays like *Death of a Salesman* or *Our Town*.

Patterns Were Set ✳ July 25

After some discussion mainly of childhood and boyhood reading, Buechner comments:

NOTHING WAS MORE remote from my thought at this period than theological speculation—except for Greene's, these books were all childhood or early boyhood reading—but certain patterns were set, certain rooms were made ready, so that when, years later, I came upon Saint Paul for the first time and heard him say, "God chose what is foolish in the world to shame the wise, God chose what is weak in the world to shame the strong, God chose what is low and despised in the world, even things that are not, to bring to nothing things that are," I had the feeling that I knew something of what he was talking about. Something of the divine comedy that we are all of us involved in. Something of grace.

Parable ✳ July 26

A PARABLE IS A small story with a large point. Most of the ones Jesus told have a kind of sad fun about them. The parables of the Crooked Judge (Luke 18:1–8), the Sleepy Friend (Luke 11:5–8), and the Distraught Father (Luke 11:11–13) are really jokes in their way, at least part of whose point seems to be that a silly question deserves a silly answer. In the Prodigal Son (Luke 15:11–32) the elder brother's pious pique when the returning prodigal gets the red-carpet treatment is worthy of Molière's *Tartuffe*, as is the outraged legalism of the Laborers in the Vineyard (Matthew 20:1–16) when Johnny-Come-Lately gets as big a slice of the worm as the Early Bird. The point of the Unjust Steward is that it's better to be a resourceful rascal than a saintly schlemiel (Luke 16:1–8), and of the Talents that, spiritually speaking, playing the market will get you further than playing it safe (Matthew 25:14–30).

Both the sadness and the fun are at their richest, however, in the parable of the Great Banquet (Luke 14:16–24). The Beautiful People all send in their excuses, of course—their real estate, their livestock, their sex lives—so the host sends his social secretary out into the streets to bring in the poor, the maimed, the blind, the lame.

The string ensemble strikes up the overture to *The Bartered Bride,* the champagne glasses are filled, the cold pheasant is passed round, and there they sit by candlelight with their white canes and their empty sleeves, their Youngstown haircuts, their orthopedic shoes, their sleazy clothes, their aluminum walkers. A woman with a harelip proposes a toast. An old man with the face of Lear on the heath and a party hat does his best to rise to his feet. A deaf-mute thinks people are starting to go home and pushes back from the table. Rose petals float in the finger bowls. The strings shift into the *Liebestod.*

With parables and jokes both, if you've got to have it explained, don't bother.

Neighbor ✳ July 27

WHEN JESUS SAID to love your neighbor, a lawyer who was present asked him to clarify what he meant by *neighbor.* He wanted a legal definition he could refer to in case the question of loving one ever happened to come up. He presumably wanted something on the order of: "A neighbor (hereinafter referred to as the party of the first part) is to be construed as meaning a person of Jewish descent whose legal residence is within a radius of no more than three statute miles from one's own legal residence unless there is another person of Jewish descent (hereinafter to be referred to as the party of the second part) living closer to the party of the first part than one is oneself, in which case the party of the second part is to be construed as neighbor to the party of the first part and one is oneself relieved of all responsibility of any sort or kind whatsoever."

Instead Jesus told the story of the Good Samaritan (Luke 10:25–37), the point of which seems to be that your neighbor is to be construed as meaning anybody who needs you. The lawyer's response is left unrecorded.

Aging ❋ *July 28*

WHEN YOU HIT SIXTY or so, you start having a new feeling about your own generation. Like you they can remember the Trilon and Perisphere, Lum and Abner, ancient Civil War veterans riding in open cars at the rear of Memorial Day parades, the Lindbergh kidnapping, cigarettes in flat fifties which nobody believed then could do any more to you than cut your wind. Like you they know about blackouts, Bond Rallies, A-stickers, Kilroy was Here. They remember where they were when the news came through that FDR was dead of a stroke in Warm Springs, and they could join you in singing "Bei Mir Bist Du Schön" and "The Last Time I Saw Paris." They wept at Spencer Tracy with his legs bitten off in *Captains Courageous*.

As time goes by, you start picking them out in crowds. There aren't as many of them around as there used to be. More likely than not, you don't say anything, and neither do they, but something seems to pass between you anyhow. They have come from the same beginning. They have seen the same sights along the way. They are bound for the same end and will get there about the same time you do. There are some who by the looks of them you wouldn't invite home for dinner on a bet, but they are your *compagnons de voyage* even so. You wish them well.

It is sad to think that it has taken you so many years to reach so obvious a conclusion.

Absalom ✳ *July 29*

ALMOST FROM THE start, Absalom had a number of strikes against him. For one thing, he was much too handsome for his own good, and his special pride was such a magnificent head of hair that once a year when he had it trimmed, the trimmings alone tipped the scales at three and a half pounds. For another thing, his father, King David, was always either spoiling him rotten or reading him the riot act. This did not promote stability of character. He murdered his lecherous brother Amnon for fooling around with their sister Tamar, and when the old war-horse Joab wouldn't help him patch things up with David afterwards, he set fire to his hay field. All Israel found this kind of derring-do irresistible, of course, and when he eventually led a revolt against his father, a lot of them joined him.

On the eve of the crucial battle, David was a wreck. If he was afraid he might lose his throne, he was even more afraid he might lose Absalom. The boy was the thorn in his flesh, but he was also the apple of his eye, and before the fighting started, he told the chiefs of staff till they were sick of hearing it that if Absalom fell into their clutches, they must promise to go easy on him for his father's sake. Remembering what had happened to his hay field, old Joab kept his fingers crossed, and when he found Absalom caught in the branches of an oak tree by his beautiful hair, he ran him through without blinking an eye. When they broke the news to David, it broke his heart, just as simple as that, and he cried out in words that have echoed down the centuries ever since. "O my son Absalom, my son, my son," he said. "Would I had died instead of you, O Absalom, my son, my son" (2 Samuel 18:33).

He meant it, of course. If he could have done the boy's dying for him, he would have done it. If he could have paid the price for the boy's betrayal of him, he would have paid it. If he could have given his own life to make the boy alive again, he would have given it. But even a king can't do things like that. As later history was to prove, it takes a God.

(2 SAMUEL 13–19)

Hidden Gifts ❋ July 30

Yes, time heals all wounds or at least dresses them, makes them endurable. Yes, at the king's death, the grief of the prince is mitigated by becoming king himself. Yes, the great transfiguring power of sex stirs early and seismically in all of us. Which of us can look at our own religion or lack of it without seeing in it the elements of wish-fulfillment? Which of us can look back at our own lives without seeing in them the role of blind chance and dumb luck? But faith, says the author of the Epistle to the Hebrews, is "the assurance of things hoped for, the conviction of things not seen," and looking back at those distant years I choose not to deny, either, the compelling sense of an unseen giver and a series of hidden gifts as not only another part of their reality, but the deepest part of all.

Humility ❋ July 31

Humility is often confused with the gentlemanly self-deprecation of saying you're not much of a bridge player when you know perfectly well you are. Conscious or otherwise, this kind of humility is a form of gamesmanship.

If you really *aren't* much of a bridge player, you're apt to be rather proud of yourself for admitting it so humbly. This kind of humility is a form of low comedy.

True humility doesn't consist of thinking ill of yourself but of not thinking of yourself much differently from the way you'd be apt to think of anybody else. It is the capacity for being no more and no less pleased when you play your own hand well than when your opponents do.

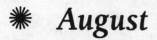 *August*

Zaccheus ❋ August 1

Z ACCHEUS APPEARS JUST once in the New Testament, and his story is brief (Luke 19:1–10). It is also one of the few places in the Gospels where we're given any visual detail. Maybe that is part of what makes it stand out.

We're told that Zaccheus was a runt, for one thing. That is why when Jesus was reported to be en route into Jericho and the crowds gathered to see what they could see, Zaccheus had to climb a tree to get a look himself. Luke says the tree he climbed was a sycamore tree.

We're also told that Zaccheus was a crook—a Jewish legman for the Roman IRS who, following the practice of the day, raked in as much more than the going tax as he could get and pocketed the difference. When people saw Zaccheus oiling down the street, they crossed to the other side.

The story goes like this. The sawed-off shyster is perched in the sycamore tree. Jesus opens his mouth to speak. All Jericho hugs itself in anticipation of hearing him give the man Holy Hell. *Woe unto you! Repent! Wise up!* is the least of what they expect. What Jesus says is, "Come down on the double. I'm staying at your house." The mob points out that the man he's talking to is a public disaster. Jesus' silence is deafening.

It is not reported how Zaccheus got out of the sycamore, but the chances are good that he fell out in pure astonishment. He said, "I'm giving everything back. In spades." Maybe he even meant it. Jesus said, "Three cheers for the Irish!"

The unflagging lunacy of God. The unending seaminess of man. The meeting between them that is always a matter of life or death and usually both. The story of Zaccheus is the Gospel in sycamore. It is the best and oldest joke in the world.

Poverty ✳ August 2

IN A SENSE WE are all hungry and in need, but most of us don't recognize it. With plenty to eat in the deepfreeze, with a roof over our heads and a car in the garage, we assume that the empty feeling inside must be just a case of the blues that can be cured by a weekend in the country or an extra martini at lunch or the purchase of a color TV.

The poor, on the other hand, are under no such delusion. When Jesus says, "Come unto me all ye who labor and are heavy laden, and I will give you rest" (Matthew 11:28), the poor stand a better chance than most of knowing what he's talking about and knowing that he's talking to them. In desperation they may even be willing to consider the possibility of accepting his offer. This is perhaps why Jesus on several occasions called them peculiarly blessed.

Wine ✳ August 3

UNFERMENTED GRAPE juice is a bland and pleasant drink, especially on a warm afternoon mixed half-and-half with ginger ale. It is a ghastly symbol of the life blood of Jesus Christ, especially when served in individual antiseptic, thimble-sized glasses.

Wine is booze, which means it is dangerous and drunk-making. It makes the timid brave and the reserved amorous. It loosens the tongue and breaks the ice especially when served in a loving cup. It kills germs. As symbols go, it is a rather splendid one.

Old Age ✳ August 4

IT'S NOT, AS THE saying goes, for sissies. There are some lucky ones who little by little slow down to be sure but otherwise go on to the end pretty much as usual. For the majority, however, it's like living in a house that's in increasing need of repairs. The plumbing doesn't work right any more. There are bats in the attic. Cracked and dusty, the windows are hard to see through, and there's a lot of creaking and groaning in bad weather. The exterior could use a coat of paint. And so on. The odd thing is that the person living in the house may feel, humanly speaking, much as always. The eighty-year-old body can be in precarious shape yet the spirit within as full of beans as ever. If that leads senior citizens to think of all the things they'd still love to do but can't anymore, it only makes things worse. But it needn't work that way.

Second childhood commonly means something to steer clear of, but it can also mean something else. It can mean that if your spirit is still more or less intact, one of the benefits of being an old crock is that you can enjoy again something of what it's like being a young squirt.

Eight-year-olds like eighty-year-olds have lots of things they'd love to do but can't because their bodies aren't up to it, so they learn to *play* instead. Eighty-year-olds might do well to take notice. They can play at being eighty-year-olds for instance. Stiff knees and hearing aids, memory loss and poor eyesight, are no fun, but there are those who marvelously survive them by somehow managing to see them as, among other things and in spite of all, a little funny.

Another thing is that if part of the pleasure of being a child the first time round is that you don't have to prove yourself yet, part of the pleasure of being a child the second time round is that you don't have to prove yourself any longer. You can be who you are and say what you feel, and let the chips fall where they may.

Very young children and very old children also have in common the advantage of being able to sit on the sideline of things. While everybody else is in there jockeying for position and sweating it out, they can lean back, put their feet up, and like the octogenarian King Lear "pray, and sing, and tell old tales, and laugh at gilded butterflies."

Very young children and very old children also seem to be in touch with something that the rest of the pack has lost track of. There is something bright and still about them at their best, like the sun before breakfast. Both the old and the young get scared sometimes about what lies ahead of them, and with good reason, but you can't help feeling that whatever inner goldenness they're in touch with will see them through in the end.

X ✳ August 5

X IS THE GREEK letter *chi*, which is the first letter of the word Christ. Thus Xmas is shorthand for Christmas, taking only about one-sixth as long to write. If you do your cards by hand, it is possible to save as much as seventy-five or eighty minutes a year.

It is tempting to say that what you do with this time that you save is your own business. Briefly stated, however, the Christian position is that there's no such thing as your own business.

Transfiguration ✳ *August 6*

H IS FACE SHONE like the sun," Matthew says, "and his garments became white as light." Moses and Elijah were talking to him. There was a bright cloud overshadowing him and out of it a voice saying, "This is my beloved son, with whom I am well pleased; listen to him." The three disciples who witnessed the scene "fell on their faces, and were filled with awe" (Matthew 17:1–6).

It is as strange a scene as there is in the Gospels. Even without the voice from the cloud to explain it, they had no doubt what they were witnessing. It was Jesus of Nazareth all right, the man they'd tramped many a dusty mile with, whose mother and brothers they knew, the one they'd seen as hungry, tired, footsore as the rest of them. But it was also the Messiah, the Christ, in his glory. It was the holiness of the man shining through his humanness, his face so afire with it they were almost blinded.

Even with us something like that happens once in a while. The face of a man walking his child in the park, of a woman picking peas in the garden, of sometimes even the unlikeliest person listening to a concert, say, or standing barefoot in the sand watching the waves roll in, or just having a beer at a Saturday baseball game in July. Every once and so often, something so touching, so incandescent, so alive transfigures the human face that it's almost beyond bearing.

"The Time Is Fulfilled" ✳ August 7

THERE IS NO GREAT mystery about what "the time is fulfilled" means, I think. "The time is fulfilled" means the time is up. That is the dark side of it anyway, saving the bright side of it till later. It means that it is possible we are living in the last days. There was a time when you could laugh that kind of message off if you saw some bearded crazy parading through the city streets with it painted on a sandwich board, but you have to be crazy yourself to laugh at it in our nuclear age. What with glasnost and perestroika and what seems to be the gradual break-up of world communism, things look more hopeful than they have for a long time, but the world is still a powder keg. The missiles are still in their silos, the vast armies are still under arms. And there are other dangers potentially more dangerous now than even nuclear war. There is AIDS. There is terrorism. There are drugs and more to the point the darkness of our time that makes people seek escape in drugs. There is the slow poisoning of what we call "the environment" of all things as if with that absurdly antiseptic phrase we can conceal from ourselves that what we are really poisoning is home, is here, is us.

It is no wonder that the books and newspapers we read, the movies and TV we watch, are obsessed with the dark and demonic, are full of death and violence. It is as if the reason we wallow in them is that they help us keep our minds off the real death, the real violence. And God knows the church of Christ has its darkness and demons too. On television and in cults it is so discredited by religious crooks and phonies and vaudevillians, and in thousands of respectable pulpits it is so bland and banal and without passion, that you wonder sometimes not only if it will survive but if it even deserves to survive. As a character in Woody Allen's *Hannah and Her Sisters* puts it, "If Jesus came back and saw what was going on in his name, he'd never stop throwing up."

Alcoholics Anonymous ❋ *August 8*

ALCOHOLICS ANONYMOUS or A.A. is the name of a group of men and women who acknowledge that addiction to alcohol is ruining their lives. Their purpose in coming together is to give it up and help others do the same. They realize they can't pull this off by themselves. They believe they need each other, and they believe they need God. The ones who aren't so sure about God speak instead of their Higher Power.

When they first start talking at a meeting, they introduce themselves by saying, "I am John. I am an alcoholic," "I am Mary. I am an alcoholic," to which the rest of the group answers each time in unison, "Hi, John," "Hi, Mary." They are apt to end with the Lord's Prayer or the Serenity Prayer. Apart from that they have no ritual. They have no hierarchy.

They have no dues or budget. They do not advertise or pros-elytize. Having no buildings of their own, they meet wherever they can.

Nobody lectures them, and they do not lecture each other. They simply tell their own stories with the candor that ano-nymity makes possible. They tell where they went wrong and how day by day they are trying to go right. They tell where they find the strength and understanding and hope to keep trying. Sometimes one of them will take special respon-sibility for another—to be available at any hour of day or night if the need arises. There's not much more to it than that, and it seems to be enough. Healing happens. Miracles are made.

You can't help thinking that something like this is what the Church is meant to be and maybe once was before it got to be Big Business. Sinners Anonymous. "I can will what is right but I cannot do it," is the way Saint Paul put it, speaking for all of us. "For I do not do the good I want, but the evil I do not want is what I do" (Romans 7:19).

"I am me. I am a sinner."

"Hi, you."

Hi, every Sadie and Sal. Hi, every Tom, Dick, and Harry. It is the forgiveness of sins, of course. It is what the Church is all about.

No matter what far place alcoholics end up in, either in this country or virtually anywhere else, they know that there will be an A.A. meeting nearby to go to and that at that meet-ing they will find strangers who are not strangers to help and to heal, to listen to the truth and to tell it. That is what the Body of Christ is all about.

Would it ever occur to Christians in a far place to turn to a church nearby in hope of finding the same? Would they find it? If not, you wonder what is so Big about the Church's Business.

Abortion ✸ August 9

SPEAKING AGAINST abortion, someone has said, "No one should be denied access to the great feast of life," to which the rebuttal, obviously enough, is that life isn't much of a feast for the child born to people who don't want it or can't afford it or are one way or another incapable of taking care of it and will one way or another probably end up abusing or abandoning it.

And yet, and yet. Who knows what treasure life may hold for even such a child as that, or what a treasure even such a child as that may grow up to become? To bear a child even under the best of circumstances, or to abort a child even under the worst—the risks are hair-raising either way and the results incalculable.

How would Jesus himself decide, he who is hailed as Lord of Life and yet who says that it is not the ones who, like an abortionist, can kill the body we should fear but the ones who can kill body and soul together the way only the world into which it is born can kill the unloved, unwanted child (Matthew 10:28)?

There is perhaps no better illustration of the truth that in an imperfect world there are no perfect solutions. All we can do, as Luther said, is *sin bravely,* which is to say (a) know that neither to have the child nor not to have the child is without the possibility of tragic consequences for everybody yet (b) be brave in knowing also that not even that can put us beyond the forgiving love of God.

Thomas ✸ August 10

IMAGINATION WAS NOT Thomas's long suit. He called a spade a spade. He was a realist. He didn't believe in fairy tales, and if anything else came up that he didn't believe in or couldn't understand, his questions could be pretty direct.

There was the last time he and the others had supper with Jesus, for instance. Jesus was talking about dying, and he said he would be leaving them soon, but it wouldn't be forever. He said he'd get things ready for them as soon as he got where he was going, and when their time finally came too, they'd all be together again. They knew the way he was going, he said, and some day they'd be there with him themselves.

Nobody else breathed a word, but Thomas couldn't hold back. When you got right down to it, he said, he personally had no idea where Jesus was going, and he didn't know the way to get there either. "I am the way," was what Jesus said to him (John 14:6), and although Thomas let it go at that, you can't help feeling that he found the answer less than satisfactory. Jesus wasn't a way, he was a man, and it was too bad he so often insisted on talking in riddles.

Then in the next few days all the things that everybody could see were going to happen happened, and Jesus was dead just as he'd said he'd be. That much Thomas was sure of. He'd been on hand himself. There was no doubt about it. And then the thing that nobody had ever been quite able to believe would happen happened too.

Thomas wasn't around at the time, but all the rest of them were. They were sitting crowded together in a room with the door locked and the shades drawn, scared sick they'd be the ones to get it next, when suddenly Jesus came in. He wasn't a ghost you could see the wallpaper through, and he wasn't just a figment of their imagination because they were all too busy imagining the horrors that were all too likely in store for themselves to imagine anything much about anybody else. He said *shalom* and then showed them enough of where the Romans had let him have it to convince them he was as real as they were if not more so. He breathed the Holy Spirit on them and gave them a few instructions to go with it, and then left.

Nobody says where Thomas was at the time. One good thing about not having too much of an imagination is that you're not apt to work yourself up into quite as much of a panic as Thomas's friends had, for example, and maybe he'd gone out for a cup of coffee or just to sit in the park for a while and watch the pigeons. Anyway, when he finally returned and they told him what had happened, his reaction was just about what they might have expected. He said that unless Jesus came back again so he could not only see the nail marks for himself but actually touch them, he was afraid that, much as he hated to say so, he simply couldn't believe that what they had seen was anything more than the product of wishful thinking or an optical illusion of an unusually vivid kind.

Eight days later, when Jesus did come back, Thomas was there and got his wish. Jesus let him see him and hear him and touch him, and not even Thomas could hold out against evidence like that. He had no questions left to ask and not enough energy left to ask them with even if he'd had a couple. All he could say was, "My Lord and my God!" (John 20:28), and Jesus seemed to consider that under the circumstances that was enough.

Then Jesus asked a question of his own. "Have you believed because you have seen me?" he said and then added, addressing himself to all the generations that have come since, "Blessed are those who have not seen and yet believe" (John 20:29).

Even though he said the greater blessing is for those who can believe without seeing, it's hard to imagine that there's a believer anywhere who wouldn't have traded places with Thomas, given the chance, and seen that face and heard that voice and touched those ruined hands.

(JOHN 14:1–7, 20:19–29)

YHWH ✳ August 11

IN EXODUS 3:13-14 when Moses asks God his name, God says his name is YHWH, which is apparently derived from the Hebrew verb *to be* and means something like "I am what I am" or "I will be what I will be." The original text of the Old Testament didn't include vowels, so YHWH is all that appears.

Since it was believed that God's name was too holy to be used by just anybody, over the years it came to be used only by the high priest on special occasions. When other people ran across it in their reading, they simply substituted for it the title Lord. The result of this pious practice was that in time no one knew any longer what vowels belonged in between the four consonants, and thus the proper pronunciation of God's name was lost. The best guess is that it was something like YaHWeH, but there's no way of being sure.

Like the bear in Thurber's fable, sometimes the pious lean so far over backward that they fall flat on their face.

It All Happened ✳ August 12

IT WAS A COUPLE of springs ago. I was driving into New York City from New Jersey on one of those crowded, fast-moving turnpikes you enter it by. It was very warm. There was brilliant sunshine, and the cars glittered in it as they went tearing by. The sky was cloudless and blue. Around Newark a huge silver plane traveling in the same direction as I was made its descent in a slow diagonal and touched down soft as a bird on the airstrip just a few hundred yards away from me as I went driving by. I had music on the radio, but I didn't need it. The day made its own music—the hot spring sun and the hum of the road, the roar of the great trucks passing and of my own engine, the hum of my own thoughts. When I came out of the Lincoln Tunnel, the city was snarled and seething with traffic as usual; but at the same time there was something about it that was not usual.

It was gorgeous traffic, it was beautiful traffic—that's what was not usual. It was a beauty to see, to hear, to smell, even to be part of. It was so dazzlingly alive it all but took my breath away. It rattled and honked and chattered with life— the people, the colors of their clothes, the marvelous hodge-podge of their faces, all of it; the taxis, the shops, the blinding sidewalks. The spring day made everybody a celebrity— blacks, whites, hispanics, every last one of them. It made even the litter and clamor and turmoil of it a kind of miracle.

There was construction going on as I inched my way east along 54th Street; and some wino, some bum, was stretched out on his back in the sun on a pile of lumber as if it was an alpine meadow he was stretched out on and he was made of money. From the garage where I left the car, I continued my way on foot. In the high-ceilinged, public atrium on the ground floor of a large office building there were people on benches eating their sandwiches. Some of them were dressed to kill. Some of them were in jeans and sneakers. There were young ones and old ones. Daylight was flooding in on them, and there were green plants growing and a sense of deep peace as they ate their lunches mostly in silence. A big man in a clown costume and whiteface took out a tubular yellow balloon big round as a noo-dle, blew it up and twisted it squeakily into a dove of peace which he handed to the bug-eyed child watching him. I am not making this up. It all happened.

Prayer ✳ August 13

EVERYBODY PRAYS whether he thinks of it as praying or not. The odd silence you fall into when something very beau-tiful is happening or something very good or very bad. The ah-h-h-h! that sometimes floats up out of you as out of a

Fourth of July crowd when the sky-rocket bursts over the water. The stammer of pain at somebody else's pain. The stammer of joy at somebody else's joy. Whatever words or sounds you use for sighing with over your own life. These are all prayers in their way. These are all spoken not just to yourself but to something even more familiar than yourself and even more strange than the world.

According to Jesus, by far the most important thing about praying is to keep at it. The images he uses to explain this are all rather comic, as though he thought it was rather comic to have to explain it at all. He says God is like a friend you go to borrow bread from at midnight. The friend tells you in effect to drop dead, but you go on knocking anyway until finally he gives you what you want so he can go back to bed again (Luke 11:5–8). Or God is like a crooked judge who refuses to hear the case of a certain poor widow, presumably because he knows there's nothing much in it for him. But she keeps on hounding him until finally he hears her case just to get her out of his hair (Luke 18:1–8). Even a stinker, Jesus says, won't give his own child a black eye when he asks for peanut butter and jelly, so how all the more will God when *his* children . . . (Matthew 7:9–11).

Be importunate, Jesus says—not, one assumes, because you have to beat a path to God's door before he'll open it, but because until you beat the path maybe there's no way of getting to *your* door. "Ravish my heart," John Donne wrote. But God will not usually ravish. He will only court.

A Glimpse of Someone ✳ August 14

Buechner recalls a Da Vinci reproduction that greatly impressed him as a boy:

BUT OF ALL OF them, the one I remember best turns out not to be in Craven's book at all, but some other collection that must have come my way at the same time, and that is a

212

pastel of the head of Jesus that Leonardo da Vinci did as a study for *The Last Supper*. The head is tipped slightly to one side and down. He looks Jewish. He looks very tired. Some of the color has flaked away. His eyes are closed. That was the face that moved me and stayed with me more in a way than all the others, though not because it was Jesus' face, as far as I can remember, but just because it seemed the face of a human being to whom everything had happened that can happen. It was a face of great stillness, a face that had survived.

It was as if in the picture I caught a glimpse of someone whose presence I noted in a different way from the others. In the case of Hogarth's shrimp girl, for instance, what delighted me was the sense of seeing in her astonished young face a beauty that I had never seen anywhere else. In the case of Da Vinci's Jesus, on the other hand, what haunted me was so strong a feeling of the painter's having in some unimaginable way caught the likeness just right that it was as if, without knowing it, I had already seen deep within myself some vision of what he looked like or what I hoped he looked like on the basis of which I could affirm the picture's authenticity. I had come across many other representations of Jesus' face in my day, but this was one that I could somehow vouch for, and although I set it aside and gave no special thought to it, somewhere in the back of my mind I seem always to have kept track of it as though to have a way of recognizing him if ever our paths happened to cross again.

Dreams ✳ August 15

No MATTER HOW prosaic, practical, and ploddingly un-imaginative we may be, we have dreams like everybody else. All of us do. In them even the most down-to-earth and pedestrian of us leave earth behind and go flying, not walk-ing, through the air like pelicans. Even the most respectable go strolling along crowded pavements naked as truth. Even the confirmed disbelievers in an afterlife hold converse with the dead just as the most dyed-in-the-wool debunkers of the supernatural have adventures to make Madame Blavatsky's hair stand on end.

The tears of dreams can be real enough to wet the pillow and the passions of them fierce enough to make the flesh burn. There are times we dream our way to a truth or an insight so overwhelming that it startles us awake and haunts us for years to come. As easily as from room to room, we move from things that happened so long ago we had forgotten them to things lying ahead that may be waiting to happen or trying to happen still. On our way we are as likely to meet old friends as perfect strangers. Sometimes, inexplicably, we meet casual acquaintances who for decades haven't so much as once crossed our minds.

Freudians and Jungians, prophets and poets, philosophers, fortunetellers, and phonies all have their own claims about what dreams mean. Others claim they don't mean a thing. But there are at least two things they mean that seem incontrovertible.

One of them is that we are in constant touch with a world that is as real to us while we are in it, and has as much to do with who we are, and whose ultimate origin and destiny are as unknown and fascinating, as the world of waking reality. The other one is that our lives are a great deal richer, deeper, more intricately interrelated, more mysterious, and less limited by time and space than we commonly suppose.

People who tend to write off the validity of the religious experience in general and the experience of God in particular on the grounds that in the Real World they can find no evidence for such things should take note. Maybe the Real World is not the only reality, and even if it should turn out to be, maybe they are not really looking at it realistically.

Joseph and His Brethren ✳ August 16

JOSEPH'S BROTHERS tried to murder him by throwing him into a pit, but if they had ever been brought to trial, they wouldn't have needed Clarence Darrow to get them an acquittal in any court in the land. Not only did Joseph have offensive dreams in which he was Mr. Big and they were all groveling at his feet but he recounted them in sickening detail at the breakfast table the next morning. He was also his father's pet, and they seethed at the sight of the many-colored coat he flaunted while they were running around in T-shirts and dirty jeans.

After tossing him into the pit, the brothers decided to tell Jacob, their father, that his fair-haired boy had had a fatal tangle with bob-cats, and in order to convince him, they produced a shirt that they'd dipped in goat's blood. Jacob was convinced, and they didn't even have to worry too much about the lie they'd told him because by the time they got around to telling it, they figured that one way or another it, or something like it, must have come true.

Unknown to them, however, Joseph was rescued from the pit by some traveling salesmen who happened to be passing by and eventually wound up as a slave in Egypt where he was bought by an Army man named Potiphar. He got into trouble over an embarrassing misunderstanding with Potiphar's prehensile wife and did some time in jail for it as a result, but Pharaoh got wind of the fact that he was big on dream interpretations and had him sprung to see what he could do with a couple of wild ones he'd had himself. When Joseph passed with flying colors, Pharaoh promoted him to be head of the Department of Agriculture and eventually his right-hand man.

Years later, Joseph's brothers, who had long since succeeded in putting him out of their minds, turned up in Egypt too, looking for something to eat because they were having a famine back home. Joseph knew who they were right off the bat, but because he was wearing his fancy uniform and speaking Egyptian, they didn't recognize him.

Joseph couldn't resist getting a little of his own back for a while. He pretended he thought they were spies. He gave them some grain to take home but made one of them stay behind as a hostage. He planted some silverware in their luggage and accused them of copping it. But though with part of himself he was presumably getting a kick out of all this, with another part he was so moved and pleased to be back in touch with his own flesh and blood after so long that every once in a while he had to get out of the room in a hurry so they wouldn't see how choked up he was and discover his true identity.

Finally he'd had enough. He told them who he was, and they all fell into each other's arms and wept. He then invited them to come live with him in Egypt and to bring old Jacob along with them too who was so delighted to find Joseph alive after all these years that he didn't even seem too upset about the trick that had been played on him with the bloody shirt.

The real moment of truth came, however, when Jacob finally died. Generous and forgiving as Joseph had been, his brothers couldn't avoid the nasty suspicion that once the old man wasn't around any more to put in a good word for them, Joseph might start thinking again about what it had felt like when they tossed him into that pit and decide to pay them back as they deserved. So they went to see him, fell down on their knees, and begged his pardon.

Joseph's answer rings out like a bell. "Don't be scared. Of course you're pardoned," he said. "Do you think I'm God to grovel before me like that?" In the old days, of course, God was just who he'd rather suspected he was and the dreams where they groveled were his all-time favorites.

Almost as much as it is the story of how Israel was saved from famine and extinction, it is the story of how Joseph was saved as a human being. It would be interesting to know which of the two achievements cost God the greater effort and which was the one he was prouder of.

(GENESIS 37–50)

Kingdom of God ✸ August 17

IT IS NOT A place, of course, but a condition. *Kingship* might be a better word. "Thy kingdom come, thy will be done," Jesus prayed. The two are in apposition.

Insofar as here and there, and now and then, God's kingly will is being done in various odd ways among us even at this moment, the kingdom has come already.

Insofar as all the odd ways we do his will at this moment are at best half-baked and halfhearted, the kingdom is still a long way off—a hell of a long way off, to be more precise and theological.

As a poet, Jesus is maybe at his best in describing the feeling you get when you glimpse the Thing Itself—the kingship of the king official at last and all the world his coronation. It's like finding a million dollars in a field, he says, or a jewel worth a king's ransom. It's like finding something you hated to lose and thought you'd never find again—an old keepsake, a stray sheep, a missing child. When the kingdom really comes, it's as if the thing you lost and thought you'd never find again is you.

Observance ✸ August 18

A RELIGIOUS OBSERVANCE can be a wedding, a christening, a Memorial Day service, a bar mitzvah, or anything like that you might be apt to think of. There are lots of things going on at them. There are lots of things you can learn from them if you're in a receptive state of mind. The word "observance" itself suggests what is perhaps the most important thing about them.

A man and a woman are getting married. A child is being given a name. A war is being remembered and many deaths. A boy is coming of age.

It is life that is going on. It is always going on, and it is always precious. It is God that is going on. It is you who are there that is going on.

As Henry James advised writers, be one on whom nothing is lost.

OBSERVE!! There are few things as important, as religious, as that.

Unbelief ❋ August 19

UNBELIEF IS AS much of a choice as belief is. What makes it in many ways more appealing is that whereas to believe in something requires some measure of understanding and effort, not to believe doesn't require much of anything at all.

Communion of Saints ❋ August 20

AT THE ALTAR TABLE, the overweight parson is doing something or other with the bread as his assistant stands by with the wine. In the pews, the congregation sits more or less patiently waiting to get into the act. The church is quiet. Outside, a bird starts singing. It's nothing special, only a handful of notes angling out in different directions. Then a pause. Then a trill or two. A chirp. It is just warming up for the business of the day, but it is enough.

The parson and his assistant and the usual scattering of senior citizens, parents, teenagers are not alone in whatever they think they're doing. Maybe that is what the bird is there to remind them. In its own slapdash way the bird has a part in it too. Not to mention "Angels and Archangels and all the company of heaven" if the prayer book is to be believed. Maybe we should believe it. Angels and Archangels. Cherubim and seraphim. They are all in the act together. It must look a little like the great *jeu de son et lumière* at Versailles when all the fountains are turned on at once and the night is ablaze with fireworks. It must sound a little like the last movement of Beethoven's *Choral Symphony* or the Atlantic in a gale.

And "all the company of heaven" means everybody we ever loved and lost, including the ones we didn't know we loved until we lost them or didn't love at all. It means people we never heard of. It means everybody who ever did—or at some unimaginable time in the future ever will—come together at something like this table in search of something like what is offered at it.

Whatever other reasons we have for coming to such a place, if we come also to give each other our love and to give God our love, then together with Gabriel and Michael, and the fat parson, and Sebastian pierced with arrows, and the old lady whose teeth don't fit, and Teresa in her ecstasy, we are the communion of saints.

Adversaries ❊ August 21

IN THIS WAR OF conquest that we all must wage, there are also the adversaries with whom we have to wage it; and they are adversaries of flesh and blood. They are human beings like ourselves, each of whom is fighting the same war toward the same end and under a banner emblazoned with the same word that our banners bear, and that word is of course Myself, or Myself and my Family, or Myself and my Country, Myself and my Race, which are all really MYSELF writ large. It can be the most ruthless of all wars, but on the other hand it need not be. Saints and sinners fight it both. Genghis Khan fought such a war under such a banner, but so did Martin Luther King, Jr. It can be the naked war of the jungle, my ambition against your ambition, my will against your will, or it can be war more in the sense of the knight at arms who abides by the rules of chivalry. If often it is the war of the unjust against the just, it can also be a war of the just against the unjust. But whichever it is, it is the war of flesh against flesh: to get ahead, to win, to gain or regain power, to survive in a world where not even survival is had without struggle.

Anxiety ✳ *August 22*

"HAVE NO ANXIETY about anything," Paul writes to the Philippians. In one sense it is like telling a woman with a bad head cold not to sniffle and sneeze so much or a lame man to stop dragging his feet. Or maybe it is more like telling a wino to lay off the booze or a compulsive gambler to stay away from the track.

Is anxiety a disease or an addiction? Perhaps it is something of both. Partly, perhaps, because you can't help it, and partly because for some dark reason you choose not to help it, you torment yourself with detailed visions of the worst that can possibly happen. The nagging headache turns out to be a malignant brain tumor. When your teenage son fails to get off the plane you've gone to meet, you see his picture being tacked up in the post office among the missing and his disappearance never accounted for. As the latest mid-East crisis boils, you wait for the TV game show to be interrupted by a special bulletin to the effect that major cities all over the country are being evacuated in anticipation of nuclear attack. If Woody Allen were to play your part on the screen, you would roll in the aisles with the rest of them, but you're not so much as cracking a smile at the screen inside your own head.

Does the terrible fear of disaster conceal an even more terrible hankering for it? Do the accelerated pulse and the knot in the stomach mean that, beneath whatever their immediate cause, you are acting out some ancient and unresolved drama of childhood? Since the worst things that happen are apt to be the things you don't see coming, do you think there is a kind of magic whereby, if you only *can* see them coming, you will be able somehow to prevent them from happening? Who knows the answer? In addition to Novocain and indoor plumbing, one of the few advantages of living in the twentieth century is the existence of psychotherapists, and if you can locate a good one, maybe one day you will manage to dig up an answer that helps.

But answer or no answer, the worst things will happen at last even so. "All life is suffering" says the first and truest of the Buddha's Four Noble Truths, by which he means that sorrow, loss, death await us all and everybody we love. Yet "the Lord is at hand. Have no anxiety about anything," Paul writes, who was evidently in prison at the time and with good reason to be anxious about everything, "but in everything by prayer and supplication with thanksgiving let your requests be made known to God."

He does not deny that the worst things will happen finally to all of us, as indeed he must have had a strong suspicion they were soon to happen to him. He does not try to minimize them. He does not try to explain them away as God's will or God's judgment or God's method of testing our spiritual fiber. He simply tells the Philippians that in spite of them—even in the thick of them—they are to keep in constant touch with the One who unimaginably transcends the worst things as he also unimaginably transcends the best.

"In everything," Paul says, they are to keep on praying. Come Hell or high water, they are to keep on asking, keep on thanking, above all keep on making themselves known. He does not promise them that as a result they will be delivered from the worst things any more than Jesus himself was delivered from them. What he promises them instead is that "the peace of God, which passes all understanding, will keep your hearts and your minds in Christ Jesus."

The worst things will surely happen no matter what—that is to be understood—but beyond all our power to understand, he writes, we will have peace both in heart and in mind. We are as sure to be in trouble as the sparks fly upward, but we will also be "in Christ," as he puts it. Ultimately not even sorrow, loss, death can get at us there.

That is the sense in which he dares say without risk of occasioning ironic laughter, "Have no anxiety about anything." Or, as he puts it a few lines earlier, "Rejoice in the Lord always. Again I will say, Rejoice!"

(PHILIPPIANS 4:4–7)

Descent into Hell ✳ August 23

THERE IS AN obscure passage in the First Epistle of Peter where the old saint writes that after the crucifixion, Jesus went and preached to "the spirits in prison, who formerly did not obey" (1 Peter 3:19–20) and it's not altogether clear just what spirits he had in mind. Later on, however, he is not obscure at all. "The gospel was preached even to the dead," he says, "that though judged in the flesh like men, they might live in the spirit like God" (1 Peter 4:5–6).

"He descended into Hell," is the way the Apostles' Creed puts it, of course. It has an almost blasphemous thud to it,

sandwiched there between the muffled drums of "was crucified, dead, and buried" and the trumpet blast of "the third
day he rose again from the dead." Christ of all people, in Hell
of all places! It strains the imagination to picture it, the Light
of the World making his way through the terrible dark to save
whatever ones he can. Yet in view of what he'd seen of the
world during his last few days in the thick of it, maybe the
transition wasn't as hard as you might think.

The fancifulness of the picture gives way to what seems,
the more you turn it over in your mind, the inevitability of it.
Of course that is where he would have gone. Of course that
is what he would have done. Christ is always descending and
redescending into Hell.

He is talking not just to other people when he says you
must be prepared to forgive not seven times but seventy times
seven, and "Come unto me, all ye that labor and are heavy
laden" is spoken to *all,* whatever they've done or left undone,
whichever side of the grave their Hell happens to be on.

Beginning of a Story ✻ *August 24*

IN THE SIXTH month the angel Gabriel was sent from God to
a city of Galilee named Nazareth, to a virgin betrothed to a
man whose name was Joseph, of the house of David; and
the virgin's name was Mary," and that is the beginning of a
story—a time, a place, a set of characters, and the implied
promise, which is common to all stories, that something is
coming, something interesting or significant or exciting is
about to happen. And I would like to start out by reminding
my reader that in essence this is what Christianity is. If we
whittle away long enough, it is a story that we come to at
last. And if we take even the fanciest and most metaphysical
kind of theologian or preacher and keep on questioning him

far enough—Why is this so? All right, but why is *that* so? Yes, but how do we know that it's so?—even he is forced finally to take off his spectacles and push his books off to one side and say, "Once upon a time there was . . . ," and then everybody leans forward a little and starts to listen. Stories have enormous power for us, and I think that it is worth speculating why they have such power. Let me suggest two reasons.

One is that they make us want to know what is coming next, and not just out of idle curiosity either because if it is a good story, we *really* want to know, almost fiercely so, and we will wade through a lot of pages or sit through a lot of endless commercials to find out. There was a young woman named Mary, and an angel came to her from God, and what did he say? And what did she say? And then how did it all turn out in the end? But the curious thing is that if it is a good story, we want to know how it all turns out in the end even if we have heard it many times before and know the outcome perfectly well already. Yet why? What is there to find out if we already know?

And that brings me to the second reason why I think stories have such power for us. They force us to consider the question, "Are stories true?" Not just, "Is *this* story true?"—was there really an angel? Did he really say, "Do not be afraid"?—but are any stories true? Is the claim that all stories make a true claim? Every storyteller, whether he is Shakespeare telling about Hamlet or Luke telling about Mary, looks out at the world much as you and I look out at it and sees things happening—people being born, growing up, working, loving, getting old, and finally dying—only then, by the very process of taking certain of these events and turning them into a story, giving them form and direction, does he make a sort of claim about events in general, about the nature of life itself. And the storyteller's claim, I believe, is that life has

meaning—that the things that happen to people happen not just by accident like leaves being blown off a tree by the wind but that there is order and purpose deep down behind them or inside them and that they are leading us not just anywhere but somewhere. The power of stories is that they are telling us that life adds up somehow, that life itself is like a story. And this grips us and fascinates us because of the feeling it gives us that if there is meaning in any life—in Hamlet's, in Mary's, in Christ's—then there is meaning also in our lives. And if this is true, it is of enormous significance in itself, and it makes us listen to the storyteller with great intensity because in this way all his stories are about us and because it is always possible that he may give us some clue as to what the meaning of our lives is.

Only One Life ✳ *August 25*

M Y WIFE AND I were buying groceries one day, and I was on one side of the store and she was on the other, and over a shelf of breakfast cereal and cake mix I said, "Don't forget the cream," and she said, "All right, but don't you forget you're trying to lose weight," and I said, "Oh well, you only live once." And then it happened, this thing that broke for a moment through my deafness. The store was nearly empty so that the woman at the checkout counter had no trouble hearing us. It was a hot, muggy afternoon, and she had been working hard all day and looked flushed and hectic there behind her cash register and the racks of Life Savers and chewing gum and TV guides, and when I said, "Oh well, you only live once," she broke into the conversation, and what she said was, "Don't you think once is enough?" That was it.

It was a mild jest and I laughed mildly and so did the boy carrying up some empty cartons from the cellar, but it was also very much not a jest because I had a feeling that what by some rare chance I had happened to hear was a human being saying something like this: "People come and people go, most of them strangers. I'm sick of them, and I'm sick of myself too. One day's very much like another." What I thought I heard was a human being saying, "I'll live my life out to the last, and I expect to have good days as well as bad. But when the end comes, I won't complain. One life will do me very nicely." Then somebody plunked a bottle of something down on the counter and the cash register rang open and the check-out clerk with her hair damp on her forehead said, "Don't you think once is enough?" Jesus said, "I am the resurrection and the life; he who believes in me, though he die, yet shall he live." It was life and death that she was talking about too, her own life and her own death, and by some fluke I happened to hear her despite that hardness of hearing that we all share. Even the Lord Jesus Christ somehow made himself heard that steamy August day among the detergents and floor waxes. "Whoever lives and believes in me shall never die." "Don't you think once is enough?" the woman said.

There are so many things to say, of course. One thing is that whether one life is enough or not enough, one life is all we get, at least only one life *here,* only one life in this gorgeous and hair-raising world, only one life with the range of possibilities for doing and being that are open to us now. William Hazlitt wrote that no young man believes that he will ever die, and the truth of the matter, I think, is that in some measure that is true of all men. Intellectually we all know that we will die, but we do not really know it in the sense that the knowledge becomes part of us. We do not really know it in the sense of living as though it were true. On the contrary, we tend to live as though our lives would go on forever. We spend our lives like drunken sailors.

Evil ✳ August 26

- God is all-powerful.
- God is all-good.
- Terrible things happen.

YOU CAN RECONCILE any two of these propositions with each other, but you can't reconcile all three. The problem of evil is perhaps the greatest single problem for religious faith.

There have been numerous theological and philosophical attempts to solve it, but when it comes down to the reality of evil itself they are none of them worth much. When a child is raped and murdered, the parents are not apt to take much comfort from the explanation (better than most) that since God wants man to love him, man must be free to love or not to love and thus free to rape and murder a child if he takes a notion to.

Christian Science solves the problem of evil by saying that it does not exist except as an illusion of mortal mind. Buddhism solves it in terms of reincarnation and an inexorable law of cause and effect whereby the raped child is merely reaping the consequences of evil deeds it committed in another life.

Christianity, on the other hand, ultimately offers no theoretical solution at all. It merely points to the cross and says that, practically speaking, there is no evil so dark and so obscene—not even this—but that God can turn it to good.

Greater Freedom ✳ August 27

I KNOW SEVERAL thoughtful and highly principled young couples living together without benefit of clergy or of anybody else who argue eloquently against the institution of marriage. "As long as ye both shall live" is transformed into "As long as you both shall love," and their view seems to be that to institutionalize such a relationship as theirs is to rob it of much that is most authentic and spontaneous and human about it. They point out that for a man and woman to commit themselves legally to honor and cherish each other for the rest of their lives is unrealistic at best and hypocritical at worst. Their love for each other should be bond enough to hold them together, and when the love ends, then the bond should end with it, and they should go their separate ways.

As for me, I find much in this that is persuasive. Who can deny that many a man and woman have married for no motive more edifying than that it was the only respectable way to enter into a full sexual relationship and that, as things turned out, they would have done better in every sense that one can imagine mattering much either to themselves or to God simply to have had the relationship and forgotten about the respectability which, once the first, careless rapture was passed, became a cheerless if respectable prison to them both? Who would argue that the vows exchanged at weddings are anything other than wild and improbable? Who can look at the apparent devotion and well-being of many an unmarried pair who live together, even have children together, and call them simply wrong in either religious terms or any other?

All I can say in response is that it was within the bonds of marriage that I, for one, found a greater freedom to be and to become and to share myself than I can imagine ever having found in any other kind of relationship, and that—absurdly hopeful and poorly understood and profoundly unrealistic as the commitment was that the girl in the white dress and I made to each other in the presence, we hoped, not only of most of the people we loved best in the world, but of God as well, in whose name Dr. Muilenburg somewhat shakily blessed us—my life would have been incalculably diminished without it.

To Become a Human Being ✳ August 28

IN 1963 I WENT on that famous March on Washington, and the clearest memory that I have of it is standing near the Lincoln Memorial hearing the song "We Shall Overcome" sung by the quarter of a million or so people who were there. And while I listened, my eye fell on one very old Negro man, with a face like shoe leather and a sleazy suit and an expression that was more befuddled than anything else; and I wondered to myself if, quite apart from the whole civil-rights question, that poor old bird could ever conceivably overcome anything. He was there to become a human being. Well, and so were the rest of us. And so are we all, no less befuddled than he when you come right down to it. Poor old bird, poor young birds, every one of us. And deep in my heart I do believe we shall overcome some day, as he will, by God's grace, by helping the seed of the kingdom grow in ourselves and in each other until finally in all of us it becomes a tree where the birds of the air can come and make their nests in our branches. That is all that matters really.

Bigger Than Both of Us ✳ August 29

HERE IS A PLACE to remember that for Christianity, the final affirmation about the nature of God is contained in the verse from the First Epistle of John: *God is love.* So another way of saying what I have just said is that man's deepest longing is for this love of God of which every conceivable form of human love is a reflection, however distorted a reflection it may be—"the smallest glass of love mixed with a pint pot of ditch-water," as Graham Greene says somewhere. And it is just for this reason that part of man's longing for the love of God can be satisfied simply by the love of man—the love of friend for friend, parent for child, sexual love—and thank

God for that, literally thank him, because for many people human love is all there is, if that, because that is all they can believe in.

But notice this: that love is not really one of man's *powers.* Man cannot achieve love, generate love, wield love, as he does his powers of destruction and creation. When I love someone, it is not something that I have achieved, but something that is happening through me, something that is happening to me as well as to him. To use the old soap-opera cliché seriously, it is something bigger than both of us, infinitely bigger, because wherever love enters this world, God enters.

Tourist Preaching ✳ August 30

ENGLISH-SPEAKING TOURISTS abroad are inclined to believe that if only they speak English loudly and distinctly and slowly enough, the natives will know what's being said even though they don't understand a single word of the language.

Preachers often make the same mistake. They believe that if only they speak the ancient verities loudly and distinctly and slowly enough, their congregations will understand them.

Unfortunately, the only language people really understand is their own language, and unless preachers are prepared to translate the ancient verities into it, they might as well save their breath.

Not for the Wise ✳ August 31

I AM AFRAID THAT prayer is really not for the wise. The wise avoid it on two bases, at least two. In the first place, if there really is a God who has this power to heal, to make whole, then it is wise to be very cautious indeed because if you go to him for healing, healing may be exactly what you will receive, and are you entirely sure that you want to be healed? By all accounts, after all, the process is not necessarily either quick or easy. And in the meanwhile, things could be a great deal worse. "Lord, take my sin from me—but not yet," Saint Augustine is said to have prayed. It is a wise man who bewares of God bearing gifts. In the second place, the wise look at twentieth-century man—civilized, rational, and at great cost emancipated from the dark superstitions of the past—and suggest that to petition some unseen power for special favors is a very childish procedure indeed.

In a way, "childish" is the very word to describe it. A child has not made up his mind yet about what is and what is not possible. He has no fixed preconceptions about what reality is; and if someone tells him that the mossy place under the lilac bush is a magic place, he may wait until he thinks that no one is watching him, but then he will very probably crawl in under the lilac bush to see for himself. A child also knows how to accept a gift. He does not worry about losing his dignity or becoming indebted if he accepts it. His conscience does not bother him because the gift is free and he has not earned it and therefore really has no right to it. He just takes it, with joy. In fact, if it is something that he wants very much, he may even ask for it. And lastly, a child knows how to trust. It is late at night and very dark and there is the sound of sirens as his father wakes him. He does not explain anything but just takes him by the hand and gets him up, and the child is scared out of his wits and has no idea what is going on, but he takes his father's hand anyway and lets his father lead him wherever he chooses into the darkness.

In honesty you have to admit to a wise man that prayer is not for the wise, not for the prudent, not for the sophisticated. Instead it is for those who recognize that in face of their deepest needs, all their wisdom is quite helpless. It is for those who are willing to persist in doing something that is both childish and crucial.

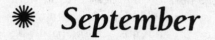 *September*

Today ✳ September 1

IT IS A MOMENT of light surrounded on all sides by darkness
and oblivion. In the entire history of the universe, let alone
in your own history, there has never been another just like it
and there will never be another just like it again. It is the
point to which all your yesterdays have been leading since the
hour of your birth. It is the point from which all your tomor-
rows will proceed until the hour of your death. If you were
aware of how precious it is, you could hardly live through it.
Unless you are aware of how precious it is, you can hardly be
said to be living at all.

"This is the day which the Lord has made," says the 118th
Psalm. "Let us rejoice and be glad in it." Or weep and be sad
in it for that matter. The point is to see it for what it is because
it will be gone before you know it. If you waste it, it is your
life that you're wasting. If you look the other way, it may
be the moment you've been waiting for always that you're
missing.

All other days have either disappeared into darkness and
oblivion or not yet emerged from them. Today is the only day
there is.

Immortality ✳ September 2

IMMORTAL MEANS death-proof. To believe in the immortality
of the soul is to believe that though John Brown's body lies
a-mouldering in the grave, his soul goes marching on simply
because marching on is the nature of souls just the way pro-
ducing apples is the nature of apple trees. Bodies die, but
souls don't.

True or false, this is not the biblical view, although many
who ought to know better assume it is. The biblical view
differs in several significant ways:

1. As someone has put it, the biblical understanding of man is not that he *has* a body but that he *is* a body. When God made Adam, he did it by slapping some mud together to make a body and then breathing some breath into it to make a living soul. Thus the body and soul which make up a man are as inextricably part and parcel of each other as the leaves and flames that make up a bonfire. When you kick the bucket, you kick it one hundred per cent. All of you. There is nothing left to go marching on with.

2. The idea that the body dies and the soul doesn't is an idea which implies that the body is something rather gross and embarrassing like a case of hemorrhoids. The Greeks spoke of it as the prison house of the soul. The suggestion was that to escape it altogether was something less than a disaster.

The Bible, on the other hand, sees the body in particular and the material world in general as a good and glorious invention.

3. Those who believe in the immortality of the soul believe that life after death is as natural a function of man as digestion after a meal.

The Bible instead speaks of resurrection. It is entirely unnatural. Man does not go on living beyond the grave because that's how he is made. Rather, he goes to his grave as dead as a doornail and is given his life back again by God (i.e., resurrected) just as he was given it by God in the first place, because that is the way God is made.

4. All the major Christian creeds affirm belief in resurrection *of the body*. In other words they affirm the belief that what God in spite of everything prizes enough to bring back to life is not just some disembodied echo of a human being but a new and revised version of all the things which made him the particular human being he was and which he needs something like a body to express: his personality, the way he looked, the sound of his voice, his peculiar capacity for creating and loving, in some sense his *face*.

5. The idea of the immortality of the soul is based on the experience of man's indomitable spirit. The idea of the resurrection of the body is based on the experience of God's unspeakable love.

La Vie ✳ September 3

ONE OF MY FAVORITE definitions of life was spoken by a comic actress in some musical of years ago. "La vie, la vie!" she cried out, rolling her big, dark eyes. "We'd be dead without it!" And maybe that is all that we can say about it ever finally. Life is what we would be dead without. Life is what we are. Life is our little portion of Being itself. But that is only to define one mystery in terms of another. You and I and the most distant star and the dragonfly's wing and the rustle of leaves as they fall—these all have one thing in common, which is that they all *are,* we all are, part of Being. What is Being?

Think of this world. Think of the great globe itself, the cloud-capped towers, the gorgeous palaces, the solemn temples, and all the people of this world. Then take it all away, take the world itself away and us away so that not a rack is left behind. Think of the universe itself. Then take away all the planets and the stars, take away every form of matter and energy, take away space itself and take away time. What is left? All that one might say is left is the absence of all these things. Now take away this absence. Nothing is left. Non-Being. So Being is what we have instead of this. Your Being and mine, the Being of our world.

Tears ✳ September 4

YOU NEVER KNOW what may cause them. The sight of the Atlantic Ocean can do it, or a piece of music, or a face you've never seen before. A pair of somebody's old shoes can do it. Almost any movie made before the great sadness that came over the world after the Second World War, a horse cantering across a meadow, the high school basketball team running out onto the gym floor at the start of a game. You can never be sure. But of this you can be sure. Whenever you find tears in your eyes, especially unexpected tears, it is well to pay the closest attention.

They are not only telling you something about the secret of who you are, but more often than not God is speaking to you through them of the mystery of where you have come from and is summoning you to where, if your soul is to be saved, you should go to next.

A Word of Great Power ✳ September 5

A N OLD MAN SITS alone in his tent. Outside, the day is coming to a close so that the light in the tent is poor, but that is of no concern to the old man because he is virtually blind, and all he can make out is a brightness where the curtain of the tent is open to the sky. He is looking that way now, his head trembling under the weight of his great age, his eyes cobwebbed around with many wrinkles, the ancient, sightless eyes. A fly buzzes through the still air, then lands somewhere.

For the old man there is no longer much difference between life and death, but for the sake of his family and his family's destiny, there are things that he has to do before the last day comes, the loose ends of a whole long life to gather together and somehow tie up. And one of these in particular will not let him sleep until he has done it: to call his eldest son to him and give him his blessing, but not a blessing in our sense of the word—a pious formality, a vague expression of good will that we might use when someone is going on a journey and we say, "God bless you." For the old man, a blessing is the speaking of a word of great power; it is the conveying of something of the very energy and vitality of his soul to the one he blesses; and this final blessing of his first-born son is to be the most powerful of all, so much so that once it is given it can never be taken back. And here even for us something of this remains true: we also know that words spoken in deep love or deep hate set things in motion within the human heart that can never be reversed.

"Good Guy" ✸ September 6

AND THE WORLD is full of Isaacs, of people who cannot help loving us no matter what we do and whose love we are free to use pretty much as we please, knowing perfectly well that they will go on loving us anyway—and without really hurting them either, or at least not in a way that they mind, feeling the way they do. One is not doing anything wrong by all this, not in a way the world objects to, and if he plays it with any kind of sensitivity, a man is not going to be ostracized by anybody or even much criticized. On the contrary, he can remain by and large what the world calls a "good guy," and I do not use that term altogether ironically either. I mean "gooder" than many, good enough so that God in his infinite mercy can still touch that man's heart with blessed dreams.

Only what does it all get him? I know what you expect the preacher to say: that it gets him nothing. But even preachers must be honest. I think it can get him a good deal, this policy of dishonesty where necessary. It can get him the invitation or the promotion. It can get him the job. It can get him the pat on the back and the admiring wink that mean so much. And these, in large measure, are what we mean by happiness. Do not underestimate them.

To Suffer in Love ✳ September 7

WHAT MAN AND WOMAN, if they gave serious thought to what having children inevitably involves, would ever have them? Yet what man and woman, once having had them and loved them, would ever want it otherwise? Because side by side with the Buddha's truth is the Gospel truth that "he who does not love remains in death." If by some magic you could eliminate the pain you are caused by the pain of someone you love, I for one cannot imagine working such magic because the pain is so much a part of the love that the love would be vastly diminished, unrecognizable, without it. To suffer in love for another's suffering is to live life not only at its fullest but at its holiest. "One mustn't have human affections—or rather one must love every soul as if it were one's own child," the whiskey priest thinks to himself as he says good-bye for the last time to his own daughter in Greene's novel, *The Power and the Glory*.

Peace ✳ September 8

PEACE HAS COME to mean the time when there aren't any wars or even when there aren't any major wars. Beggars can't be choosers; we'd most of us settle for that. But in Hebrew peace, *shalom,* means fullness, means having everything you need to be wholly and happily yourself.

One of the titles by which Jesus is known is Prince of Peace, and he used the word himself in what seem at first glance to be two radically contradictory utterances. On one occasion he said to the disciples, "Do not think that I have come to bring peace on earth; I have not come to bring peace, but a sword" (Matthew 10:34). And later on, the last time they ate together, he said to them, "Peace I leave with you; my peace I give to you" (John 14:27).

The contradiction is resolved when you realize that for Jesus peace seems to have meant not the absence of struggle but the presence of love.

No Theological Axe ✳ September 9

AS I HAVE LONG since discovered, the world is full of people—many of them, I regret to say, book reviewers—who, if they hear that a minister has written a novel, feel that they know, even without reading it, what sort of a novel it must be. It must be essentially a sermon with illustrations in the form of character and dialogue, and, as such, its view of life must be one-sided, simplistic, naive, with everything subordinated to the one central business of scoring some kind of homiletical bull's-eye. I protest that, in my case anyway, this simply is not so. Since my ordination, as well as before, novels, for me, start—as Robert Frost said his poems did—with a lump in the throat. I don't start with some theological axe to grind, but with a deep, wordless feeling for some aspect of my own experience that has moved me. Then, out of the shadows, a handful of characters starts to emerge, then various possible relationships between them, then a setting maybe, and lastly, out of those relationships, the semblance at least of a plot. Like any other serious novelist, I try to be as true as I can to life as I have known it. I write not as a propagandist but as an artist.

On the other hand—and here is where I feel I must be so careful—since my ordination I have written consciously as a Christian, as an evangelist, or apologist, even. That does not mean that I preach in my novels, which would make for neither good novels nor good preaching. On the contrary, I lean over backwards not to. I choose as my characters (or out of my dreams do they choose me?) men and women whose feet are as much of clay as mine are because they are the only people I can begin to understand. As a novelist no less than as a teacher, I try not to stack the deck unduly but always let doubt and darkness have their say along with faith and hope, not just because it is good apologetics—woe to him who tries to make it look simple and easy—but because to do it any other way would be to be less than true to the elements of doubt and darkness that exist in myself no less than in others. I am a Christian novelist in the same sense that somebody from Boston or Chicago is an American novelist. I must be as true to my experience as a Christian as black writers to their experience as blacks or women writers to their experience as women. It is no more complicated, no more sinister than that. As to *The Final Beast,* the part of the Christian experience that I particularly tried to make real was the one I found so conspicuously absent in most of the books I searched through for readings to assign my Exeter classes, and that was the experience of salvation as grace, as the now-and-thenness and here-and-thereness of the New Being.

Love ✳ September 10

THE FIRST STAGE is to believe that there is only one kind of love. The middle stage is to believe that there are many kinds of love and that the Greeks had a different word for each of them. The last stage is to believe that there is only one kind of love.

The unabashed *eros* of lovers, the sympathetic *philia* of friends, *agape* giving itself away freely no less for the murderer than for his victim (the King James version translates it as *charity*)—these are all varied manifestations of a single reality. To lose yourself in another's arms, or in another's company, or in suffering for all men who suffer, including the ones who inflict suffering upon you—to lose yourself in such ways is to find yourself. Is what it's all about. Is what love is.

Of all powers, love is the most powerful and the most powerless. It is the most powerful because it alone can conquer that final and most impregnable stronghold which is the human heart. It is the most powerless because it can do nothing except by consent.

To say that love is God is romantic idealism. To say that God is love is either the last straw or the ultimate truth.

In the Christian sense, love is not primarily an emotion but an act of the will. When Jesus tells us to love our neighbors, he is not telling us to love them in the sense of responding to them with a cozy emotional feeling. You can as well produce a cozy emotional feeling on demand as you can a yawn or a sneeze. On the contrary, he is telling us to love our neighbors in the sense of being willing to work for their well-being even if it means sacrificing our own well-being to that end, even if it means sometimes just leaving them alone. Thus in Jesus' terms we can love our neighbors without necessarily liking them. In fact liking them may stand in the way of loving them by making us overprotective sentimentalists instead of reasonably honest friends.

When Jesus talked to the Pharisees, he didn't say, "There, there. Everything's going to be all right." He said, "You brood of vipers! how can you speak good when you are evil!" (Matthew 12:34). And he said that to them because he loved them.

This does not mean that liking may not be a part of loving, only that it doesn't have to be. Sometimes liking follows on the heels of loving. It is hard to work for somebody's well-being very long without coming in the end to rather like him too.

Born Again ✳ *September 11*

T HE PHRASE COMES, of course, from a scene in John's Gospel where Jesus tells a Pharisee named Nicodemus that he will never see the Kingdom of God unless he is born again.

Somewhat testily prodded by Nicodemus to make himself clearer, Jesus says, "That which is born of the flesh is flesh, and that which is born of the Spirit is spirit." In other words, spiritual rebirth by the power of the Holy Spirit is what Jesus is talking about.

He then goes one step further, playing on the word *pneuma*, which means both "spirit" and "wind" in Greek. "The wind blows where it will, and you hear the sound of it, but you do not know whence it comes or whither it goes; so it is with everyone who is born of the Spirit," he says (John 3:1–8). The implication seems to be that the kind of rebirth he has in mind is (*a*) elusive and mysterious and (*b*) entirely God's doing. There's no telling when it will happen or to whom.

Presumably those to whom it does happen feel themselves filled, as a sheer gift, with that love, joy, peace which Saint Paul singles out as the principal fruits of the experience. In some measure, however fleetingly, it is to be hoped that most Christians have had at least a taste of them.

Some of those who specifically refer to themselves as "Born Again Christians," however, seem to use the term in a different sense. You get the feeling that to them it means Super Christians. They are apt to have the relentless cheerfulness of car salesmen. They tend to be a little too friendly a little too soon and the women to wear more make-up than they need. You can't imagine any of them ever having had a bad moment or a lascivious thought or used a nasty word when they bumped their head getting out of the car. They speak a great deal about "the Lord" as if they have him in their hip pocket and seem to feel that it's no harder to figure out what he wants them to do in any given situation than to look up in Fanny Farmer how to make brownies. The whole shadow side of human existence—the suffering, the doubt, the frustration, the ambiguity—appears as absent from their view of things as litter from the streets of Disneyland. To hear them speak of God, he seems about as elusive and mysterious as a Billy

243

Graham rally at Madison Square Garden, and on their lips the Born Again experience often sounds like something we can all make happen any time we want to, like fudge, if only we follow their recipe.

It is not for anybody to judge the authenticity of the Born Again's spiritual rebirth or anybody else's, but my guess is that by the style and substance of their witnessing to it, the souls they turn on to Christ are apt to be fewer in number than the ones they turn off.

Truly Human ✳ September 12

In addition to the battle to "get ahead," there is another:

THIS OTHER WAR is the war not to conquer but the war to become whole and at peace inside our skins. It is a war not of conquest now but of liberation because the object of this other war is to liberate that dimension of selfhood which has somehow become lost, that dimension of selfhood that involves the capacity to forgive and to will the good not only of the self but of all other selves. This other war is the war to become a human being. This is the goal that we are really after and that God is really after. This is the goal that power, success, and security are only forlorn substitutes for. This is the victory that not all our human armory of self-confidence and wisdom and personality can win for us—not simply to be treated as human but to become at last truly human.

Two Answers ✳ September 13

WHAT DOES IT mean to be a human being? There are two fine novels, written over twenty-five years ago, one by a Roman Catholic, the other by an atheist, both of which are much involved with this question. In *The Power and the Glory*, by Graham Greene, the hero, or nonhero, is a seedy, alcoholic

Catholic priest who after months as a fugitive is finally caught by the revolutionary Mexican government and condemned to be shot. On the evening before his execution, he sits in his cell with a flask of brandy to keep his courage up and thinks back over what seems to him the dingy failure of his life. "Tears poured down his face," Greene writes. "He was not at the moment afraid of damnation—even the fear of pain was in the background. He felt only an immense disappointment because he had to go to God empty-handed, with nothing done at all. It seemed to him at that moment that it would have been quite easy to have been a saint. It would only have needed a little self-restraint, and a little courage. He felt like someone who has missed happiness by seconds at an appointed place. He knew now that at the end there was only one thing that counted—to be a saint." And in the other novel, *The Plague,* by Albert Camus, there is a scrap of conversation that takes place between two atheists, one of them a journalist and the other a doctor who has been trying somehow to check the plague that has been devastating the North African city where they live. "It comes to this," says one of them. "What interests me is learning to become a saint."

The One Good Reason ✳ *September 14*

To anyone who is looking for good reasons for being a Christian, let me suggest the only really good one that I know. What does the faith mean by taking this man who was really a man, perhaps the only man, and calling him the Son of God, the Word of God, the Christ, all these metaphors so alien to our whole way of thinking? What is the reality about him other than the reality of his manhood that these metaphors are so clumsily, hopelessly, beautifully trying to convey? Just this, I believe, and it is much: that in this man there is power to turn goats into tigers, to give life to the half-alive, even to the dead; that what he asks of us when he says "Follow me" is what he also has the power to give, and this is the power of God that he has, that he is, and that is why men have called him the Christ.

Hell ❋ September 15

PEOPLE ARE FREE in this world to live for themselves alone if they want to and let the rest go hang, and they are free to live out the dismal consequences as long as they can stand it. The doctrine of Hell proclaims that they retain this same freedom in whatever world comes next. Thus the possibility of making damned fools of ourselves would appear to be limitless.

Or maybe Hell is the limit. Since the damned are said to suffer as dismally in the next world as they do in this one, they must still have enough life left in them to suffer with, which means that in their flight from Love, God apparently stops them just this side of extinguishing themselves utterly. Thus the bottomless pit is not really bottomless. Hell is the bottom beyond which God in his terrible mercy will not let them go.

Dante saw written over the gates of Hell the words "Abandon all hope ye who enter here," but he must have seen wrong. If there is suffering life in Hell, there must also be hope in Hell, because where there is life there is the Lord and giver of life, and where there is suffering he is there too because the suffering of the ones he loves is also his suffering.

"He descended into Hell," the Creed says, and "If I make my bed in Sheol, thou art there," the Psalmist (139:8). It seems there is no depth to which he will not sink. Maybe not even Old Scratch will be able to hold out against him forever.

David ✳ September 16

To see what there was about David that made Israel adore him like no other king she ever had, as good a place to look as any is the account of how he captured Jerusalem and moved in the ark.

Jerusalem was a major plum for the new young king, a hill town considered so untakable that the inhabitants had a saying to the effect that a blind man and a cripple could hold it against the U.S. Marines (2 Samuel 5:6). Just to remind people who it was that had nevertheless finally taken it, David's first move was to change its name to the City of David. His second move was a brilliant maneuver for giving his victory the stamp of divine approval by trotting out that holy box of acacia wood overlaid with gold which was known as the ark and contained who knows what but was as close as Israel ever officially got to a representation in space of their God who dwelled in eternity. David had the ark loaded onto a custom-built cart and made a regular circus parade of it, complete with horns, harps, cymbals, and psalteries, not to mention himself high-stepping out front like the Mayor of Dublin on Saint Patrick's Day. When they finally made it into town, he set up a big tent to keep out the weather, had refreshments passed around on the house, and, just so nobody would forget who was picking up the tab, did the lion's share of the praying himself and personally took up the collection afterwards.

So far it was none of it anything a good public relations man couldn't have dreamed up for him, but the next thing was something else again. He stripped down to his skivvies, and then with everybody looking on including his wife—a high-class girl named Michal who gave his administration tone as the late King Saul's daughter—he did a dance. Maybe it started out as just another Madison Avenue ploy, but not for long.

With trumpets blaring and drums beating, it was Camelot all over again, and for once that royal young red-head didn't have to talk up the bright future and the high hopes because he was himself the future at its brightest, and there were no hopes higher than the ones his people had in him. And for once he didn't have to drag God in for politics' sake either because it was obvious to everybody that this time God was there on his own. How they cut loose together, David and Yahweh, whirling around before the ark in such a passion that they caught fire from each other and blazed up in a single flame of such magnificence that not even the dressing-down David got from Michal afterwards could dim the glory of it.

He had feet of clay like the rest of us if not more so—self-serving and deceitful, lustful and vain—but on the basis of that dance alone, you can see why it was David more than anybody else that Israel lost her heart to and why, when Jesus of Nazareth came riding into Jerusalem on his flea-bitten mule a thousand years later, it was as the Son of David that they hailed him.

(2 SAMUEL 5–6)

A Man's Face ✴ September 17

Jesus had a face . . .

WHOEVER HE WAS or was not, whoever he thought he was, whoever he has become in the memories of men since and will go on becoming for as long as men remember him— exalted, sentimentalized, debunked, made and remade to the measure of each generation's desire, dread, indifference—he was a man once, whatever else he may have been. And he had a man's face, a human face. So suppose, as the old game goes, that we could return in time and see it for ourselves, see the face of Jesus as it actually was two thousand years of faces back. *Ecce homo,* Pilate said—*Behold the man*—yet whatever our religion or lack of it, we tend to shrink from beholding him and play our game instead with Shakespeare's face or Helen of Troy's because with them the chances are we could survive almost anything—Shakespeare's simper, say, or a cast in Helen's eye. But with Jesus the risk is too great; the risk that his face would be too much for us if not enough, either a face like any other face to see, pass by, forget, or a face so unlike any other that we would have no choice but to remember it always and follow or flee it to the end of our days and beyond. Like you and me he had a face his life gave shape to and that shaped his life and others' lives, and with part of ourselves I think we might turn away from the mystery of that face, that life, as much of the time we turn away from the mystery of life itself. With part of ourselves I think we might avoid meeting his real eyes, if such a meeting were possible, the way that at certain moments we avoid meeting our own real eyes in mirrors because for better or worse they threaten to tell us more than we want to know.

Before Abraham ✳ September 18

BEFORE ABRAHAM WAS," Jesus said, "I am." Who can say what he meant? Perhaps that just as his death was not the end of him, so his birth was not the beginning of him.

Whatever it is that history has come to see in him over the centuries, seen or unseen it was there from the start of history, he seems to be saying, and even before the start. Before Abraham was—before any king rose up in Israel or any prophet to bedevil him, before any patriarch or priest, Temple or Torah—something of Jesus existed no less truly for having no name yet or face, something holy and hidden, something implicit as sound is implicit in silence, as the Fall of Rome is implicit in the first atom sent spinning through space at the creation. And more than that.

Jesus does not say that before Abraham was, he was, but before Abraham was, he *is*. No past, no future, but only the present, because only the present is real. Named or unnamed, known or unknown, there neither has been nor ever will be a real time without him. If he is the Savior of the world as his followers believe, there never has been nor ever will be a world without salvation.

The Plain Sense ❈ *September 19*

THE AUTHOR OF the Epistle to the Hebrews describes Jesus as "one who in every respect has been tempted as we are yet without sinning"—tempted to be a demagogue, a spellbinder, a mere humanitarian, we are told in the account of his encounter in the wilderness with Satan, who offered him all the kingdoms of the earth if he would only settle for them and no more; tempted to escape martyrdom as Peter urged him to, saying, "God forbid, Lord. This shall never happen to you," to which Jesus replied, "Get behind me, Satan. You are a hindrance to me"; tempted, ultimately, to doubt the very faithfulness of God as he howls out his *Eloi, Eloi* from the cross.

And yet without sinning, Hebrews says. However great the temptation to abandon once and for all both his fellow men and his God—who together he had good reason to believe had abandoned him—he never ceased to reach out to them in love, forgiving finally his own executioners. He addressed his cry of dereliction to a God who, in spite of everything, he believed to the end was near enough, and counted him dear enough, to hear it. The paradoxical assertion that Jesus was both fully man and in some way also fully God seems to many the unnecessary and obfuscating doctrine of later theologians, but the truth of the matter is that like all doctrines it was an experience first, in this case the experience of the simple men who had actually known him. Having talked with him and eaten with him, having seen him angry, sad, merry, tired, and finally dead, they had no choice but to say that he was a man even as they themselves were men. But having found in him an undying power to heal and transform their lives, they had no choice but to say that he was God too if only because there was no other way of saying it.

If the doctrine of the divinity of Christ is paradoxical, it is only because the experience was paradoxical first. Much as we may wish it otherwise, reality seldom comes to us simple, logical, all of a piece. Man is an animal, we must say if we are honest, but he is also more than animal. In honesty we must say that too. If we are determined to speak the plain sense of our experience, we must be willing to risk the charge of speaking what often sounds like nonsense.

History ✳ September 20

UNLIKE BUDDHISM OR Hinduism, biblical faith takes history very seriously because God takes it very seriously. He took it seriously enough to begin it and to enter it and to promise that one day he will bring it to a serious close. The biblical view is that history is not an absurdity to be endured or an illusion to be dispelled or an endlessly repeating cycle to be escaped. Instead it is for each of us a series of crucial, precious, and unrepeatable moments that are seeking to lead us somewhere.

The true history of mankind and the true history of each individual man has less to do than we tend to think with the kind of information that gets into most histories, biographies, and autobiographies. True history has to do with the saving and losing of souls, and both of these are apt to take place when most people including the one whose soul is at stake are looking the other way. The real turning point in a man's life is less likely to be the day he wins the election or marries the girl than the morning he decides not to mail the letter or the afternoon he watches the woods fill up with snow. The real turning point in human history is less apt to be the day the wheel is invented or Rome falls than the day a boy is born to a couple of hick Jews.

John the Evangelist ✹ *September 21*

JOHN WAS A POET, and he knew about words. He knew that all men and all women are mysteries known only to themselves until they speak a word that opens up the mystery. He knew that the words people speak have their life in them just as surely as they have their breath in them. He knew that the words people speak have dynamite in them and that a word may be all it takes to set somebody's heart on fire or break it in two. He knew that words break silence and that the word that is spoken is the word that is heard and may even be answered. And at the beginning of his gospel he wrote a poem about the Word that God spoke.

When God speaks, things happen because the words of God aren't just as good as his deeds, they are his deeds. When God speaks his word, John says, creation happens, and when God speaks to his creation, what comes out is not ancient Hebrew or the King James Version or a sentiment suitable for framing in the pastor's study. On the contrary. "The word became flesh," John says (1:14), and that means that when God wanted to say what God is all about and what man is all about and what life is all about, it wasn't a sound that emerged but a man. Jesus was his name. He was dynamite. He was the Word of God.

As this might lead you to expect, the Gospel of John is as different from the other three as night from day. Matthew quotes Scripture, Mark lists miracles, Luke reels off parables, and each has his own special axe to grind too, but the one thing they all did in common was to say something also about the thirty-odd years Jesus lived on this earth, the kinds of things he did and said and what he got for his pains as well as what the world got for his pains too. John, on the other hand, clearly has something else in mind, and if you didn't happen to know, you'd hardly guess that his Jesus and the Jesus of the other three gospels are the same man.

John says nothing about when or where or how he was born. He says nothing about how the baptist baptized him. There's no account of the temptation in John, or the transfiguration, nothing about how he told people to eat bread and drink wine in his memory once in a while, or how he sweated blood in the garden the night they arrested him, or how he was tried before the Sanhedrin as well as before Pilate. There's nothing in John about the terrible moment when he cried out that God had forsaken him at the very time he needed him most. Jesus doesn't tell even a single parable in John. So what then, according to John, does Jesus do?

He speaks words. He speaks poems that sound much like John's poems, and the poems are about himself. Even when he works his miracles, you feel he's thinking less about the human needs of the people he's working them for than about something else he's got to say about who he is and what he's there to get done. When he feeds a big, hungry crowd on hardly enough to fill a grocery bag, for instance, he says, "I am the bread of life. He who comes to me shall not hunger, and he who believes in me shall never thirst" (6:35). When he raises his old friend Lazarus from the dead, he says, "I am the resurrection and the life. He who believes in me, though he die, yet shall he live, and whoever lives and believes in me shall never die" (11:25–26). "I am the door," he says, "and if any one enters by me, he will be saved" (10:9). "I am the good shepherd" (10:14), "the light of the world" (8:12), "I am the way, the truth, and the life," he says (14:6) and "I and the Father are one" (10:30).

You miss the Jesus of Matthew, Mark, and Luke of course—the one who got mad and tired and took naps in boats. You miss the Jesus who healed people because he felt sorry for them and made jokes about camels squeezing through the eyes of needles and had a soft spot in his heart for easy-going ladies and children who didn't worry about Heaven like the disciples because in a way they were already there. There's nothing he doesn't know in John, nothing he can't do, and when they take him in the end, you feel he could blow them right off the map if he felt like it. Majestic, mystical, aloof almost, the Jesus of the Fourth Gospel walks three feet off the ground, you feel, and you can't help wishing that once in a while he'd come down to earth.

But that's just the point, of course—John's point. It's not the Jesus people knew on earth that he's mainly talking about, and everybody agrees that the story about how he saved the adulteress's skin by saying, "Let him who is without sin cast the first stone" (8:7) must have been added by somebody else, it seems so out of place with all the rest.

Jesus, for John, is the Jesus he knew in his own heart and the one he believed everybody else could know too if they only kept their hearts open. He is Jesus as the Word that breaks the heart and sets the feet to dancing and stirs tigers in the blood. He is the Jesus John loved not just because he'd healed the sick and fed the hungry but because he'd saved the world. Jesus as the *mot juste* of God.

Gluttony ✳ September 22

A GLUTTON IS ONE who raids the icebox for a cure for spiritual malnutrition.

This Way ✳ September 23

BUT ON THE REALLY crucial decisions of life—Do I love her enough to marry her? Is it worth dying for? Can I give my life to this?—when it comes to decisions like these, it is not just the pro-and-con-listing part of me or the coin-tossing and advice-seeking parts that are involved. It is all of me, heart, mind, will, and when the moment comes and I find myself moving out for good and all, one way or another, there is a kind of relentless spontaneity about it, a kind of terrific sense of conviction, so that if you are Matthew in the tax office, you lay down your slide rule and your pencil, do not even finish the form that you happened to be working on at the moment, but just push back your chair and start heading for the door without even bothering to pick up your coat hanging over by the water cooler. And then you step out of there forever without once looking back over your shoulder, and start following the way you have chosen: not that way over there or that way right here, but *this* way. Of all the ten million and one ways in the world, you choose this way. Or maybe it chooses you—to put it a better way. Or you choose each other, your way and you.

Possibility ✳ September 24

IN THE SPRING of 1953, I had left my job at Lawrenceville to be a full-time writer in New York, and it was that fall, with my third novel failing to come to life for me, that in some sense my life itself started to come to life for me—the possibility, at least, of a life in Christ, with Christ, and, on some fine day conceivably, even a life for Christ, if I could ever find out what such a life involved, could find somewhere in myself courage enough, faith enough, craziness and grace enough, to undertake the living of it.

Beatitudes ✳ *September 25*

IF WE DIDN'T already know but were asked to guess the kind of people Jesus would pick out for special commendation, we might be tempted to guess one sort or another of spiritual hero—men and women of impeccable credentials morally, spiritually, humanly, and every which way. If so, we would be wrong. Maybe those aren't the ones he picked out because he felt they didn't need the shot in the arm his commendation would give them. Maybe they're not the ones he picked out because he didn't happen to know any. Be that as it may, it's worth noting the ones he did pick out.

Not the spiritual giants but "the poor in spirit" as he called them, the ones who spiritually speaking have absolutely nothing to give and absolutely everything to receive like the Prodigal telling his father "I am not worthy to be called thy son" only to discover for the first time all he had in having a father.

Not the champions of faith who can rejoice even in the midst of suffering but the ones who mourn over their own suffering because they know that for the most part they've brought it down on themselves, and over the suffering of others because that's just the way it makes them feel to be in the same room with them.

Not the strong ones but the meek ones in the sense of the gentle ones, i.e., the ones not like Caspar Milquetoast but like Charlie Chaplin, the little tramp who lets the world walk over him and yet, dapper and undaunted to the end, somehow makes the world more human in the process.

Not the ones who are righteous but the ones who hope they will be someday and in the meantime are well aware that the distance they still have to go is even greater than the distance they've already come.

Not the winners of great victories over Evil in the world but the ones who, seeing it also in themselves every time they comb their hair in front of the bathroom mirror, are merciful when they find it in others and maybe that way win the greater victory.

Not the totally pure but the "pure in heart," to use Jesus' phrase, the ones who may be as shop-worn and clay-footed as the next one but have somehow kept some inner freshness and innocence intact.

Not the ones who have necessarily found peace in its fullness but the ones who, just for that reason, try to bring it about wherever and however they can—peace with their neighbors and God, peace with themselves.

Jesus saved for last the ones who side with Heaven even when any fool can see it's the losing side and all you get for your pains is pain. Looking into the faces of his listeners, he speaks to them directly for the first time. "Blessed are you," he says.

You can see them looking back at him. They're not what you'd call a high-class crowd—peasants and fisherfolk for the most part, on the shabby side, not all that bright. It doesn't look as if there's a hero among them. They have their jaws set. Their brows are furrowed with concentration.

They are blessed when they are worked over and cursed out on his account he tells them. It is not his hard times to come but theirs he is concerned with, speaking out of his own meekness and mercy, the purity of his own heart.

(MATTHEW 5:1–12)

To Go On Trying ✳ September 26

WE TRY SO HARD as Christians. We think such long thoughts, manipulate such long words, and both listen to and preach such long sermons. Each one of us somewhere, somehow, has known, if only for a moment or so, something of what it is to feel the shattering love of God, and once that has happened, we can never rest easy again for trying somehow to set that love forth not only in words, myriads of words, but in our lives themselves. And when, as must always happen, we sometimes give up this trying either because for a moment it seems unreal or because we are tired or bored or because we forget or choose to forget, we cannot even enjoy our moment's release for the sense of failure that chokes us. This is of course as it should be. Fruitless and destructive as so much of our trying must always be, and tormented as we are by knowing this and by beholding the shallowness and duplicity of our motives, we have scarcely any choice but to go on trying no matter what, and there is much that is beautiful and brave and true about it. Yet we must remember this other word too: "Unless you turn and become like children. . . ."

Vocation ✳ September 27

IN THE YEAR THAT King Uzziah died, or in the year that John F. Kennedy died, or in the year that somebody you loved died, you go into the temple if that is your taste, or you hide your face in the little padded temple of your hands, and a voice says, "Whom shall I send into the pain of a world where people die?" and if you are not careful, you may find yourself answering, "Send me." You may hear the voice say, "Go." Just *go*.

Like "duty," "law," "religion," the word "vocation" has a dull ring to it, but in terms of what it means, it is really not dull at all. *Vocare,* to call, of course, and a man's vocation is a man's calling. It is the work that he is called to in this world, the thing that he is summoned to spend his life doing. We can speak of a man's choosing his vocation, but perhaps it is at least as accurate to speak of a vocation's choosing the man, of a call's being given and a man's hearing it, or not hearing it. And maybe that is the place to start: the business of listening and hearing. A man's life is full of all sorts of voices calling him in all sorts of directions. Some of them are voices from inside and some of them are voices from outside. The more alive and alert we are, the more clamorous our lives are. Which do we listen to? What kind of voice do we listen for?

Dream ✳ September 28

A FRIEND OF mine dreamed that he was standing in an open place out under the sky, and there was a woman also standing there dressed in some coarse material like burlap. He could not see her face distinctly, but the impression that he had was that she was beautiful, and he went up to her and asked her a question. This friend of mine described himself to me once as a believing unbeliever, and the question that he asked her was the same one that Pontius Pilate asked Jesus, only he did not ask it the way you can imagine Pilate did—urbanely, with his eyes narrowed—but instead he asked it with great urgency as if his life depended on the answer, as perhaps it did. He went up to the woman in his dream and asked, "What is the truth?" Then he reached out for her hand, and she took it. Only instead of a hand, she had the claw of a bird, and as she answered his question, she grasped his hand so tightly in that claw that the pain was almost unendurable and prevented him from hearing her answer. So again he asked her, "What is the truth?" and again she pressed his hand, and again the pain drowned out her words. And then once more, a third time, and once more the terrible pain and behind it the answer that he could not hear. And the dream ended. What is the truth for the man who believes and cannot believe that there is a truth beyond all truths, to know which is to be himself made whole and true?

Good Works ✳ September 29

BUT IF GOOD WORKS are not the cause of salvation, they are nonetheless the mark and effect of it. If the forgiven man does not become forgiving, the loved man loving, then he is only deceiving himself. "You shall know them by their fruits," Jesus says, and here Gentle Jesus Meek and Mild becomes Christ the Tiger, becomes both at once, this stern and loving man. "Every tree that does not bear good fruit is cut down and thrown into the fire," he says, and Saint Paul is only echoing him when he writes to the Galatians, "The fruit of the Spirit is love, joy, peace, patience, kindness, goodness, faithfulness, gentleness, self-control; against such there is no law."

More Than Symbol ✳ September 30

IN ITS FULLEST sense, remembering is far more than the long backward glance of nostalgia, and in its fullest sense the symbol of bread and wine is far more than symbol. It is part of the mystery of any symbol always to contain something of the power of the thing symbolized just as it is more than a mere piece of painted cloth that makes your pulse quicken when you come upon your country's flag in a foreign land, more than a mere sound that gladdens your spirit when you hear someone speak the name of an absent friend. When in remembrance of Jesus, the disciples ate the bread and drank the wine, it was more than mere bread and wine they were dealing with, and for all the tragic and ludicrous battles Christians have fought with each other for centuries over what actually takes place at the Mass, the Eucharist, Communion, or whatever they call it, they would all seem to agree that something extraordinary takes place. Even if the priest is a fraud, the bread a tasteless wafer, the wine not wine at all but temperance grapejuice, the one who comes to this outlandish meal in faith may find there something to feed his deepest hunger, may feel stirring within himself a life even more precious, more urgent, more near than his own.

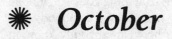 *October*

Anything Goes? ✳ October 1

MOST OF THE OLD restraints are gone or going. Such purely practical restraints as the fear of pregnancy and venereal disease have been all but eliminated by the ingenuity of modern science. Pornography is available to anybody who has the money to buy it at the newsstand. As much as you can generalize about such matters, in the realm of sexual behavior the word seems to be increasingly, "Anything goes," or, among the more responsible, "Anything goes as long as nobody gets hurt," the trouble with which is how can anybody know in advance, in any complex human relationship, sexual or otherwise, who is going to get hurt psychologically, emotionally, spiritually? Or the word is, "Anything goes as long as you love each other," the trouble with which is that love here is likely to mean a highly romanticized, sentimental sort of enterprise that comes and goes like the pink haze it is.

What makes this a tragic situation, I believe, is not so much that by one set of standards or another it is morally wrong, but that in terms of the way human life is, it just does not work very well. Our society is filled with people for whom the sexual relationship is one where body meets body but where person fails to meet person; where the immediate need for sexual gratification is satisfied but where the deeper need for companionship and understanding is left untouched. The result is that the relationship leads not to fulfillment but to a half-conscious sense of incompleteness, of inner loneliness, which is so much the sickness of our time. The desire to know another's nakedness is really the desire to know the other fully as a person. It is the desire to know and to be known, not just sexually but as a total human being. It is the desire for a relationship where each gives not just of his body but of his self, body and spirit both, for the other's gladness.

Isaiah ✳ October 2

THERE WERE BANKS of candles flickering in the distance and clouds of incense thickening the air with holiness and stinging his eyes, and high above him, as if it had always been there but was only now seen for what it was (like a face in the leaves of a tree or a bear among the stars), there was the Mystery Itself whose gown was the incense and the candles a dusting of gold at the hem. There were winged creatures shouting back and forth the way excited children shout to each other when dusk calls them home, and the whole vast, reeking place started to shake beneath his feet like a wagon going over cobbles, and he cried out, "O God, I am done for! I am foul of mouth and the member of a foul-mouthed race. With my own two eyes I have seen him. I'm a goner and sunk." Then one of the winged things touched his mouth with fire and said, "There, it will be all right now," and the Mystery Itself said, "Who will it be?" and with charred lips he said, "Me," and Mystery said "GO."

Mystery said, "Go give the deaf Hell till you're blue in the face and go show the blind Heaven till you drop in your tracks because they'd sooner eat ground glass than swallow the bitter pill that puts roses in the cheeks and a gleam in the eye. Go do it."

Isaiah said, "Do it till when?"

Mystery said, "Till Hell freezes over."

Mystery said, "Do it till the cows come home."

And that is what a prophet does for a living, and, starting from the year that King Uzziah died when he saw and heard all these things, Isaiah went and did it.

(ISAIAH 6)

265

Darkness ✻ October 3

"The people who walked in darkness have seen a great light."

IN ONE RESPECT if in no other this metaphor of Isaiah's is a very relevant one for us and our age because we are also, God knows, a people who walk in darkness. There seems little need to explain. If darkness is meant to suggest a world where nobody can see very well—either themselves, or each other, or where they are heading, or even where they are standing at the moment; if darkness is meant to convey a sense of uncertainty, of being lost, of being afraid; if darkness suggests conflict, conflict between races, between nations, between individuals each pretty much out for himself when you come right down to it; then we live in a world that knows much about darkness. Darkness is what our newspapers are about. Darkness is what most of our best contemporary literature is about. Darkness fills the skies over our own cities no less than over the cities of our enemies. And in our single lives, we know much about darkness too. If we are people who pray, darkness is apt to be a lot of what our prayers are about. If we are people who do not pray, it is apt to be darkness in one form or another that has stopped our mouths.

Eternity ✻ October 4

ETERNITY IS NOT endless time or the opposite of time. It is the essence of time.

If you spin a pinwheel fast enough, then all its colors blend into a single color—white—which is the essence of all the colors of the spectrum combined.

If you spin time fast enough, then time-past, time-present, and time-to-come all blend into a single timelessness or eternity, which is the essence of all times combined.

As human beings we know time as a passing of unrepeatable events in the course of which everything passes away including ourselves. As human beings, we also know occasions when we stand outside the passing of events and glimpse their meaning. Sometimes an event occurs in our lives (a birth, a death, a marriage—some event of unusual beauty, pain, joy) through which we catch a glimpse of what our lives are all about and maybe even what life itself is all about, and this glimpse of what "it's all about" involves not just the present but the past and future too.

Inhabitants of time that we are, we stand on such occasions with one foot in eternity. God, as Isaiah says (57:15) "inhabiteth eternity" but stands with one foot in time. The part of time where he stands most particularly is Christ, and thus in Christ we catch a glimpse of what eternity is all about, what God is all about, and what we ourselves are all about too.

"Remember Me" ✳ October 5

ONE OF THE CRIMINALS who were hanged taunted him, saying, 'Are you not the Christ? Save yourself and us!' But the other rebuked him, saying, 'Have you no fear of God? For us it is plain justice, but this man has done nothing wrong.' And he said, 'Jesus, remember me when you come in your kingly power.' And Jesus said to him, 'Today you will be with me in Paradise.'"

We can imagine the soldiers smiling as simple men do when they encounter the unforeseen—these three criminals with their swollen tongues, like frogs croaking to each other of Paradise.

God ✸ October 6

THERE MUST BE A God because (a) since the beginning of history the most variegated majority of people have intermittently believed there was; (b) it is hard to consider the vast and complex structure of the universe in general and of the human mind in particular without considering the possibility that they issued from some ultimate source, itself vast, complex, and somehow mindful; (c) built into the very being of even the most primitive man there seems to be a profound psychophysical need or hunger for something like truth, goodness, love, and—under one alias or another—for God himself; and (d) every age and culture has produced mystics who have experienced a Reality beyond reality and have come back using different words and images but obviously and without collusion describing with awed adoration the same Indescribability.

Statements of this sort and others like them have been advanced for several thousand years as proofs of the existence of God. A twelve-year-old child can see that no one of them is watertight. And even all of them taken together won't convince anybody unless his predisposition to be convinced outweighs his predisposition not to be.

It is as impossible to prove or disprove that God exists beyond the various and conflicting ideas people have dreamed up about him as it is to prove or disprove that Goodness exists beyond the various and conflicting ideas people have dreamed up about what is good.

It is as impossible for man to demonstrate the existence of God as it would be for even Sherlock Holmes to demonstrate the existence of Arthur Conan Doyle.

All-wise. All-powerful. All-loving. All-knowing. We bore to death both God and ourselves with our chatter. God cannot be expressed but only experienced.

In the last analysis, you cannot pontificate but only point. A Christian is one who points at Christ and says, "I can't prove a thing, but there's something about his eyes and his voice. There's something about the way he carries his head, his hands, the way he carries his cross—the way he carries me."

You ❋ October 7

IN THE BOOK OF Genesis, the first word God speaks to a human being is *you* (Genesis 2:15), and in the Book of Revelation, the last word a human being speaks in effect to God is "Come, Lord Jesus!" which is to say "Come, *you!*" (Revelation 22:20).

It is possible that the whole miracle of Creation is to bridge the immeasurable distance between Creator and Creature with that one small word, and every time human beings use it to bridge the immeasurable distances between one another, something of that miracle happens again.

Chanting ❋ October 8

IT IS A FORM of high-church Popery that is supposed to set mainline Protestant teeth on edge. It shouldn't.

Words wear out after a while, especially religious words. We've said them so many times. We've listened to them so often. They are like voices we know so well we no longer hear them.

When a prayer or a psalm or a passage from the Gospels is chanted, we hear the words again. We hear them in a new way. We remember that they are not only meaning but music and mystery. The chanting italicizes them. The prose becomes poetry. The prosaic becomes powerful.

Of course chanting wears out after a while too.

A ND FINALLY THERE was Lazarus, the friend from Bethany whom he loved and whose sisters he loved. When word was brought to him that Lazarus was ill, he said, "This illness is not unto death," and when on the contrary it killed him, Jesus was still able to speak words which his followers to this day treasure as among the most precious he ever spoke: "I am the resurrection and the life; he who believes in me, though he dies, yet shall he live, and whoever lives and believes in me shall never die." But when he went to Bethany and actually faced the sisters in their terrible grief, he could find for the moment no more such brave and hopeful words. "He was deeply moved in spirit," the evangelist writes, and then that shortest, bluntest verse in the entire New Testament: "Jesus wept."

If we could understand all that lay behind those tears, we would understand much about him, more maybe than it is well for us to understand; but to the degree that he was, whatever else, a human being like ourselves, we can understand at least something. It was presumably the naked fact itself that staggered him there in Bethany—death not as a distant darkness that his great faith was light enough to see him through; death not as a universal condition; but death as *this* death and darkness which he saw written across the swollen faces of the two women who stood there before him. Whatever Jesus may at other moments have seen as rising bright as hope beyond it, at this particular moment death was a darkness he had no heart to see beyond. Maybe it was more than that. "Could not he who opened the eyes of the blind have kept this man from dying?" some of the bystanders muttered in his hearing. It is hard not to believe that in the abyss of his being Jesus was asking himself the same dark question.

Truly Ourselves ❋ October 10

THE FACE OF JESUS is a face that belongs to us the way our past belongs to us. It is a face that we belong to if only as to the one face out of the past that has perhaps had more to do with the shaping of our present than any other. According to Paul, the face of Jesus is our own face finally, the face we will all come to look like a little when the kingdom comes and we are truly ourselves at last, truly the brothers and sisters of one another and the children of God.

Another Reason ❋ October 11

A TANNED, SOFT-SPOKEN man has something wrong with his blood which is not at all soft-spokenly killing him. He is my friend, and when he was not dying, I always sought him out especially to be with, but now I go to see him only because I am—was it your own idea, or were you poorly advised?—a priest of sorts, and if the interlocutor, that prosecuting attorney, should press me for another reason for believing in God, I would say that I believe in him because it is only by the grace of something like God that I can do something as much braver than my face as visiting this good man whose pain makes awkward strangers of us. But if grace gets me there, it gets me no further. We cannot make ourselves known to each other; we are not healed and forgiven by each other's presence. With words as valueless as poker chips, we play games whose object it is to keep us from seeing each other's cards. Chit-chat games in which "How are you?" means "Don't tell me who you are," and "I'm alone and scared" becomes "Fine thanks." Games where the players create the illusion of being in the same room but where the reality of it is that each is alone inside a skin in that room, like bathyspheres at the bottom of the sea. Blind man's buff games where everyone is blind.

It is no wonder that we have had to invent other games to counteract these. Encounter groups, T groups, the multisensory techniques of William Schutz and the Esalen Institute and the Living Theater. After all these years of playing games whose purpose it is to keep us at arm's length from one another, to hide from each other our nakedness and our humanity, we turn at last to games no less pathetic and foolish in their ways but whose purpose is nonetheless to help us meet without disguise, to touch without embarrassment, to be human without fear. The sacrament of the Lord's Supper was such a game, I imagine, was once such a supper, such a breakfast, with bread being broken, people praying with their mouths full, and the priest thumping the table for a little silence, all of them caught up in some hallowed middle ground where God knows what was celebrated—the breadness of bread, the transfiguring miracle of bread shared, the passing of a common cup from lip to lip and tipsy kiss of peace, breath laden with bread, wine, miracle.

Rejoice Is the Last Word ✳ October 12

A YOUNG MINISTER acquaintance of mine said not long ago, "There are two kinds of Christians in the world. There are gloomy Christians and there are joyful Christians," and there wasn't the shadow of a doubt which kind he preferred with his smile as bright as his clerical collar, full of bounce and zip and the gift of gab, and there is little doubt as to which we all prefer. And why not? Joy is at the end of it, after all. Astonishment and joy are what our faith finally points to, and even Saint Paul, that in a way gloomiest of Christians, said as much though he was hardly less battered than the

Jesus he preached by the time he had come through his forty lashes less one, his stonings and shipwrecks and sleepless nights. Yet at the end, licking his wounds in a Roman lock-up, he wrote, "Rejoice in the Lord always. Again I will say, rejoice" (Philippians 4:4). But it is at the end that he wrote it. *Rejoice* is the last word and can be spoken only after the first word. The sheltering word can be spoken only after the word that leaves us without a roof over our heads, the answering word only after the word it answers.

A Doorway Opens ✳ *October 13*

AT ITS HEART, I think, religion is mystical. Moses with his flocks in Midian, Buddha under the Bo tree, Jesus up to his knees in the waters of Jordan: each of them responds to something for which words like *shalom,* oneness, God even, are only pallid, alphabetic souvenirs. "I have seen things," Aquinas told a friend, "that make all my writings seem like straw." Religion as institution, as ethics, as dogma, as social action—all of this comes later and in the long run maybe counts for less. Religions start, as Frost said poems do, with a lump in the throat, to put it mildly, or with the bush going up in flames, the rain of flowers, the dove coming down out of the sky.

As for the man in the street, any street, wherever his own religion is a matter of more than custom, it is likely to be because, however dimly, a doorway opened in the air once to him too, a word was spoken, and, however shakily, he responded. The debris of his life continues to accumulate, the Vesuvius of the years scatters its ashes deep and much gets buried alive, but even under many layers the tell-tale heart can go on beating still. Where it beats strong, there starts pulsing out from it a kind of life that is marked by, above all things perhaps, compassion: that sometimes fatal capacity for feeling what it is like to live inside another's skin and for knowing that there can never really be peace and joy for any until there is peace and joy finally for all. Where it stops beating altogether, little is left religiously speaking but a good man, not perhaps in Mark Twain's "the worst sense of the word" but surely in the grayest and saddest: the good man whose goodness has become cheerless and finicky, a technique for working off his own guilts, a gift with no love in it which neither deceives nor benefits any for long.

Novelist at Work * October 14

ON MICHELANGELO'S ceiling, the old man reaches down out of the cloud to touch Adam's finger and give him life. Here the situation is reversed. I am Adam reaching up to touch an old man's finger and give life to a cloud. I am writing about an old man who exists only in my mind. I have put him together out of scraps and pieces, most of them forgotten. There's some of Mark Twain in him, the old Mark they brought back in a wheel chair from Bermuda to die at Stormfield. There's some of the old man Isak from Bergman's *Wild Strawberries* in him who at the end of the film looks across a little inlet and sees a young man and a young woman in Victorian dress—the man in a straw hat fishing, the woman sitting on the grass beside him with a white parasol—and recognizing them as his parents, raises one hand in greeting as across the water one of them raises a hand to him. There's some of an old German cousin in him who looked like the Kaiser and walked through forests with his cane in the air naming trees. No need to list more of what went into my old man's making. It is enough to say that it is I who made him and not he himself. I speak not of Michelangelo's old man in the cloud but of the old man in the novel I am here to try to write. He is my old man, and it is in me that he lives and moves and has such being as he may be said to have.

It is true that he has never run away with the book as novelists are fond of saying their characters do, but he has on occasion lived and moved in ways other than those I had in mind for him. For instance, he weeps from time to time. I had imagined him as crustier and more remote than that. Also, although I intended him to see ghosts, I did not intend the particular ghosts that he saw—Elizabethan ghosts mainly. He saw Shakespeare's ghost whispering on and on with a faint lisp about forgotten rooms and forgotten faces, and he saw the ghost of Elizabeth herself. "She had the worst set of teeth I ever saw," my old man said, "as if she'd been eating blueberry pie. Now, the dress and all could have been a figment of my imagination," he went on. "The dress I could have dreamed, but not the teeth. It would have taken a dentist to dream a set of teeth like that." It was I obviously who put those words into the old man's mouth, but I had not planned on his saying them any more than the old man planned on the Queen's bad teeth. It is the same way, I suppose, as with people you dream about. They have only your dream to move around in and they are your creatures, but they move with a curious freedom. It is my godlike task this morning to start the old man moving again.

With the rain beginning to let up a little, I read back over the work of the last few days, an absurdly small amount for all the hours of my life I spent on it, only three or four pages in a script so nearly unreadable even to myself that I assume that at some level of my being I do not want it read, sentences written and rewritten and then so befuddled with interlineations that I have to copy them out all over again in order to read them and then in the process of copying rewrite them into illegibility again. I read it all over only to discover when I am finished that it is apparently not the words that I have been listening to but the silence in between the words maybe or the silence in this familiar room where I have spoken the name of Christ and signed myself with his cross. I have understood nothing of what I have read so I have to go back and read it all over again.

From Afar ✻ October 15

THE WOMAN AT THE desk calls out my name. She mispronounces it. Maybe with the lectern and the limelight what I want more than anything else is simply for people to know how to pronounce my name. Maybe, as Dostoevski said about old Karamazov, "even the wicked are much more naive and simple-hearted than we suppose. And we ourselves are too." I could always change the spelling of my name to be phonetic, but then it would no longer be my name. The umlauts of the fathers are visited upon the heads of the sons. My name is mispronounced, but it is my name, it is me, and I rise from my seat at the sound of it. The message that the woman gives me is that someone has called to say that my friend cannot make it for lunch. The one I have been waiting for is not going to come, and I am Estragon waiting for Godot, I am the old man in the woods reaching up to a shape of air and closing his fingers down on emptiness. But in many disguises he has come before, and in many disguises he will come again before he comes finally, and once or twice I have even thought I recognized him. I watch the waiter suspiciously as I eat my lunch alone. I decide against the shrimp cocktail.

And what more shall I say? For time would fail me to tell of Gideon, Barak, Samson, Jephthah, of David and Samuel and the prophets. All these also did not receive what was promised but greeted it from afar, and then there are all those who did not much believe in the promise to begin with, and it is not always possible to tell the two apart.

Worth Dying For   ✹   October 16

I HEAR YOU ARE entering the ministry," the woman said down the long table, meaning no real harm. "Was it your own idea or were you poorly advised?" And the answer that she could not have heard even if I had given it was that it was not an idea at all, neither my own nor anyone else's. It was a lump in the throat. It was an itching in the feet. It was a stirring in the blood at the sound of rain. It was a sickening of the heart at the sight of misery. It was a clamoring of ghosts. It was a name which, when I wrote it out in a dream, I knew was a name worth dying for even if I was not brave enough to do the dying myself and could not even name the name for sure. Come unto me, all ye who labor and are heavy laden, and I will give you a high and driving peace. I will condemn you to death.

I pick the children up at the bottom of the mountain where the orange bus lets them off in the wind. They run for the car like leaves blowing. Not for keeps, to be sure, but at least for the time being, the world has given them back again, and whatever the world chooses to do later on, it can never so much as lay a hand on the having-beenness of this time. The past is inviolate. We are none of us safe, but everything that has happened is safe. In all the vast and empty reaches of the universe it can never be otherwise than that when the orange bus stopped with its red lights blinking, these two children were on it. Their noses were running. One of them dropped a sweater. I drove them home.

Is It True?   ✹   October 17

S LEEP IS A threshold I drift toward like leaves. Brown and sere as a leaf, a face drifts toward me, the eyes buzzard-amber and burning. Is it true, my dear dead dear? Is all of it true? Is any of it true? If there's anywhere to be now, you must be there. If there's anything to know now wherever you are, then you must know it. But I can dream no sure and certain answer onto the old lips, just the faintest inclination of the black-felt tricorne. The face becomes a map of the world, becomes the world itself seen from a great height.

◆ ◆ ◆

Half drowned in my pillow, a sleepy, shiftless prayer at the end. Rejoice in the Lord always; again I will say, Rejoice. O Thou. Thou who didst call us this morning out of sleep and death. I come, we all of us come, down through the litter and the letters of the day. On broken legs. Sweet Christ, forgive and mend. Of thy finally unspeakable grace, grant to each in his own dark room valor and an unnatural virtue. Amen.

Virtue ✳ October 18

NEXT TO THE Seven Deadly Sins, the Seven Cardinal Virtues are apt to look pale and unenterprising, but appearances are notoriously untrustworthy.

Prudence and *temperance* taken separately may not be apt to get you to your feet cheering, but when they go together, as they almost always do, that's a different matter. The chain smoker or the junkie, for instance, who exemplifies both by managing to kick the habit, can very well have you throwing your hat in the air, especially if it happens to be somebody whom for personal reasons you'd like to have around a few years longer. And the *courage* involved isn't likely to leave you cold either. Often it's the habit-kicker's variety that seems the most courageous.

If you think of *justice* as sitting blindfolded with a scale in her hand, you may have to stifle a yawn, but if you think of a black judge acquitting a white racist of a false murder charge, it can give you gooseflesh.

The *faith* of a child taking your hand in the night is as moving as the faith of Mother Teresa among the untouchables, or Bernadette facing the skeptics at Lourdes, or Abraham, age seventy-five, packing up his bags for the Promised Land. And *hope* is the glimmer on the horizon that keeps faith plugging forward, of course, the wings that keep it more or less in the air.

Maybe it's only *love* that turns things around and makes the Seven Deadly Sins be the ones to look pale and unenterprising for a change. Greed, gluttony, lust, envy, pride are no more than sad efforts to fill the empty place where love belongs, and anger and sloth just two things that may happen when you find that not even all seven of them at their deadliest ever can.

Sleep ✸ October 19

IT'S A SURRENDER, a laying down of arms. Whatever plans you're making, whatever work you're up to your ears in, whatever pleasures you're enjoying, whatever sorrows or anxieties or problems you're in the midst of, you set them aside, find a place to stretch out somewhere, close your eyes, and wait for sleep.

All the things that make you the particular person you are stop working—your thoughts and feelings, the changing expressions of your face, the constant moving around, the yammering will, the relentless or not so relentless purpose. But all the other things keep on working with a will and purpose of their own. You go on breathing in and out. Your heart goes on beating. If some faint thought stirs somewhere in the depths of you, it's converted into a dream so you can go on sleeping and not have to wake up to think it through before it's time.

Whether you're just or unjust, you have the innocence of a cat dozing under the stove. Whether you're old or young, homely or fair, you take on the serenity of marble. You have given up being in charge of your life. You have put yourself into the hands of the night.

It is a rehearsal for the final laying down of arms, of course, when you trust yourself to the same unseen benevolence to see you through the dark and to wake you when the time comes—with new hope, new strength—into the return again of light.

Goodbye ✳ October 20

A WOMAN WITH A scarf over her head hoists her six-year-old up onto the first step of the school bus. "Goodbye," she says.

A father on the phone with his freshman son has just finished bawling him out for his poor grades. There is mostly silence at the other end of the line. "Well, goodbye," the father says.

When the girl at the airport hears the announcement that her plane is starting to board, she turns to the boy who is seeing her off. "I guess this is goodbye," she says.

The noise of the traffic almost drowns out the sound of the word, but the shape of it lingers on the old man's lips. He tries to look vigorous and resourceful as he holds out his hand to the other old man. "Goodbye." This time they say it so nearly in unison that it makes them both smile.

It was a long while ago that the words God be with you disappeared into the word goodbye, but every now and again some trace of them still glimmers through.

Extraordinary Things ✳ *October 21*

T HE GOSPEL IS BAD news before it is good news. It is the news that man is a sinner, to use the old word, that he is evil in the imagination of his heart, that when he looks in the mirror all in a lather what he sees is at least eight parts chicken, phony, slob. That is the tragedy. But it is also the news that he is loved anyway, cherished, forgiven, bleeding to be sure, but also bled for. That is the comedy. And yet, so what? So what if even in his sin the slob is loved and forgiven when the very mark and substance of his sin and of his slobbery is that he keeps turning down the love and forgiveness because he either doesn't believe them or doesn't want them or just doesn't give a damn? In answer, the news of the Gospel is that extraordinary things happen to him just as in fairy tales extraordinary things happen. Henry Ward Beecher cheats on his wife, his God, himself, but manages to keep on bringing the Gospel to life for people anyway, maybe even for himself. Lear goes berserk on a heath but comes out of it for a few brief hours every inch a king. Zaccheus climbs up a sycamore tree a crook and climbs down a saint. Paul sets out a hatchet man for the Pharisees and comes back a fool for Christ. It is impossible for anybody to leave behind the darkness of the world he carries on his back like a snail, but for God all things are possible. That is the fairy tale. All together they are the truth.

The Stones Do Cry Out ✳ *October 22*

W HEN HE COMES riding into the city on a mule, the cry goes up, "Blessed be the king that cometh in the name of the Lord" (Luke 19:38), and the Pharisees say, "Master, rebuke thy disciples" (Luke 29:38), and Jesus says, "I tell you, if these were silent, the very stones would cry out" (Luke

19:40). The point is, of course, that the stones do cry out. The mountain, the flames, cry out, the pretty girl at the piano cries out, and the child being born into his first summer, the old man smoking his last summer down to the butt like a cigar without knowing that it is his last summer. They all cry out truth, and their cry is wordless and silent and devastating. As somebody said, God does not sign his sunsets the way Turner did, nor does he arrange the stars to spell out messages of comfort. What is truth? Life is truth, the life of the world, your own life, and the life inside the world you are. The task of the preacher is to hold up life to us; by whatever gifts he or she has of imagination, eloquence, simple candor, to create images of life through which we can somehow see into the wordless truth of our lives. Before the Gospel is good news, it is simply the news that that's the way it is, whatever day it is of whatever year.

Finding the Words ✳ October 23

A T THE LEVEL OF words, what do they say, these prophet-preachers? They say this and they say that. They say things that are relevant, lacerating, profound, beautiful, spine-chilling, and more besides. They put words to both the wonder and the horror of the world, and the words can be looked up in the dictionary or the biblical commentary and can be interpreted, passed on, understood, but because these words are poetry, are image and symbol as well as meaning, are sound and rhythm, maybe above all are passion, they set echoes going the way a choir in a great cathedral does, only it is we who become the cathedral and in us that the words echo.

Ethically, politically, religiously, the prophets say what they ought to say, to use Shakespeare's phrase again, but beyond and even more crucial than that they say what they feel in a language that even across all the centuries and through all the translations and mistranslations causes us to feel them, too. At their most truly prophetic they speak things that my guess is that even they themselves did not entirely understand because they are things that are of truth itself rather than of particular truths, truth itself which cannot finally be understood but only experienced. It is the experience that they stun us with, speaking it out in poetry which transcends all other language in its power to open the doors of the heart. The man of sorrows and acquainted with grief. The one with the cauliflower ear and the split lip. By whose swollen eye and ruptured spleen we are somehow healed. Who can put a word to him and who needs to? They simply hold him up to our gaze. At their most poetic and powerful they do not say something as much as they make something happen.

Out of the Silence ✳ *October 24*

THE PREACHER PULLS the little cord that turns on the lectern light and deals out his note cards like a riverboat gambler. The stakes have never been higher. Two minutes from now he may have lost his listeners completely to their own thoughts, but at this minute he has them in the palm of his hand. The silence in the shabby church is deafening because everybody is listening to it. Everybody is listening including even himself. Everybody knows the kind of things he has told them before and not told them, but who knows what this time, out of the silence, he will tell them?

Let him tell them the truth. Before the Gospel is a word, it is silence. It is the silence of their own lives and of his life. It is life with the sound turned off so that for a moment or two you can experience it not in terms of the words you make it bearable by but for the unutterable mystery that it is. Let him say, "Be silent and know that I am God, saith the Lord" (Psalm

46:10). Be silent and know that even by my silence and absence I am known. Be silent and listen to the stones cry out.

Out of the silence let the only real news come, which is sad news before it is glad news and that is fairy tale last of all. The preacher is not brave enough to be literally silent for long, and since it is his calling to speak the truth with love, even if he were brave enough, he would not be silent for long because we are none of us very good at silence. It says too much. So let him use words, but, in addition to using them to explain, expound, exhort, let him use them to evoke, to set us dreaming as well as thinking, to use words as at their most prophetic and truthful, the prophets used them to stir in us memories and longings and intuitions that we starve for without knowing that we starve. Let him use words which do not only try to give answers to the questions that we ask or ought to ask but which help us to hear the questions that we do not have words for asking and to hear the silence that those questions rise out of and the silence that is the answer to those questions. Drawing on nothing fancier than the poetry of his own life, let him use words and images that help make the surface of our lives transparent to the truth that lies deep within them, which is the wordless truth of who we are and who God is and the Gospel of our meeting.

Holocaust ✻ *October 25*

IT IS IMPOSSIBLE to think about it. It is impossible not to think about it. Nothing in history equals the horror of it. There is no way to imagine it. There is no way to speak of it without diminishing it. Thousands upon thousands of them were taken away in Nazi Germany during the Second World War. They were gassed. Their corpses were burned. Many were old men. Many were small children. Many were women. They were charged with nothing except being Jews. In the end there were apparently something like six million of them who died, six thousand thousands.

Anyone who claims to believe in an all-powerful, all-loving God without taking into account this devastating evidence either that God is indifferent or powerless, or that there is no God at all, is playing games.

Anyone who claims to believe in the inevitable perfectibility of the human race without taking this into account is either a fool or a lunatic.

That many of the people who took part in the killings were professing Christians, not to mention many more who knew about the killings but did nothing to interfere, is a scandal which the Church of Christ perhaps does not deserve to survive.

For people who don't believe in God, suffering can be understood simply as part of the way the world works. The Holocaust is no more than an extreme example of the barbarities that human beings have been perpetrating on each other since the start. For people who do believe in God, it must remain always a dark and awful mystery.

If Love itself is really at the heart of all, how can such things happen? What do such things mean? The Old Testament speaks of the elusive figure of the Suffering Servant who though "despised and rejected of men" and brutally misused has nonetheless willingly "borne our griefs and carried our sorrows" and thereby won an extraordinary victory in which we all somehow share (Isaiah 52:13–53:12). The New Testament speaks of the Cross, part of whose meaning is that even out of the worst the world can do, God is still able to bring about the best.

But all such explanations sound pale and inadequate before the gas chambers of Buchenwald and Ravensbrück, the ovens of Treblinka.

Wishful Thinking ✳ October 26

CHRISTIANITY IS mainly wishful thinking. Even the part about Judgment and Hell reflects the wish that somewhere the score is being kept.

Dreams are wishful thinking. Children playing at being grown-up is wishful thinking. Interplanetary travel is wishful thinking.

Sometimes wishing is the wings the truth comes true on.

Sometimes the truth is what sets us wishing for it.

Myth ✳ October 27

THE RAW MATERIAL of a myth, like the raw material of a dream, may be something that actually happened once. But myths, like dreams, do not tell us much about that kind of actuality. The creation of man, Adam and Eve, the Tower of Babel, Oedipus—they do not tell us primarily about events. They tell us about ourselves.

In popular usage, a myth has come to mean a story that is not true. Historically speaking that may well be so. Humanly speaking, a myth is a story that is always true.

Touched with Joy ✳ October 28

THERE IS NOT ONE of us whose life has not already been touched somewhere with joy, so that in order to make it real to us, to show it forth, it should be enough for Jesus simply to remind us of it, to make us remember the joyous moments of our own lives. Yet this is not easy because, ironically enough, these are likely to be precisely the moments that we do not associate with religion. We tend to think that joy is not only not properly religious but that it is even the opposite of religion. We tend to think that religion is sitting stiff and antiseptic and a little bored and that joy is laughter and freedom and reaching out our arms to embrace the whole wide and preposterous earth which is so beautiful that sometimes it nearly breaks our hearts. We need to be reminded that at its heart Christianity is joy and that laughter and freedom and the reaching out of arms are the essence of it. We need to be reminded too that joy is not the same as happiness. Happiness is man-made—a happy home, a happy marriage, a happy relationship with our friends and within our jobs. We work for these things, and if we are careful and wise and lucky, we can usually achieve them. Happiness is one of the highest achievements of which we are capable, and when it is ours, we take credit for it, and properly so. But we never take credit for our moments of joy because we know that they are not man-made and that we are never really responsible for them. They come when they come. They are always sudden and quick and unrepeatable. The unspeakable joy sometimes of just being alive. The miracle sometimes of being just who we are with the blue sky and the green grass, the faces of our friends and the waves of the ocean, being just what they are. The joy of release, of being suddenly well when before we were sick, of being forgiven when before we were ashamed and afraid, of finding ourselves loved when we were lost and alone. The joy of love, which is the joy of the flesh as well as the spirit. But each of us can supply his own moments, so just two more things. One is that joy is always all-encompassing; there is nothing of us left over to hate with or to be afraid with, to feel guilty with or to be selfish about. Joy is where the whole being is pointed in one direction, and it is something that by its nature a man never hoards but always wants to share. The second thing is that joy is a mystery because it can happen anywhere, anytime, even under the most unpromising circumstances, even in the midst of suffering, with tears in its eyes. Even nailed to a tree.

What Jesus is saying is that men are made for joy and that anyone who is truly joyous has a right to say that he is doing God's will on this earth. Where you have known joy, you have known him.

Every Wedding a Dream ✳ October 29

A DREAM IS A compression of time where the dreamer can live through a whole constellation of events in no more time than it takes a curtain to rustle in the room where he sleeps. In dreams time does not flow on so much as it flows up, like water from a deep spring. And in this way every wedding is a dream, and every word that is spoken there means more than it says, and every gesture—the clasping of hands, the giving of rings—is rich with mystery. Part of the mystery is that Christ is there as he was in Cana once, and the joy of a wedding, and maybe even sometimes the tears, are a miracle that he works. But when the wedding feast was over, he set his face toward Jerusalem and started out for the hour that had not yet come but was to come soon enough, the hour when he too was to embrace the whole earth and water it with more than his tears.

And so it was also, we hope, with the bride and groom at Cana and with every bride and groom—that the love they bear one another and the joy they take in one another may help them grow in love for this whole troubled world.

Grace ✳ October 30

A FTER CENTURIES OF handling and mishandling, most religious words have become so shopworn nobody's much interested any more. Not so with *grace,* for some reason. Mysteriously, even derivatives like *gracious* and *graceful* still have some of the bloom left.

Grace is something you can never get but only be given. There's no way to earn it or deserve it or bring it about any more than you can deserve the taste of raspberries and cream or earn good looks or bring about your own birth.

A good sleep is grace and so are good dreams. Most tears are grace. The smell of rain is grace. Somebody loving you is grace. Loving somebody is grace. Have you ever *tried* to love somebody?

A crucial eccentricity of the Christian faith is the assertion that people are saved by grace. There's nothing *you* have to do. There's nothing you *have* to do. There's nothing you have to *do*.

The grace of God means something like: Here is your life. You might never have been, but you *are* because the party wouldn't have been complete without you. Here is the world. Beautiful and terrible things will happen. Don't be afraid. I am with you. Nothing can ever separate us. It's for you I created the universe. I love you.

There's only one catch. Like any other gift, the gift of grace can be yours only if you'll reach out and take it.

Maybe being able to reach out and take it is a gift too.

Not Just the Saints ✳ October 31

Buechner is remembering his days at Lawrenceville:

AND I LOVED THEM, these others, those friends and teachers. I would never have used the word *love,* saving that for what I had felt for the girl with the mouth that turned up at the corners, and for Naya, my mother and brother, but love of a kind it nonetheless was. Even the ones I did not all that much like I think I knew I would miss when the time came. I sensed in them, as in myself, an inner battle against loneliness and the great dark, and to know that they were also battling was to be no longer alone in the same way within myself. I loved them for that. I wished them well. And then there was Jimmy, my first fast friend; and Huyler, who of all of them heard out most healingly the secret of my father; and Bill, skinny and full of life and the brightest of us all, who would have added God only knows what richness to the great ragbag of things if the war had not ended him before he more than got started. I could not imagine who I would have been without them, nor can I imagine it to this day because they are in so many ways a part of me still.

◆　◆　◆

On All Saints' Day, it is not just the saints of the church that we should remember in our prayers, but all the foolish ones and wise ones, the shy ones and overbearing ones, the broken ones and whole ones, the despots and tosspots and crackpots of our lives who, one way or another, have been our particular fathers and mothers and saints, and whom we loved without knowing we loved them and by whom we were helped to whatever little we may have, or ever hope to have, of some kind of seedy sainthood of our own.

And I found work to do. By the time I was sixteen, I knew as surely as I knew anything that the work I wanted to spend my life doing was the work of words. I did not yet know what I wanted to say with them. I did not yet know in what form I wanted to say it or to what purpose. But if a vocation is as much the work that chooses you as the work you choose, then I knew from that time on that my vocation was, for better or worse, to involve that searching for, and treasuring, and telling of secrets which is what the real business of words is all about.

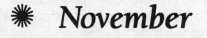 *November*

How They Do Live On ✳ November 1

How THEY DO LIVE on, those giants of our childhood, and how well they manage to take even death in their stride because although death can put an end to them right enough, it can never put an end to our relationship with them. Wherever or however else they may have come to life since, it is beyond a doubt that they live still in us. Memory is more than a looking back to a time that is no longer; it is a looking out into another kind of time altogether where everything that ever was continues not just to be, but to grow and change with the life that is in it still. The people we loved. The people who loved us. The people who, for good or ill, taught us things. Dead and gone though they may be, as we come to understand them in new ways, it is as though they come to understand us—and through them we come to understand ourselves—in new ways too. Who knows what "the communion of saints" means, but surely it means more than just that we are all of us haunted by ghosts because they are not ghosts, these people we once knew, not just echoes of voices that have years since ceased to speak, but saints in the sense that through them something of the power and richness of life itself not only touched us once long ago, but continues to touch us. They have their own business to get on with now, I assume—"increasing in knowledge and love of Thee," says the Book of Common Prayer, and moving "from strength to strength," which sounds like business enough for anybody—and one imagines all of us on this shore fading for them as they journey ahead toward whatever new shore may await them; but it is as if they carry something of us on their way as we assuredly carry something of them on ours. That is perhaps why to think of them is a matter not only of remembering them as they used to be but of seeing and hearing them as in some sense they are now. If they had things to say to us then, they have things to say to us now too, nor are they by any means always things we expect or the same things.

God's Demands ❋ November 2

ISRAEL DID NOT want to be a holy nation. Israel wanted to be a nation like all the other nations, a nation like Egypt, like Syria. She wanted clout. She wanted security. She wanted a place in the sun. It was her own way she wanted, not God's way; and when the prophets got after her for it, she got rid of the prophets, and when God's demands seemed too exorbitant, God's promises too remote, she took up with all the other gods who still get our votes and our money and our 9 A.M. to 5 P.M. energies, because they are gods who could not care less whether we are holy or not, and promise absolutely everything we really want and absolutely nothing we really need.

Three Rules ❋ November 3

WHEN HENRY JAMES, of all people, was saying goodbye once to his young nephew Billy, his brother William's son, he said something that the boy never forgot. And of all the labyrinthine and impenetrably subtle things that that most labyrinthine and impenetrable old romancer could have said, what he did say was this: "There are three things that are important in human life. The first is to be kind. The second is to be kind. The third is to be kind."

Friends ❋ November 4

FRIENDS ARE PEOPLE you make part of your life just because you feel like it. There are lots of other ways people get to be part of each other's lives like being related to each other, living near each other, sharing some special passion with each other like P. G. Wodehouse or jogging or lepidopterology, and so on, but though all or any of those may be involved in a friendship, they are secondary to it.

Basically your friends are not your friends for any particular reason. They are your friends for no particular reason. The job you do, the family you have, the way you vote, the major achievements and blunders of your life, your religious convictions or lack of them, are all somehow set off to one side when the two of you get·together. If you are old friends, you know all those things about each other and a lot more besides, but they are beside the point. Even if you talk about them, they are beside the point. Stripped, humanly speaking, to the bare essentials, you are yourselves the point. The usual distinctions of older-younger, richer-poorer, smarter-dumber, male-female even, cease to matter. You meet with a clean slate every time, and you meet on equal terms. Anything may come of it or nothing may. That doesn't matter either. Only the meeting matters.

"The Lord used to speak to Moses face to face, as a man speaks to his friend," the Book of Exodus says (Exodus 33:11), and in the Book of Isaiah it is God himself who says the same thing of Abraham. "Abraham, my friend," he calls him (Isaiah 41:8). It is a staggering thought.

The love of God. The mercy of God. The judgment of God. You take the shoes off your feet and stand as you would before a mountain or at the edge of the sea. But the *friendship* of God?

It is not something God does. It is something Abraham and God, or Moses and God, do together. Not even God can be a friend all by himself apparently. You see Abraham, say, not standing at all but sitting down, loosening his prayer shawl, trimming the end off his cigar. He is not being Creature for the moment, and God is not being Creator. There is no agenda. They are simply being together, the two of them, and being themselves.

Is it a privilege only for patriarchs? Not as far as Jesus is concerned at least. "You are my friends," he says, "if you do what I command you." The command, of course, is "to love one another," as he puts it. To be his friends, that is to say, we have to be each other's friends, conceivably even lay down our lives for each other. You never know (John 15:12–15). It is a high price to pay, and Jesus does not pretend otherwise, but the implication is that it's worth every cent.

Theology ✳ November 5

THEOLOGY IS THE study of God and his ways. For all we know, dung beetles may study man and his ways and call it humanology. If so, we would probably be more touched and amused than irritated. One hopes that God feels likewise.

Meditation ✳ November 6

WHEN NOT FOCUSING on anything in particular, the mind skitters around mindlessly among whatever thoughts happen to present themselves. To *think* is to direct the mind in a more or less systematic way along a specific sequence of thoughts toward a specific end. To *meditate* is to open the mind to a single thought until it fills the mind so completely that there is no room left for anything else.

If you compare the mind to a balloon, *meditation* as a religious technique is the process of inflating it with a single thought to the point where the balloon finally bursts and there is no longer even the thinnest skin between what is inside it and what is outside it. The thinker and the thought become one in much the same way that if you concentrate long enough on watching a fire burn, after a while the distinction between you as the one that is watching and the fire as the one that is being watched disappears, and you yourself burst into flames.

Fool ✳ November 7

THE WISDOM OF men is the kind of worldly wisdom that more or less all men have been living by since the cave man. It is best exemplified by such homely utterances as *You've got your own life to lead, Business is business, Charity begins at home, Don't get involved, God helps those who help themselves, Safety first,* and so forth.

Although this wisdom can lead on occasion to ruthlessness and indifference, it is by no means incompatible with Niceness, as the life of anyone apt to read (or write) a book like this bears witness. A man can be basically interested in nothing so much as feathering his own nest and still give generously to the Cancer Fund, be on the Board of Deacons, run for town office, and have a soft spot in his heart for children and animals.

It is in contrast to all this that what St. Paul calls "the foolishness of God" looks so foolish. Inspection stickers used to have printed on the back "Drive carefully—the life you save may be your own." That is the wisdom of men in a nutshell.

What God says, on the other hand, is "The life you save is the life you lose." In other words, the life you clutch, hoard, guard, and play safe with is in the end a life worth little to anybody, including yourself, and only a life given away for love's sake is a life worth living. To bring his point home, God shows us a man who gave his life away to the extent of dying a national disgrace without a penny in the bank or a friend to his name. In terms of men's wisdom, he was a Perfect Fool, and anybody who thinks he can follow him without making something like the same kind of a fool of himself is laboring under not a cross but a delusion.

There are two kinds of fools in the world: damned fools and what St. Paul calls "fools for Christ's sake."

Love Each Other ❋ November 8

MATTHEW THE TAX-COLLECTOR and Thomas the doubter. Peter the Rock and Judas the traitor. Mary Magdalene and Lazarus's sister Martha. And the popcorn-eating old woman. And the fat man in the pick-up. They are all our family, and you and I are their family and each other's family, because that is what Jesus has called us as the Church to be. Our happiness is all mixed up with each other's happiness and our peace with each other's peace. Our own happiness, our own peace, can never be complete until we find some way of sharing it with people who the way things are now have no happiness and know no peace. Jesus calls us to show this truth forth, live this truth forth. Be the light of the world, he says. Where there are dark places, be the light especially there. Be the salt of the earth. Bring out the true flavor of what it is to be alive truly. Be truly alive. Be life-givers to others. That is what Jesus tells the disciples to be. That is what Jesus tells his Church, tells us, to be and do. Love each other. Heal the sick, he says. Raise the dead. Cleanse lepers. Cast out demons. That is what loving each other means. If the Church is doing things like that, then it is being what Jesus told it to be. If it is not doing things like that—no matter how many other good and useful things it may be doing instead— then it is not being what Jesus told it to be. It is as simple as that.

A Secret Understood ✳ November 9

A LARGE PART of the truth that *Godric* had for me was the truth that although death ended my father, it has never ended my relationship with my father—a secret that I had never so clearly understood before. So forty-four years after the last time I saw him, it was to my father that I dedicated the book—*In memoriam patris mei.* I wrote the dedication in Latin solely because at the time it seemed appropriate to the medieval nature of the tale, but I have come to suspect since that Latin was also my unconscious way of remaining obedient to the ancient family law that the secret of my father must be at all costs kept secret.

"For Christ and His Kingdom" ✳ November 10

Buechner accepted an invitation to teach at Wheaton College (Illinois) during the Fall semester, 1985.

I KNEW WHEATON was Billy Graham's alma mater. I knew it was evangelical though without any clear idea as to what that meant. I knew that, although as only a visiting professor I would myself be exempt from it, everyone had to sign a pledge not to smoke or drink for as long as they either taught or studied there. If I had known that they had to pledge also not to dance, of all things, I think that I would probably have been horrified enough to turn down the invitation on principle. The irony is that if I had done so, my life would have been immeasurably impoverished.

The famous pledge sends out highly misleading signals not only as to what Christianity is all about but also as to what Wheaton College is all about. Because of those signals I was apprehensive about having my students read *The Brothers*

Karamazov as I had planned. I was afraid that Ivan's devastating attack on belief in a loving God might constitute a heresy that the administration would not tolerate, and then I discovered that it was one of the standard texts used in the English Department. Whatever evangelical meant, in other words, it did not mean closed-minded. On the contrary I found the college as open to what was going on in the world and as generally sophisticated as any I have known. What made it different from any I have known can perhaps best be suggested by the college motto, which is more in evidence there than such mottos usually are. It is not in Latin like most of the other mottos I can think of but in English plain enough for anybody to read and understand. "For Christ and his Kingdom" is the way it goes—as plain as that.

I Had Been Starving ✳ November 11

ONE DAY I WAS having lunch with two Wheaton students who were talking about whatever they were talking about—the weather, the movies—when without warning one of them asked the other as naturally as he would have asked the time of day what God was doing in his life. If there is anything in this world I believe, it is that God is indeed doing all kinds of things in the lives of all of us including those who do not believe in God and would have nothing to do with him if they did, but in the part of the East where I live, if anybody were to ask a question like that, even among religious people, the sky would fall, the walls would cave in, the grass would wither. I think the very air would stop my mouth if I opened it to speak such words among just about any group of people I can think of in the East because their faith itself, if they happen to have any, is one of the secrets that they have kept so long that it might almost as well not exist. The result was that to find myself at Wheaton among people who, although they spoke about it in different words from mine and expressed it in their lives differently, not only believed in Christ and his Kingdom more or less as I did but were also not ashamed or embarrassed to say so was like finding something which, only when I tasted it, I realized I had been starving for for years.

Who Jesus Is ✳ November 12

While he was at Wheaton, Buechner went often to what someone described as "an evangelical high Episcopal church," St. Barnabas in Glen Ellyn. He found the rector, the Rev. Robert MacFarlane, a rewarding preacher.

ONE PARTICULAR SERMON I will always remember though I cannot be sure that it is exactly the sermon he preached because of course it is the sermons we preach to ourselves around the preacher's sermons that are the ones that we hear most powerfully. He was talking about Saint Peter in any case, how Peter was sitting outside in the high priest's courtyard while Jesus was inside being interrogated. A maidservant came up and asked him if it wasn't true that he was a follower of this man who was at the root of all the trouble. Then Peter said, "I do not know the man." It was Peter's denial, of course, MacFarlane said: *I do not even know who he is.* It was the denial that Jesus himself had predicted, and the cock raised his beak into the air and crowed just as Jesus had foretold. But it was something else too, MacFarlane said. It was a denial, but it was also the truth. Peter really did not know who Jesus was, did not really know, and neither do any of us really know who Jesus is either. Beyond all we can find to say about him and believe about him, he remains always beyond our grasp, except maybe once in a while the hem of his garment. We should never forget that. We can love him, we can learn from him, but we can come to know him only by following him—by searching for him in his church, in his Gospels, in each other.

Caiaphas ✳ November 13

THE HIGH PRIEST Caiaphas was essentially a mathematician. When the Jews started worrying that they might all get into hot water with the Romans because of the way Jesus was carrying on, Caiaphas said that in that case they should dump him like a hot potato. His argument ran that it is better for one man to get it in the neck for the sake of many than for many to get it in the neck for the sake of one man. His grim arithmetic proved unassailable.

The arithmetic of Jesus, on the other hand, was atrocious. He said that Heaven gets a bigger kick out of one sinner who repents than out of ninety-nine saints who don't need to. He said that God pays as much for one hour's work as for one day's. He said that the more you give away, the more you have.

It is curious that in the matter of deciding his own fate, he reached the same conclusion as Caiaphas and took it in the neck for the sake of many, Caiaphas included. It was not, however, the laws of mathematics that he was following.

Funeral ✳ November 14

IN ARAMAIC *talitha cumi* means "little girl, get up." It's the language Jesus and his friends probably used when they spoke to each other, so these may well be his actual words, among the very few that have come down to us verbatim. He spoke them at a child's funeral, the twelve-year-old daughter of a man named Jairus (Mark 5:35–43).

The occasion took place at the man's house. There was plenty of the kind of sorrow you expect when anybody that young dies. And that's one of the great uses of funerals surely, to be cited when people protest that they're barbaric holdovers from the past, that you should celebrate the life rather than mourn the death, and so on. Celebrate the life by all means but face up to the death of that life. Weep all the tears you have in you to weep because whatever may happen next, if anything does, this has happened. Something precious and irreplaceable has come to an end and something in you has come to an end with it. Funerals put a period after the sentence's last word. They close a door. They let you get on with your life.

The child was dead, but Jesus, when he got there, said she was only asleep. He said the same thing when his friend Lazarus died. Death is not any more permanent than sleep is permanent is what he meant apparently. That isn't to say he took death lightly. When he heard about Lazarus, he wept, and it's hard to imagine him doing any differently here. But if death is the closing of one door, he seems to say, it is the opening of another one. *Talitha cumi.* He took the little girl's hand, and he told her to get up, and she did. The mother and father were there, Mark says. The neighbors, the friends. It is a scene to conjure with.

Old woman, get up. Young man. The one you don't know how you'll ever manage to live without. The one you don't know how you ever managed to live with. Little girl. "Get up," he says.

The other use of funerals is to remind us of those two words. When the last hymn has been sung, the benediction given, and the immediate family escorted out a side door, they may be the best we have to make it possible to *get up* ourselves.

Love ✸ November 15

THE LOVE FOR equals is a human thing—of friend for friend, brother for brother. It is to love what is loving and lovely. The world smiles.

The love for the less fortunate is a beautiful thing—the love for those who suffer, for those who are poor, the sick, the failures, the unlovely. This is compassion, and it touches the heart of the world.

The love for the more fortunate is a rare thing—to love those who succeed where we fail, to rejoice without envy with those who rejoice, the love of the poor for the rich, of the black man for the white man. The world is always bewildered by its saints.

And then there is the love for the enemy—love for the one who does not love you but mocks, threatens, and inflicts pain. The tortured's love for the torturer. This is God's love. It conquers the world.

A Book About Us * November 16

IT IS POSSIBLE to say that in spite of all its extraordinary variety, the Bible is held together by having a single plot. It is one that can be simply stated: God creates the world; the world gets lost; God seeks to restore the world to the glory for which he created it. That means that the Bible is a book about you and me, whom he also made and lost and continually seeks, so you might say that what holds it together more than anything else is us. You might add to that, of course, that of all the books that humanity has produced, it is the one which more than any other—and in more senses than one—also holds us together.

The Kingdom * November 17

IF WE ONLY HAD eyes to see and ears to hear and wits to understand, we would know that the Kingdom of God in the sense of holiness, goodness, beauty is as close as breathing and is crying out to be born both within ourselves and within the world; we would know that the Kingdom of God is what we all of us hunger for above all other things even when we don't know its name or realize that it's what we're starving to death for. The Kingdom of God is where our best dreams come from and our truest prayers. We glimpse it at those moments when we find ourselves being better than we are and wiser than we know. We catch sight of it when at some moment of crisis a strength seems to come to us that is greater than our own strength. The Kingdom of God is where we belong. It is home, and whether we realize it or not, I think we are all of us homesick for it.

Sloth ✻ November 18

SLOTH IS NOT TO be confused with laziness. A lazy man, a man who sits around and watches the grass grow, may be a man at peace. His sun-drenched, bumblebee dreaming may be the prelude to action or itself an act well worth the acting.

A slothful man, on the other hand, may be a very busy man. He is a man who goes through the motions, who flies on automatic pilot. Like a man with a bad head cold, he has mostly lost his sense of taste and smell. He knows something's wrong with him, but not wrong enough to do anything about. Other people come and go, but through glazed eyes he hardly notices them. He is letting things run their course. He is getting through his life.

Miracle ✻ November 19

A CANCER INEXPLICABLY cured. A voice in a dream. A statue that weeps. A miracle is an event that strengthens faith. It is possible to look at most miracles and find a rational explanation in terms of natural cause and effect. It is possible to look at Rembrandt's *Supper at Emmaus* and find a rational explanation in terms of paint and canvas.

Faith in God is less apt to proceed from miracles than miracles from faith in God.

Forgiveness ✳ November 20

WHEN SOMEBODY you've wronged forgives you, you're spared the dull and self-diminishing throb of a guilty conscience.

When you forgive somebody who has wronged you, you're spared the dismal corrosion of bitterness and wounded pride.

For both parties, forgiveness means the freedom again to be at peace inside their own skins and to be glad in each other's presence.

The Truth of Our Stories ✳ November 21

IN THE LONG RUN the stories all overlap and mingle like searchlights in the dark. The stories Jesus tells are part of the story Jesus is, and the other way round. And the story Jesus is is part of the story you and I are because Jesus has become so much a part of the world's story that it is impossible to imagine how any of our stories would have turned out without him, even the stories of people who don't believe in him or even know who he is or care about knowing. And my story and your story are all part of each other too if only because we have sung together and prayed together and seen each other's faces so that we are at least a footnote at the bottom of each other's stories.

In other words all our stories are in the end one story, one vast story about being human, being together, being here. Does the story point beyond itself? Does it mean something? What is the truth of this interminable, sprawling story we all of us are? Or is it as absurd to ask about the truth of it as it is to ask about the truth of the wind howling through a crack under the door?

Sudden Snow ✸ November 22

YOU WAKE UP ON a winter morning and pull up the shade, and what lay there the evening before is no longer there—the sodden gray yard, the dog droppings, the tire tracks in the frozen mud, the broken lawn chair you forgot to take in last fall. All this has disappeared overnight, and what you look out on is not the snow of Narnia but the snow of home, which is no less shimmering and white as it falls. The earth is covered with it, and it is falling still in silence so deep that you can hear its silence. It is snow to be shoveled, to make driving even worse than usual, snow to be joked about and cursed at, but unless the child in you is entirely dead, it is snow, too, that can make the heart beat faster when it catches you by surprise that way, before your defenses are up. It is snow that can awaken memories of things more wonderful than anything you ever knew or dreamed.

Glimpses of Joy ✸ November 23

THE JOY BEYOND the walls of the world more poignant than grief. Even in church you catch glimpses of it sometimes though church is apt to be the last place because you are looking too hard for it there. It is not apt to be so much in the sermon that you find it or the prayers or the liturgy but often in something quite incidental like the evening the choral society does the Mozart *Requiem,* and there is your friend Dr. X, who you know thinks the whole business of religion is for the birds, singing the Kyrie like a bird himself—*Lord, have mercy, have mercy*—as he stands there among the baritones in his wilted shirt and skimpy tux; and his workaday basset-hound face is so alive with if not the God he wouldn't be caught dead believing in then at least with his twin brother that for a moment nothing in the whole world matters less than what he believes or doesn't believe—*Kyrie eleison, Christe eleison*—and as at snow, dreams, certain memories, at fairy tales, the heart leaps, the eyes fill.

The Ultimate ✳ *November 24*

JESUS DID NOT say that religion was the truth or that his own teachings were the truth or that what people taught about him was the truth or that the Bible was the truth or the Church or any system of ethics or theological doctrine. There are individual truths in all of them, we hope and believe, but individual truths were not what Pilate was after or what you and I are after either unless I miss my guess. Truths about this or that are a dime a dozen, including religious truths. THE truth is what Pilate is after: the truth about who we are and who God is if there is a God, the truth about life, the truth about death, the truth about truth itself. That is the truth we are all of us after.

"Once Upon a Time" ✳ *November 25*

JESUS DOES NOT sound like Saint Paul or Thomas Aquinas or John Calvin when we hear him teaching in the Gospels. "Once upon a time" is what he says. Once upon a time somebody went out to plant some seeds. Once upon a time somebody stubbed a toe on a great treasure. Once upon a time somebody lost a precious coin. The Gospels are full of the stories Jesus tells, stories that are alive in somewhat the way the truth is alive, the way he himself is alive when Pilate asks him about truth, and his silence is a way of saying "Look at my aliveness if you want to know! Listen to my life!" Matthew goes so far as to tell us that "he said nothing to them without a parable," that is to say without a story, and then quotes the words, "I will open my mouth in parables, I will utter what has been hidden since the foundation of the world." In stories the hiddenness and the utterance are both present, and that is another reason why they are a good way of talking about God's truth which is part hidden and part uttered too.

Giving Prodigally ✳ November 26

T O PRAY FOR YOUR enemies, to worry about the poor when you have worries enough of your own, to start becoming yourself fully by giving of yourself prodigally to whoever needs you, to love your neighbors when an intelligent 4th grader could tell you that the way to get ahead in the world is to beat your neighbors to the draw every chance you get— that was what this God asked, Paul wrote. That was who this God was. That was who Jesus was. Paul is passionate in his assertion, of course, that in the long run it is such worldly wisdom as the intelligent 4th grader's that is foolish and the sublime foolishness of God that is ultimately wise, and nobody heard him better than William Shakespeare did when he wove the rich fabric of *King Lear* around precisely this paradox. It is the Fool, Edgar, Kent, Cordelia, Gloucester— the foolish, weak, despised ones—who in their fatal loyalty to the ruined king triumph, humanly speaking, over the powerful cunning of Regan, Goneril, Edmund, and the rest of them. "Upon such sacrifices, my Cordelia, the gods themselves throw incense," Lear says to Cordelia—that is their triumph—just as, before him, Paul quoted Isaiah's "What no eye has seen, nor ear heard, nor the heart of man conceived, [that is] what God has prepared for those who love him."

A Telling Silence ✳ November 27

I REMEMBER ONCE going to see the movie *Gandhi* when it first came out. . . . We were the usual kind of noisy, restless Saturday night crowd as we sat there waiting for the lights to dim with our popcorn and soda pop, girl friends and boy friends, legs draped over the backs of the empty seats in front of us. But by the time the movie came to a close with the flames of Gandhi's funeral pyre filling the entire wide screen, there was not a sound or a movement in that whole theater, and we filed out of there—teenagers and senior citizens, blacks and whites, swingers and squares—in as deep and telling a silence as I have ever been part of.

Real People ✳ November 28

WHATEVER ELSE THEY may be, the people in the Bible are real human beings, . . . and it is not the world of the Sunday School tract that they move through but a Dostoyevskian world of darkness and light commingled, where suffering is sometimes redemptive and sometimes turns the heart to stone. It is a world where although God is sometimes to be known through his life-giving presence, there are other times when he is known only by his appalling absence. The Bible is a compilation of stories of what happened to these human beings in such a world, and the stories are not only as different from one another as the people they are about but are told in almost as many different ways. Side by side in the opening pages of Genesis, for instance, there are two stories of the creation, one of them as stately and rhythmic as plainsong, the other as homely and human as the way you might tell it to your grandchildren. The groups of stories about Jacob and his son Joseph, told in as unpretentious a style as the second creation story, are nonetheless complex, full of psychological motivation and rich with detail; and in the case of Jacob in particular, no character in fiction is more multi-faceted, fascinating, or believable.

Not Suitable for Framing ✳ November 29

I F WE THINK THE purpose of Jesus' stories is essentially to make a point as extractable as the moral at the end of a fable, then the inevitable conclusion is that once you get the point, you can throw the story itself away like the rind of an orange when you have squeezed out the juice. Is that true? How about other people's stories? What is the point of *A Midsummer Night's Dream* or *The Iliad* or *For Whom the Bell Tolls*? Can we extract the point in each case and frame it on the living room wall for our perpetual edification?

Or is the story itself the point and truth of the story? Is the point of Jesus' stories that they point to the truth about you and me and our stories? We are the ones who have been mugged, and we are also the ones who pass by pretending we don't notice. Hard as it is to believe, maybe every once in a while we are even the ones who pay an arm and a leg to help. The truth of the story is not a motto suitable for framing. It is a truth that one way or another, God help us, we live out every day of our lives. It is a truth as complicated and sad as you and I ourselves are complicated and sad, and as joyous and as simple as we are too. The stories that Jesus tells are about us. Once upon a time is *our* time, in other words.

A Visit ✳ November 30

I REMEMBER AN especially dark time of my life. One of my children was sick, and in my anxiety for her I was in my own way as sick as she was. Then one day the phone rang, and it was a man I didn't know very well then though he has become a great friend since, a minister from Charlotte, North Carolina, which is about 800 miles or so from where I live in Vermont. I assumed he was calling from home and asked him how things were going down there only to hear him say that no, he wasn't in Charlotte. He was at an inn about twenty minutes away from my house. He'd known I was having troubles, he said, and he thought maybe it would be handy to have an extra friend around for a day or two. The reason he didn't tell me in advance that he was coming must have been that he knew I would tell him for Heaven's sake not to do anything so crazy, so for Heaven's sake he did something crazier still which was to come those 800 miles without telling me he was coming so that for all he knew I might not even have been there. But as luck had it, I was there, and for a day or two he was there with me. He was there for me. I don't think anything we found to say to each other amounted to very much or had anything particularly religious about it. I don't remember even spending much time talking about my troubles with him. We just took a couple of walks, had a meal or two together and smoked our pipes, drove around to see some of the countryside, and that was about it.

I have never forgotten how he came all that distance just for that, and I'm sure he has never forgotten it either. I also believe that although as far as I can remember we never so much as mentioned the name of Christ, Christ was as much in the air we breathed those few days as the smoke of our pipes was in the air, or the dappled light of the woods we walked through. I believe that for a little time we both of us touched the hem of Christ's garment, were both of us, for a little time anyway, healed.

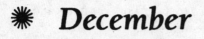 *December*

The Armor of Light ✴ December 1

The following four meditations are from a church's hundredth-anniversary sermon:

GIVE US GRACE that we may cast away the works of darkness, and put upon us the armor of light, now in the time of this mortal life in which thy son Jesus Christ came to visit us in great humility: that in the last day, when he shall come again in his glorious majesty, to judge both the quick and the dead, we may rise to the life immortal."

All the paradoxical themes of Advent are compressed into that handful of words: Christ coming at Christmas time in great humility and again at the end of time in glorious majesty—Christ coming as a child to save us and as a king to judge us—mortal life, immortal life. They clatter against each other like shutters in the wind with all their points and counterpoints. They all but deafen us with their message at one and the same time of sin and grace, justice and mercy, comfort and challenge. "Cast away the works of darkness," they say, and put on "the armor of light." Maybe those are the words that best sum up the paradox of who we are and where we are. Somewhere between the darkness and the light. That is where we are as Christians. And not just at Advent time, but at all times. Somewhere between the fact of darkness and the hope of light. That is who we are.

"Advent" means "coming" of course, and the promise of Advent is that what is coming is an unimaginable invasion. The mythology of our age has to do with flying saucers and invasions from outer space, and that is unimaginable enough. But what is upon us now is even more so—a close encounter not of the third kind but of a different kind altogether. An invasion of *holiness*. That is what Advent is about.

What is coming upon the world is the Light of the World. It is Christ. That is the comfort of it. The challenge of it is that it has not come yet. Only the hope for it has come, only the longing for it. In the meantime we are in the dark, and the dark, God knows, is also in us. We watch and wait for a holiness to heal us and hallow us, to liberate us from the dark. Advent is like the hush in a theater just before the curtain rises. It is like the hazy ring around the winter moon that means the coming of snow which will turn the night to silver. Soon. But for the time being, our time, darkness is where we are.

A Visit We Remember ✳ December 2

IT WAS THOUSANDS of years ago and thousands of miles away, but it is a visit that for all our madness and cynicism and indifference and despair we have never quite forgotten. The oxen in their stalls. The smell of hay. The shepherds standing around. That child and that place are somehow the closest of all close encounters, the one we are closest to, the one that brings us closest to something that cannot be told in any other way. This story that faith tells in the fairytale language of faith is not just that God *is,* which God knows is a lot to swallow in itself much of the time, but that God *comes.* Comes here. "In great humility." There is nothing much humbler than being born: naked, totally helpless, not much bigger than a loaf of bread. But with righteousness and faithfulness the girdle of his loins. And to *us* came. *For* us came. Is it true—not just the way fairytales are true but as the truest of all truths? Almighty God, are you true?

When you are standing up to your neck in darkness, how do you say yes to that question? You say yes, I suppose, the only way faith can ever say it if it is honest with itself. You say yes with your fingers crossed. You say it with your heart in your mouth. Maybe that way we can say yes. He visited us.

The world has never been quite the same since. It is still a very dark world, in some ways darker than ever before, but the darkness is different because he keeps getting born into it. The threat of holocaust. The threat of poisoning the earth and sea and air. The threat of our own deaths. The broken marriage. The child in pain. The lost chance. Anyone who has ever known him has known him perhaps better in the dark than anywhere else because it is in the dark where he seems to visit most often.

Like a Uniform ✳ December 3

WHAT IF ANYTHING have you and I done to do battle against the great darkness of things? As parents and the children of our own parents, as wives and husbands and friends and lovers, as players of whatever parts we have chosen to play in this world, as wielders of whatever kind of power, as possessors of whatever kind of wealth, what other human selves have we sacrificed something of our own sweet selves to help and heal?

"Bear fruit that befits repentance!" thunders the Baptist. "Give us grace that we may cast away the works of darkness and put upon us the armor of light," whispers the prayer we pray. Bear fruit. Put on light like a garment, like a uniform. That is the place to stop and also the place to start. It is the place to stop and *think*—think back, think ahead, think deep. It is the place to start and *be*.

"The Best She Could" ✳ December 4

WHEN YOU INVITED me to come speak at this anniversary of your founding as a church you had no way of knowing that the minister who founded you, a man named George Shinn, happened to be my wife's great grandfather, and it pleases me to think that maybe that was not entirely a coincidence. In any case, it was this same George Shinn who in 1880, five years before being asked to start your church here in Chestnut Hill, was summoned once at midnight to the bedside of an old woman who lived by herself without much in the way of either money or friends and was dying. She managed to convey that she wanted some other woman to come stay with her for such time as she might have left, so George Shinn and the old woman's doctor struck out in the darkness to try to dig one up for her. It sounds like a parable the way it is told, and I am inclined to believe that if someone were ever to tell the story of your lives and mine, they also would sound more like parables than we ordinarily suppose. They knocked at doors and threw pebbles at second story windows. One woman said she couldn't come because she had children. Another said she simply wouldn't know what to do, what to be, in a crisis like that. Another was suspicious of two men prowling around at that hour of night and wouldn't even talk to them. But finally, as the memoir of Dr. Shinn puts it in the prose of another age, "They rapped at the humble door of an Irish woman, the mother of a brood of children. She put her head out of the window. 'Who's there?' she said. 'And what can you want at this time of night?' They tell her the situation. Her warm, Irish heart cannot resist. 'Will you come?' 'Sure and I'll come, and I'll do the best I can.' And she did come," the account ends. "She did the best she could."

That Deep Place Inside Us ✳ December 5

I HAVE CALLED the third and most recent memoir *Telling Secrets* because I have come to believe that by and large the human family all has the same secrets, which are both very telling and very important to tell. They are telling in the sense

that they tell what is perhaps the central paradox of our condition—that what we hunger for perhaps more than anything
else is to be known in our full humanness, and yet that is
often just what we also fear more than anything else. It is
important to tell at least from time to time the secret of who
we truly and fully are—even if we tell it only to ourselves—
because otherwise we run the risk of losing track of who we
truly and fully are and little by little come to accept instead
the highly edited version which we put forth in hope that the
world will find it more acceptable than the real thing. It is
important to tell our secrets too because it makes it easier that
way to see where we have been in our lives and where we are
going. It also makes it easier for other people to tell us a secret
or two of their own, and exchanges like that have a lot to do
with what being a family is all about and what being human
is all about. Finally, I suspect that it is by entering that deep
place inside us where our secrets are kept that we come perhaps closer than we do anywhere else to the One who,
whether we realize it or not, is of all our secrets the most
telling and the most precious we have to tell.

A Secret ✳ December 6

WE DIDN'T TALK about my father with each other, and we
didn't talk about him outside the family either partly
at least because suicide was looked on as something a little
shabby and shameful in those days. Nice people weren't supposed to get mixed up with it My father had tried to keep it
a secret himself by leaving his note to my mother in a place
where only she would be likely to find it and by saying a
number of times the last few weeks of his life that there was
something wrong with the Chevy's exhaust system, which he
was going to see if he could fix. He did this partly in hopes
that his life insurance wouldn't be invalidated, which of
course it was, and partly too, I guess, in hopes that his friends

wouldn't find out how he had died, which of course they did. His suicide was a secret we nonetheless tried to keep as best we could, and after a while my father himself became such a secret. There were times when he almost seemed a secret we were trying to keep from each other. I suppose there were occasions when one of us said, "Remember the time he did this," or, "Remember the time he said that," but if so, I've long since forgotten them. And because words are so much a part of what we keep the past alive by, if only words to ourselves, by not speaking of what we remembered about him we soon simply stopped remembering at all, or at least I did.

The Last Rose ✳ December 7

M Y MOTHER EXCORIATED the ravages of old age but never accepted them as the inevitable consequence of getting old. "I don't know what's wrong with me today," she must have said a thousand days as she tried once, then again, then a third time, to pull herself out of her chair into her walker. It never seemed to occur to her that what was wrong with her was that she was on her way to pushing a hundred. Maybe that was why some part of her remained unravaged. Some surviving lightness of touch let her stand back from the wreckage and see that among other things it was absurdly funny. When I told her the last time she was mobile enough to visit us in Vermont that the man who had just passed her window was the gardener, she said, "Tell him to come in and take a look at the last rose of summer."

Summing Up ✳ December 8

I T IS SO EASY to sum up other people's lives, . . . and neces- sary too, of course, especially our parents' lives. It is a way of reducing their giant figures to a size we can manage, I suppose, a way of getting even maybe, of getting on, of saying goodbye. The day will come when somebody tries to sum you up the same way and also me. Tell me about old Buechner then. What was he really like? What made him tick? How did his story go? Well, you see, this happened and then that happened, and then that, and that is why he became thus and so, and why when all is said and done it is not so hard to understand why things turned out for him as they finally did. Is there any truth at all in the patterns we think we see, the explanations and insights that fall so readily from our tongues? Who knows. The main thing that leads me to believe that what I've said about my mother has at least a kind of partial truth is that I know at first hand that it is true of the mother who lives on in me and will always be part of who I am.

Take Care of Yourself ✳ December 9

LOVE YOUR NEIGHBOR as yourself is part of the great commandment. The other way to say it is, Love yourself as your neighbor. Love yourself not in some egocentric, self-serving sense but love yourself the way you would love your friend in the sense of taking care of yourself, nourishing yourself, trying to understand, comfort, strengthen yourself. Ministers in particular, people in the caring professions in general, are famous for neglecting their selves with the result that they are apt to become in their own way as helpless and crippled as the people they are trying to care for and thus no longer selves who can be of much use to anybody. If your daughter is struggling for life in a raging torrent, you do not save her by jumping into the torrent with her, which leads only to your both drowning together. Instead you keep your feet on the dry bank—you maintain as best you can your own inner peace, the best and strongest of who you are—and from that solid ground reach out a rescuing hand. "Mind your own business" means butt out of other people's lives because in the long run they must live their lives for themselves, but it also means pay mind to your own life, your own health and wholeness, both for your own sake and ultimately for the sake of those you love too. Take care of yourself so you can take care of them. A bleeding heart is of no help to anybody if it bleeds to death.

Our Stories ✳ December 10

THIS IS ALL PART of the story about what it has been like for the last ten years or so to be me, and before anybody else has the chance to ask it, I will ask it myself: Who cares? What in the world could be less important than who I am and who my father and mother were, the mistakes I have made together with the occasional discoveries, the bad times and good times, the moments of grace. If I were a public figure and my story had had some impact on the world at large, that might be some justification for telling it, but I am a very private figure indeed, living very much out of the mainstream of things in the hills of Vermont, and my life has had very little impact on anybody much except for the people closest to me and the comparative few who have read books I've written and been one way or another touched by them.

But I talk about my life anyway because if, on the one hand, hardly anything could be less important, on the other hand, hardly anything could be more important. My story is important not because it is mine, God knows, but because if I tell it anything like right, the chances are you will recognize that in many ways it is also yours. Maybe nothing is more important than that we keep track, you and I, of these stories of who we are and where we have come from and the people we have met along the way because it is precisely through these stories in all their particularity, as I have long believed and often said, that God makes himself known to each of us most powerfully and personally. If this is true, it means that to lose track of our stories is to be profoundly impoverished not only humanly but spiritually.

God Is Mightily Present ❋ December 11

A S I UNDERSTAND it, to say that God is mightily present even in such private events as these does not mean that he makes events happen to us which move us in certain directions like chessmen. Instead, events happen under their own steam as random as rain, which means that God is present in them not as their cause but as the one who even in the hardest and most hair-raising of them offers us the possibility of that new life and healing which I believe is what salvation is. For instance I cannot believe that a God of love and mercy in any sense willed my father's suicide; it was my father himself who willed it as the only way out available to him from a life that for various reasons he had come to find unbearable. God did not will what happened that early November morning in Essex Fells, New Jersey, but I believe that God was present in what happened. I cannot guess how he was present with my father—I can guess much better how utterly abandoned by God my father must have felt if he thought about God at all—but my faith as well as my prayer is that he was and continues to be present with him in ways beyond my guessing. I can speak with some assurance only of how God was present in that dark time for me in the sense that I was not destroyed by it but came out of it with scars that I bear to this day, to be sure, but also somehow the wiser and the stronger for it. Who knows how I might have turned out if my father had lived, but through the loss of him all those long years ago I think that I learned something about how even tragedy can be a means of grace that I might never have come to any other way.

As I see it, in other words, God acts in history and in your and my brief histories not as the puppeteer who sets the scene and works the strings but rather as the great director who no matter what role fate casts us in conveys to us somehow from the wings, if we have our eyes, ears, hearts open and sometimes even if we don't, how we can play those roles in a way to enrich and ennoble and hallow the whole vast drama of things including our own small but crucial parts in it.

Uses of Memory ✳ December 12

I AM INCLINED to believe that God's chief purpose in giving us memory is to enable us to go back in time so that if we didn't play those roles right the first time round, we can still have another go at it now. We cannot undo our old mistakes or their consequences any more than we can erase old wounds that we have both suffered and inflicted, but through the power that memory gives us of thinking, feeling, imagining our way back through time we can at long last finally finish with the past in the sense of removing its power to hurt us and other people and to stunt our growth as human beings.

The sad things that happened long ago will always remain part of who we are just as the glad and gracious things will too, but instead of being a burden of guilt, recrimination, and regret that make us constantly stumble as we go, even the saddest things can become, once we have made peace with them, a source of wisdom and strength for the journey that still lies ahead. It is through memory that we are able to reclaim much of our lives that we have long since written off by finding that in everything that has happened to us over the years God was offering us possibilities of new life and healing which, though we may have missed them at the time, we can still choose and be brought to life by and healed by all these years later.

Keeping Touch ❋ December 13

WE BELIEVE IN God—such as it is, we have faith—because certain things happened to us once and go on happening. We work and goof off, we love and dream, we have wonderful times and awful times, are cruelly hurt and hurt others cruelly, get mad and bored and scared stiff and ache with desire, do all such human things as these, and if our faith is not mainly just window dressing or a rabbit's foot or fire insurance, it is because it grows out of precisely this kind of rich human compost. The God of biblical faith is the God who meets us at those moments in which for better or worse we are being most human, most ourselves, and if we lose touch with those moments, if we don't stop from time to time to notice what is happening to us and around us and inside us, we run the tragic risk of losing touch with God too.

I Am My Secrets ❋ December 14

TO KEEP TRACK of these lives we live is not just a means of enriching our understanding and possibly improving our sermons but a truly sacred work. In these pages I tell secrets about my parents, my children, myself because that is one way of keeping track and because I believe that it is not only more honest but also vastly more interesting than to pretend that I have no such secrets to tell. I not only have my secrets, I am my secrets. And you are your secrets. Our secrets are human secrets, and our trusting each other enough to share them with each other has much to do with the secret of what it is to be human.

The Deepest Self ✳ December 15

LIFE BATTERS AND shapes us in all sorts of ways before it's done, but those original selves which we were born with and which I believe we continue in some measure to be no matter what are selves which still echo with the holiness of their origin. I believe that what Genesis suggests is that this original self, with the print of God's thumb still upon it, is the most essential part of who we are and is buried deep in all of us as a source of wisdom and strength and healing which we can draw upon or, with our terrible freedom, not draw upon as we choose. I think that among other things all real art comes from that deepest self—painting, writing music, dance, all of it that in some way nourishes the spirit and enriches the understanding. I think that our truest prayers come from there too, the often unspoken, unbidden prayers that can rise out of the lives of unbelievers as well as believers whether they recognize them as prayers or not. And I think that from there also come our best dreams and our times of gladdest playing and taking it easy and all those moments when we find ourselves being better or stronger or braver or wiser than we are.

Small Events ✳ December 16

LIFE WENT ON OF course because that is what life does. I kept on writing books, which a relatively small but faithful audience kept on reading. It was at this time that I wrote two short autobiographical volumes called *The Sacred Journey* in 1982 and *Now and Then* in 1983, and they helped let a little light and air into the dark place where I was imprisoned. They gave me more of a sense than I had ever had before of how as far back as I could remember things had been stirring in my life that I was all but totally unaware of at the time.

If anybody had predicted when I was an undergraduate at Princeton that I was going to be ordained as a minister ten years after graduation, I think I would have been flabbergasted. Yet as I wrote those two autobiographical volumes I found myself remembering small events as far back as early childhood which were even then leading me in something like that direction but so subtly and almost imperceptibly that it wasn't until decades had passed that I saw them for what they were—or thought I did because you can never be sure whether you are discovering that kind of truth or inventing it. The events were often so small that I was surprised to remember them, yet they turned out to have been road markers on a journey I didn't even know I was taking. The people involved in them were often people I had never thought of as having played particularly significant roles in my life yet looking back at them I saw that, for me, they had been life-givers, saints.

Trust ✳ December 17

I REMEMBER SITTING parked by the roadside once, terribly depressed and afraid about my daughter's illness and what was going on in our family, when out of nowhere a car came along down the highway with a license plate that bore on it the one word out of all the words in the dictionary that I needed most to see exactly then. The word was TRUST. What do you call a moment like that? Something to laugh off as the kind of joke life plays on us every once in a while? The word of God? I am willing to believe that maybe it was something of both, but for me it was an epiphany. The owner of the car turned out to be, as I'd suspected, a trust officer in a bank, and not long ago, having read an account I wrote of the incident somewhere, he found out where I lived and one afternoon brought me the license plate itself, which sits propped up on a bookshelf in my house to this day. It is rusty around the edges and a little battered, and it is also as holy a relic as I have ever seen.

What Preaching Is ✳ December 18

In the winter of 1982 Buechner accepted an invitation to teach for a term in Harvard Divinity School.

I HAD NEVER understood so clearly before what preaching is to me. Basically, it is to proclaim a Mystery before which, before whom, even our most exalted ideas turn to straw. It is also to proclaim this Mystery with a passion that ideas alone have little to do with. It is to try to put the Gospel into words not the way you would compose an essay but the way you would write a poem or a love letter—putting your heart into it, your own excitement, most of all your own life. It is to speak words that you hope may, by grace, be bearers not simply of new understanding but of new life both for the ones you are speaking to and also for you. Out of that life, who knows what new ideas about peace and honesty and social responsibility may come, but they are the fruits of the preaching, not the roots of it. Another Unitarian Universalist student said once that what he believed in was faith, and when I asked him faith in what, his answer was faith in faith. I don't mean to disparage him—he was doing the best he could—but it struck me that having faith in faith was as barren as being in love with love or having money that you spend only on the accumulation of more money. It struck me too that to attend a divinity school when you did not believe in divinity involved a peculiarly depressing form of bankruptcy, and there were times as I wandered through those corridors that I felt a little like Alice on the far side of the looking glass.

Pluralism ✳ December 19

HARVARD DIVINITY School was proud, and justly so, of what it called its pluralism—feminists, humanists, theists, liberation theologians all pursuing truth together—but the price that pluralism can cost was dramatized one day in a way that I have never forgotten. I had been speaking as candidly and personally as I knew how about my own faith and how I had tried over the years to express it in language. At the same time I had been trying to get the class to respond in kind. For the most part none of them were responding at all but just sitting there taking it in without saying a word. Finally I had to tell them what I thought. I said they reminded me of a lot of dead fish lying on cracked ice in a fish store window with their round blank eyes. There I was, making a fool of myself spilling out to them the secrets of my heart, and there they were, not telling me what they believed about anything beneath the level of their various causes. It was at that point that a black African student got up and spoke. "The reason I do not say anything about what I believe," he said in his stately African English, "is that I'm afraid it will be shot down."

At least for a moment we all saw, I think, that the danger of pluralism is that it becomes factionalism, and that if factions grind their separate axes too vociferously, something mutual, precious, and human is in danger of being drowned out and lost. I had good times as well as bad ones that winter term. I was able to say a few things that some of my students seemed to find valuable, and some of them said things that I value still, but if there was anything like a community to draw strength and comfort from there at Harvard as years before there had been at Union, I for one was not lucky enough to discover it.

"The Thoughts of Our Hearts" ✳ December 20

"CLEANSE THE THOUGHTS of our hearts by the inspiration of thy Holy Spirit," the collect goes, "that we may perfectly love" if not thee, because we are such a feckless and faithless crowd most of us, then at least ourselves, at least each other. If, as someone has said, we are as sick as our secrets, then to get well is to air those secrets if only in our own hearts, which the prayer asks God himself to air and cleanse. When our secrets are guilty secrets, like the burden [of expecting too much from them] I had unwittingly placed on my own children, we can start to make amends, to change what can be changed; we can start to heal. When they are sad and hurtful secrets, like my father's death, we can in a way honor the hurt by letting ourselves feel it as we never let ourselves feel it before, and then, having felt it, by laying it aside; we can start to take care of ourselves the way we take care of people we love. To love our neighbors as we love ourselves means also to love ourselves as we love our neighbors. It means to treat ourselves with as much kindness and understanding as we would the person next door who is in trouble.

Let Go ✳ December 21

Buechner is discussing a support group for adult children of alcoholics:

THEY COULD HARDLY be a more ill-assorted lot. Some are educated, and some never finished grade school. Some are on welfare, and some of them have hit the jackpot. Some are straight, and some are gay. There are senior citizens among them and also twenty-year-olds. Some groups are composed of alcoholics and some, like the ones I found my way to, of people who have no alcoholic problem themselves but come from families who did. The one thing they have in common can be easily stated. It is just that they all believe that they cannot live fully human lives without each other and without what they call their Higher Power. They avoid using the word *God* because some of them do not believe in God. What they all do believe in, or are searching for, is a power higher than their own which will make them well. Some of them would simply say that it is the power of the group itself.

They are apt to begin their meetings with a prayer written by my old seminary professor Reinhold Niebuhr: "God, grant me the serenity to accept the things I cannot change, the courage to change the things I can, and wisdom to know the difference." They are apt to end with the Lord's Prayer: "*thy* will be done . . . give us *this* day our daily bread . . . forgive us as we forgive . . . deliver us." "To lend each other a hand when we're falling," Brendan said. "Perhaps that's the only work that matters in the end." As they live their lives, they try to follow a kind of spiritual rule, which consists basically not only of uncovering their own deep secrets but of making peace with the people they have hurt and been hurt by. Through prayer and meditation, through seeking help from each other and from helpful books, they try to draw near any way they can to God or to whatever they call what they have instead of God. They sometimes make serious slips. They sometimes make miraculous gains. They laugh a lot. Once in a while they cry. When the meeting is over, some of them embrace. Sometimes one of them will take special responsibility for another, agreeing to be available at any hour of day or night if the need should arise.

They also have slogans, which you can either dismiss as hopelessly simplistic or cling on to like driftwood in a stormy sea. One of them is "Let go and let God"—which is so easy to say and for people like me so far from easy to follow. Let go of the dark, which you wrap yourself in like a straitjacket, and let in the light. Stop trying to protect, to rescue, to judge, to manage the lives around you—your children's lives, the lives of your husband, your wife, your friends—because that is just what you are powerless to do. Remember that the lives of other people are not your business. They are their business. They are God's business because they all have God whether they use the word God or not. Even your own life is not your business. It also is God's business. Leave it to God. It is an astonishing thought. It can become a life-transforming thought.

What Christ Meant ❋ December 22

I DO NOT BELIEVE that such groups as these which I found my way to not long after returning from Wheaton, or Alcoholics Anonymous, which is the group they all grew out of, are perfect any more than anything human is perfect, but I believe that the Church has an enormous amount to learn from them. I also believe that what goes on in them is far closer to what Christ meant his Church to be, and what it originally was, than much of what goes on in most churches I know. These groups have no buildings or official leadership or money. They have no rummage sales, no altar guilds, no every-member canvases. They have no preachers, no choirs, no liturgy, no real estate. They have no creeds. They have no program. They make you wonder if the best thing that could happen to many a church might not be to have its building burn down and to lose all its money. Then all that the people would have left would be God and each other.

The church often bears an uncomfortable resemblance to the dysfunctional family. There is the authoritarian presence of the minister—the professional who knows all of the answers and calls most of the shots—whom few ever challenge either because they don't dare to or because they feel it would do no good if they did. There is the outward camaraderie and inward loneliness of the congregation. There are the unspoken rules and hidden agendas, the doubts and disagreements that for propriety's sake are kept more or less under cover. There are people with all sorts of enthusiasms and creativities which are not often enough made use of or even recognized because the tendency is not to rock the boat but to keep on doing things the way they have always been done.

Silence of the Holy Place ✳ December 23

WHAT DEADENS US most to God's presence within us, I think, is the inner dialogue that we are continuously engaged in with ourselves, the endless chatter of human thought. I suspect that there is nothing more crucial to true spiritual *comfort*, as the huge monk in cloth of gold put it, than being able from time to time to stop that chatter including the chatter of spoken prayer. If we choose to seek the silence of the holy place, or to open ourselves to its seeking, I think there is no surer way than by keeping silent.

God knows I am no good at it, but I keep trying, and once or twice I have been lucky, graced. I have been conscious but not conscious of anything, not even of myself. I have been surrounded by the whiteness of snow. I have heard a stillness that encloses all sounds stilled the way whiteness encloses all colors stilled, the way wordlessness encloses all words stilled. I have sensed the presence of a presence. I have felt a promise promised.

I like to believe that once or twice, at times like those, I have bumbled my way into at least the outermost suburbs of the Truth that can never be told but only come upon, that can never be proved but only lived for and loved.

Search for a Face ✳ December 24

MANY YEARS AGO I was in Rome at Christmastime, and on Christmas Eve I went to St. Peter's to see the Pope celebrate mass. It happened also to be the end of Holy Year, and there were thousands of pilgrims from all over Europe who started arriving hours ahead of when the mass was supposed to begin so that they would be sure to find a good place to watch from, and it was not long before the whole enormous church was filled. I am sure that we did not look like a particularly religious crowd. We were milling around, thousands of us, elbowing each other out of the way to get as near as possible to the papal altar with its huge canopy of gilded bronze and to the aisle that was roped off for the Pope to come down. Some had brought food to sustain them through the long wait, and every once in a while singing would break out like brush fire—"Adeste Fidelis" and "Heilige Nacht" I remember especially because everybody seemed to know the Latin words to one and the German words to the other—and the singing would billow up into the great Michelangelo dome and then fade away until somebody somewhere started it up again. Whatever sense anybody might have had of its being a holy time and a holy place was swallowed up by the sheer spectacle of it—the countless voices and candles, and the marble faces of saints and apostles, and the hiss and shuffle of feet on the acres of mosaic.

Then finally, after several hours of waiting, there was suddenly a hush, and way off in the flickering distance I could see that the Swiss Guard had entered with the golden throne on their shoulders, and the crowds pressed in toward the aisle, and in a burst of cheering the procession began to work its slow way forward.

What I remember most clearly, of course, is the Pope himself, Pius XII as he was then. In all that Renaissance of

333

splendor with the Swiss Guard in their scarlet and gold, the Pope himself was vested in plainest white with only a white skullcap on the back of his head. I can still see his face as he was carried by me on his throne—that lean, ascetic face, gray-skinned, with the high-bridged beak of a nose, his glasses glittering in the candlelight. And as he passed by me he was leaning slightly forward and peering into the crowd with extraordinary intensity.

Through the thick lenses of his glasses his eyes were larger than life, and he peered into my face and into all the faces around me and behind me with a look so keen and so charged that I could not escape the feeling that he must be looking for someone in particular. He was not a potentate nodding and smiling to acknowledge the enthusiasm of the multitudes. He was a man whose face seemed gray with waiting, whose eyes seemed huge and exhausted with searching, for someone, some *one*, who he thought might be there that night or any night, anywhere, but whom he had never found, and yet he kept looking. Face after face he searched for the face that he knew he would know—was it this one? was it this one? or this one?—and then he passed on out of my sight. It was a powerful moment for me, a moment that many other things have crystallized about since, and I felt that I knew whom he was looking for. I felt that anyone else who was really watching must also have known.

And the cry of Isaiah, "O that thou wouldst rend the heavens and come down, that the mountains would quake at thy presence . . . that the nations might tremble at thy presence! . . . There is no one that calls upon thy name, that bestirs himself to take hold of thee, for thou hast hid thy face from us, and hast delivered us into the hands of our iniquities."

In one sense, of course, the face was not hidden, and as the old Pope surely knew, the one he was looking for so hard was at that very moment crouched in some doorway against

the night or leading home some raging Roman drunk or waiting for the mass to be over so he could come in with his pail
and his mop to start cleaning up that holy mess. The old Pope
surely knew that the one he was looking for was all around
him there in St. Peter's. The face that he was looking for was
visible, however dimly, in the faces of all of us who had come
there that night mostly, perhaps, because it was the biggest
show in Rome just then and did not cost a cent but also
because we were looking for the same one he was looking for,
even though, as Isaiah said, there were few of us with wit
enough to call upon his name. The one we were looking for
was there then as he is here now because he haunts the world,
and as the years have gone by since that Christmas Eve, I
think he has come to haunt us more and more until there is
scarcely a place any longer where, recognized or unrecog-
nized, his ghost has not been seen. It may well be a post-
Christian age that we are living in, but I cannot think of an
age that in its own way has looked with more wistfulness and
fervor toward the ghost at least of Christ.

So Hallowed ❋ December 25

Some say that ever 'gainst that season comes
Wherein our Saviour's birth is celebrated,
The bird of dawning singeth all night long;
And then, they say, no spirit dare stir abroad,
The nights are wholesome, then no planets strike,
No fairy takes, nor witch hath power to charm,
So hallowed and so gracious is the time.

(I, ii, 157)

So HALLOWED AND *so gracious is the time*—these lines from
the first scene of *Hamlet* in a sense say it all. We tend to
think of time as progression, as moment following moment,
day following day, in relentless flow, the kind of time a clock

or calendar can measure. But we experience time also as depth, as having quality as well as quantity—a good time, a dangerous time, an auspicious time, a time we mark not by its duration but by its content.

On the dark battlements of Elsinore, Marcellus speaks to his companions of the time of Jesus' birth. It is a *hallowed* time he says, a holy time, a time in which life grows still like the surface of a river so that we can look down into it and see glimmering there in its depths something timeless, precious, other. And a *gracious* time, Marcellus says—a time that we cannot bring about as we can bring about a happy time or a sad time but a time that comes upon us as grace, as a free and unbidden gift. Marcellus explains that Christmas is a time of such holiness that the cock crows the whole night through as though it is perpetually dawn, and thus for once, even the powers of darkness are powerless.

Horatio's answer is equally instructive. "So have I heard and do in part believe," he says to Marcellus, thus speaking, one feels, not just for himself but for Shakespeare and for us. *In part* believe it. At Christmas time it is hard even for the unbeliever not to believe in something if not in everything. Peace on earth, good will to men; a dream of innocence that is good to hold on to even if it is only a dream; the mystery of being a child; the possibility of hope—not even the canned carols piped out over the shopping center parking plaza from Thanksgiving on can drown it out entirely.

For a moment or two, the darkness of disenchantment, cynicism, doubt, draw back at least a little, and all the usual worldly witcheries lose something of their power to charm. Maybe we cannot manage to believe with all our hearts. But as long as the moments last, we can believe that this is of all things the thing most worth believing. And that may not be as far as it sounds from what belief is. For as long as the moment lasts, that hallowed, gracious time.

Birth of the Child ✳ December 26

IN THE LETTERS of St. Paul, which are the earliest New Testament writings, there is no suggestion that the birth of Jesus was accompanied by any miracle, and in the Gospel of Mark, which is probably the earliest of the four, the birth plays no part. So a great many biblical scholars would agree with the skeptics that the great nativity stories of Luke and Matthew are simply the legendary accretions, the poetry, of a later generation, and that were we to have been present, we would have seen a birth no more or less marvelous than any other birth.

But if that is the case, what do we do with the legends of the wise men and the star, the shepherds and the angels and the great hymn of joy that the angels sang? Do we dismiss them as fairy tales, the subject for pageants to sentimentalize over once a year come Christmas, the lovely dream that never came true? Only if we are fools do we do that, although there are many in our age who have done it and there are moments of darkness when each one of us is tempted to do it. A lovely dream. That is all.

Who knows what the facts of Jesus' birth actually were? As for myself, the longer I live, the more inclined I am to believe in miracle, the more I suspect that if we had been there at the birth, we might well have seen and heard things that would be hard to reconcile with modern science. But of course that is not the point, because the Gospel writers are not really interested primarily in the facts of the birth but in the significance, the meaning for them of that birth just as the people who love us are not really interested primarily in the facts of our births but in what it meant to them when we were born and how for them the world was never the same again, how their whole lives were charged with new significance. Whether there were ten million angels there or just the woman herself and her husband, when that child was born the whole course of history was changed. That is a fact as hard and blunt as any fact. Art, music, literature, our culture itself, our political institutions, our whole understanding of ourselves and our world—it is impossible to conceive of how differently world history would have developed if that child had not been born. And in terms of faith, much more must be said because for faith, the birth of the child into the darkness of the world made possible not just a new way of understanding life but a new way of living life.

So Caught Up ✳ December 27

WHETHER HE WAS born in 4 B.C. or A.D. 6, in Bethlehem or Nazareth, whether there were multitudes of the heavenly host to hymn the glory of it or just Mary and her husband—when the child was born, the whole course of human history was changed. That is a truth as unassailable as any truth. Art, music, literature, Western culture itself with all its institutions and Western man's whole understanding of himself and his world—it is impossible to conceive how differently things would have turned out if that birth had not happened whenever, wherever, however it did. And there is a truth beyond that: for millions of people who have lived since, the birth of Jesus made possible not just a new way of understanding life but a new way of living it.

For better or worse, it is a truth that, for twenty centuries, there have been untold numbers of men and women who, in untold numbers of ways, have been so grasped by the child who was born, so caught up in the message he taught and the life he lived, that they have found themselves profoundly changed by their relationship with him. And they have gone on proclaiming, as the writers of the Gospels proclaimed before them, that through the birth of Jesus a life-giving power was released into the world which to their minds could have been no less than the power of God himself. This is the central truth that Matthew and Luke are trying to convey in their accounts of the Nativity. And it was a truth which no language or legend seemed too extravagant to convey. What the birth *meant*—meant to them, to the world—was the truth that mattered to them most and, when all is said and done, perhaps the only truth that matters to anyone.

Incarnation ❋ *December 28*

"THE WORD BECAME flesh," wrote John, "and dwelt among us, full of grace and truth" (John 1:14). That is what incarnation means. It is untheological. It is unsophisticated. It is undignified. But according to Christianity it is the way things are.

All religions and philosophies which deny the reality or the significance of the material, the fleshly, the earth-bound, are themselves denied. Moses at the burning bush was told to take off his shoes because the ground on which he stood was holy ground (Exodus 3:5), and incarnation means that all ground is holy ground because God not only made it but walked on it, ate and slept and worked and died on it. If we are saved anywhere, we are saved here. And what is saved is not some diaphanous distillation of our bodies and our earth but our bodies and our earth themselves. Jerusalem becomes the New Jerusalem coming down out of Heaven like a bride adorned for her husband (Revelation 21:2). Our bodies are sown perishable and raised imperishable (1 Corinthians 15:42).

One of the blunders religious people are particularly fond of making is the attempt to be more spiritual than God.

Emmanuel ✳ December 29

BACK THEN TO THE essential message of Christmas which is Emmanuel, God with us, and to the questions it raises: Who is this God and how is he with us? "The high and lofty One who inhabits eternity" is the answer to the first. The One who is with us is the One whom none can look upon because the space-and-time human mind can no more comprehend fully the spaceless, timeless Reality of the One than the eyes of the blind can comprehend light. The One who is with us is the One who has made himself known at most only partially and dimly through the pantomime of nature and history and the eloquent but always garbled utterance of prophets, saints, and mystics.

The Wild Hope ✳ December 30

TO LOOK AT THE last great self-portraits of Rembrandt or to read Pascal or hear Bach's B-minor Mass is to know beyond the need for further evidence that if God is anywhere, he is with them, as he is also with the man behind the meat counter, the woman who scrubs floors at Roosevelt Memorial, the high-school math teacher who explains fractions to the bewildered child. And the step from "God with them" to Emmanuel, "God with us," may not be as great as it seems. What keeps the wild hope of Christmas alive year after year in a world notorious for dashing all hopes is the haunting dream that the child who was born that day may yet be born again even in us and our own snowbound, snowblind longing for him.

Lord, Jesus Christ ✸ December 31

THOU SON OF THE Most High, Prince of Peace, be born again into our world. Wherever there is war in this world, wherever there is pain, wherever there is loneliness, wherever there is no hope, come, thou long-expected one, with healing in thy wings.

Holy Child, whom the shepherds and the kings and the dumb beasts adored, be born again. Wherever there is boredom, wherever there is fear of failure, wherever there is temptation too strong to resist, wherever there is bitterness of heart, come, thou blessed one, with healing in thy wings.

Saviour, be born in each of us who raises his face to thy face, not knowing fully who he is or who thou art, knowing only that thy love is beyond his knowing and that no other has the power to make him whole. Come, Lord Jesus, to each who longs for thee even though he has forgotten thy name. Come quickly.

Amen.

Books by Frederick Buechner

FICTION

The Book of Bebb: Lion Country, Open Heart, Love Feast, Treasure Hunt. New York: Atheneum, 1979; San Francisco: HarperCollins, 1990.

Brendan. New York: Atheneum, 1987; San Francisco: Harper & Row, 1988.

The Entrance to Porlock. New York: Atheneum, 1970.

The Final Beast. New York: Atheneum, 1965; San Francisco: Harper & Row, 1982.

Godric. New York: Atheneum, 1981; San Francisco: Harper & Row, 1983.

Lion Country. New York: Atheneum, 1971; San Francisco: Harper & Row, 1984.

A Long Day's Dying. New York: Knopf, 1950.

Love Feast. New York: Atheneum, 1974; San Francisco: Harper & Row, 1984.

Open Heart. New York: Atheneum, 1972; San Francisco: Harper & Row, 1984.

The Return of Ansel Gibbs. New York: Knopf, 1958.

The Seasons' Difference. New York: Knopf, 1952.

The Son of Laughter. San Francisco: HarperCollins, in press.

Treasure Hunt. New York: Atheneum, 1977; San Francisco: Harper & Row, 1984.

The Wizard's Tide. San Francisco: HarperCollins, 1990.

NONFICTION

The Alphabet of Grace. New York: Seabury, 1970; San Francisco: Harper & Row, 1985.

The Clown in the Belfry. San Francisco: HarperCollins, 1992.

The Faces of Jesus. Croton-on-Hudson, NY: Riverwood Publishers, 1974; San Francisco: Harper & Row, 1989.

The Hungering Dark. New York: Seabury, 1969; San Francisco: Harper & Row, 1985.

The Magnificent Defeat. New York: Seabury, 1966; San Francisco: Harper & Row, 1985.

Now and Then. San Francisco: Harper & Row, 1983.

Peculiar Treasures: A Biblical Who's Who. San Francisco: Harper & Row, 1982.

A Room Called Remember: Uncollected Pieces. San Francisco: Harper & Row, 1984.

The Sacred Journey. San Francisco: Harper & Row, 1982.

Telling Secrets. San Francisco: HarperCollins, 1991.

Telling the Truth: The Gospel as Tragedy, Comedy, and Fairy Tale. San Francisco: Harper & Row, 1977.

Whistling in the Dark: An ABC Theologized. San Francisco: Harper & Row, 1988.

Wishful Thinking: A Theological ABC. New York: Harper & Row, 1973.

Sources by Book

The Alphabet of Grace (AG), March 28–April 9, October 11, October 13–17

The Book of Bebb (BB), June 3–9

Brendan (B), March 17–25, April 23

The Clown in the Belfry (CB), July 5–12, July 21–24, August 7, August 12, November 2–3, November 8, November 16–17, November 21, November 24–December 4

The Faces of Jesus (FJ), April 10–14, April 16–19, April 21, September 17–19, September 29–30, October 9–10, December 25, December 27

The Final Beast (FB), May 8–14

Godric (G), January 5–6, January 9, January 21, January 31, February 21, March 1–14

The Hungering Dark (HD), May 26–29, June 2, August 25, August 30, September 27–28, October 1, October 3, October 28–29, December 24, December 26, December 31

The Magnificent Defeat (MD), March 26, April 20, April 22, May 18–25, August 21, August 24, August 28–29, August 31, September 2–3, September 5–6, September 12–14, September 16, September 23, September 26, October 5, November 15

Now and Then (NT), January 1, February 1–19, June 1, August 27, September 7, September 9, September 24

Peculiar Treasures (PT), July 20, July 29, August 10, August 16, September 16, September 21, October 3, November 13

A Room Called Remember (RCR), January 8, April 15, June 12–13, June 16–July 1, December 29–30

The Sacred Journey (SJ), January 2–4, January 10–15, January 17–20, January 22–28, May 30, July 17, July 25, July 30, August 14, October 31–November 1

Telling Secrets (TS), November 9–12, December 5–23

Telling the Truth (TT), January 29–30, April 24–May 7, October 12, October 21–24, November 22–23

Whistling in the Dark (WD), January 16, February 20, February 22–25, March 15–16, March 27, May 15–16, May 31, June 10, July 4, July 19, July 28, August 4, August 6, August 8–9, August 15, August 18–20, August 22–23, September 1, September 4, September 8, September 11, September 25, October 7–8, October 18–20, October 25, November 4, November 14

Wishful Thinking (WT), January 7, February 26–29, March 27, May 17, June 14–15, July 2–3, July 13–14, July 18, July 26–27, July 31–August 3, August 5–6, August 11, August 13, August 17, August 26, September 2, September 8, September 10, September 15, September 20, September 22, October 4, October 6, October 26–27, October 30, November 5–7, November 18–20, December 28

25	FJ, 27–28	May	1	PT, 167
26	MD, 87		2	WT, 58
27	WD, 83–84		3	TT, 86

Sources by Day

January				
	1	NT, 92, 87	26	SJ, 108–10
	2	SJ, 1–4	27	SJ, 112
	3	SJ, 4	28	SJ, 104
	4	SJ, 77–78	29	TT, 44–45
	5	G, 57	30	TT, 28–29, 30–31
	6	PT, 172, 50–51	31	G, 90
	7	WT, 51	February	
	8	RCR, 140–41	1	NT, 4–5
	9	G, 96	2	NT, 9–10
	10	SJ, 57–58	3	NT, 12–13
	11	SJ, 6–7	4	NT, 15–16
	12	SJ, 16	5	NT, 17–18
	13	SJ, 31–32	6	NT, 20–21
	14	SJ, 41	7	NT, 29–30
	15	SJ, 46	8	NT, 27
	16	WD, 100	9	NT, 42–43
	17	SJ, 68–69	10	NT, 47–49
	18	SJ, 80–81	11	NT, 61–64
	19	SJ, 91–92	12	NT, 72–73
	20	SJ, 85	13	NT, 78–79
	21	G, 36–37	14	NT, 84–85
	22	SJ, 94–95	15	NT, 3
	23	SJ, 96–97	16	NT, 89–90
	24	SJ, 100–101	17	NT, 93
	25	SJ, 107	18	NT, 97–98

	19	NT, 108		28	AG, 3–4
	20	WD, 14–16		29	AG, 7–8
	21	G, 60		30	AG, 9–10
	22	WD, 66		31	AG, 10–12
	23	WD, 113			
	24	WD, 67	April	1	AG, 24–25
	25	WD, 98		2	AG, 26–28
	26	WT, 74–75		3	AG, 35–37
	27	WT, 82		4	AG, 39–40
	28	WT, 14		5	AG, 41–42
	29	WT, 48		6	AG, 46–47
				7	AG, 48–50
March	1	G, 24		8	AG, 50–51
	2	G, 29		9	AG, 52–53
	3	G, 41–42		10	FJ, 136
	4	G, 43		11	FJ, 136–38
	5	G, 64		12	FJ, 115
	6	G, 103		13	FJ, 144–46
	7	G, 104–5		14	FJ, 148–50
	8	G, 114		15	RCR, 44
	9	G, 118		16	FJ, 176–79
	10	G, 124		17	FJ, 184–87
	11	G, 131		18	FJ, 233–34
	12	G, 142		19	FJ, 237
	13	G, 143–44		20	MD, 77–79
	14	G, 149–50		21	FJ, 219–20
	15	WD, 33–35		22	MD, 81
	16	WD, 96		23	B, 115–16
	17	B, 10–11		24	TT, 36–37
	18	B, 24		25	TT, 40–41
	19	B, 27–28		26	TT, 43
	20	B, 34–35		27	TT, 53–54
	21	B, 47–48		28	TT, 62–63
	22	B, 49–50		29	TT, 70–71
	23	B, 134		30	TT, 71
	24	B, 217			
	25	FJ, 27–28	May	1	PT, 167
	26	MD, 87		2	WT, 58
	27	WT, 76–77		3	TT, 86

4	TT, 86–87		11	RCR, 27
5	TT, 89–90		12	RCR, 29–30
6	TT, 96–97		13	RCR, 35
7	TT, 97–98		14	WT, 10–12
8	FB, 43		15	WT, 93
9	FB, 96–97		16	RCR, 49–50
10	FB, 115		17	RCR, 56
11	FB, 117–18		18	RCR, 68–69
12	FB, 176–78		19	RCR, 45
13	FB, 181–82		20	RCR, 86
14	FB, 215–16		21	RCR, 95–96
15	WD, 57		22	RCR, 100–101
16	WD, 25			
17	WT, 77–78		23	RCR, 104–5
18	MD, 10		24	RCR, 119–20
19	MD, 24–25		25	RCR, 132–33
20	MD, 47–49		26	RCR, 152–53
21	MD, 110–11		27	RCR, 155–56
22	MD, 114–15		28	RCR, 180–81
23	MD, 126–27		29	RCR, 172–73
24	MD, 142–43		30	RCR, 187
25	MD, 105–7			
26	HD, 74–75	July	1	RCR, 189–90
27	HD, 29–31		2	WT, 73
28	HD, 45–46		3	WT, 5
29	HD, 93–94		4	WD, 92–93
30	SJ, 58		5	CB, 108–9
31	WD, 21–22		6	CB, 109–10
			7	CB, 110–11
June	1	NT, 39	8	CB, 112–13
	2	HD, 107–9	9	CB, 113
	3	BB, 128	10	CB, 113
	4	BB, 173–74	11	CB, 115–16
	5	BB, 306–7	12	CB, 116–17
	6	BB, 393	13	WT, 72–73
	7	BB, 409	14	WT, 97–98
	8	BB, 492–93	15	SJ, 9–10
	9	BB, 530	16	WD, 1–2
	10	WD, 32–33	17	HD, 104

	18	WT, 95	24	MD, 58–60
	19	WD, 5–6	25	HD, 71–72
	20	PT, 75–76	26	WT, 24
	21	CB, 74–75	27	NT, 34–35
	22	CB, 76	28	MD, 122–23
	23	CB, 77–78	29	MD, 33–34
	24	CB, 81, 78–	30	HD, 114–16
		79	31	MD, 129–30
	25	SJ, 18		
	26	WT, 66–67	September 1	WD, 105–6
	27	WT, 65–66	2	WT, 41–43
	28	WD, 3–4	3	MD, 21
	29	PT, 5–6	4	WD, 105
	30	SJ, 55–56	5	MD, 11–12
	31	WT, 40	6	MD, 16
			7	NT, 55–56
August	1	WT, 99–100	8	WT, 69
	2	WT, 69–70	9	NT, 59–60
	3	WT, 95–96	10	WT, 53–54
	4	WD, 91–92	11	WD, 22–23
	5	WT, 98	12	MD, 40–41
	6	WD, 107–8	13	MD, 118–19
	7	CB, 163–64	14	MD, 95
	8	WD, 4–5	15	WT, 37–38
	9	WD, 1	16	PT, 22–24
	10	PT, 165–66	17	FJ, 9
	11	WT, 98–99	18	FJ, 23
	12	CB, 166–67	19	FJ, 91–93
	13	WT, 70–71	20	WT, 38
	14	SJ, 61–62	21	PT, 71–73
	15	WD, 37–38	22	WT, 31
	16	PT, 77–79	23	MD, 96–97
	17	WT, 49–50	24	NT, 8
	18	WD, 90–91	25	WD, 18–19
	19	WD, 108	26	MD, 133
	20	WD, 30–31	27	HD, 27
	21	MD, 38	28	HD, 64–65
	22	WD, 10–12	29	FJ, 99–100
	23	WD, 36–37	30	FJ, 138–39

October	1	HD, 87–88		8	CB, 154–55
	2	PT, 55–56		9	TS, 22
	3	HD, 49–50		10	TS, 79–80
	4	WT, 23		11	TS, 81–82
	5	MD, 104		12	TS, 85
	6	WT, 31–32		13	PT, 18–19
	7	WD, 114–15		14	WD, 51–52
	8	WD, 24		15	MD, 105
	9	FJ, 112–15		16	CB, 44
	10	FJ, 240		17	CB, 152–53
	11	AG, 57–59		18	WT, 89–90
	12	TT, 35		19	WT, 63
	13	AG, 74–75		20	WT, 29
	14	AG, 82–84		21	CB, 137
	15	AG, 108–9		22	TT, 83
	16	AG, 109–10		23	TT, 84
	17	AG, 111–12		24	CB, 130
	18	WD, 111		25	CB, 131
	19	WD, 102–3		26	CB, 51
	20	WD, 55–56		27	CB, 144
	21	TT, 7–8		28	CB, 41
	22	TT, 16–17		29	CB, 132–33
	23	TT, 21–22		30	CB, 156–57
	24	TT, 23–24			
	25	WD, 61–62	December	1	CB, 120–22
	26	WT, 96		2	CB, 124–25
	27	WT, 65		3	CB, 126
	28	HD, 101–2		4	CB, 126–27
	29	HD, 94		5	TS, 2–3
	30	WT, 33–34		6	TS, 8–9
	31	SJ, 73–74		7	TS, 13
				8	TS, 18
November	1	SJ, 21–22		9	TS, 27–28
	2	CB, 143		10	TS, 29–30
	3	CB, 147		11	TS, 31–32
	4	WD, 49–50		12	TS, 32–33
	5	WT, 91		13	TS, 35–36
	6	WT, 57–58		14	TS, 38–39
	7	WT, 27–28		15	TS, 44–45

16	TS, 47–48	24	HD, 114–16
17	TS, 49–50	25	FJ, 38–40
18	TS, 61–62	26	HD, 52–53
19	TS, 63–64	27	FJ, 41–44
20	TS, 76	28	WT, 43
21	TS, 90–92	29	RCR, 60
22	TS, 93–94	30	RCR, 65
23	TS, 105–6	31	HD, 16

Index by Title

Abortion *August 9*
Absalom *July 29*
Adolescence *July 16*
Adversaries *August 21*
Aging *July 28*
Alcoholics Anonymous *August 8*
Algebraic Preaching *July 19*
Alive and Changing *January 14*
All Is Well *April 22*
All the Doors *March 1*
Alphabet of Grace *January 3*
Among the Poor *February 7*
Angels' Music *March 18*
Angels When They Sang *March 11*
Annunciation, The *March 25*
Another Moment *January 24*
Another Reason *October 11*
Anxiety *August 22*
Anything Goes? *October 1*
Armor of Light, The *December 1*
Art *February 20*
Artful Dodging *April 6*
At the Heart of Things *June 12*
Avarice *July 3*

Be Alive *April 4*
Beatitudes *September 25*
Beauty in It *June 4*
Before Abraham *September 18*
Beginning of a Story *August 24*
Below a Time *July 15*
"Best She Could, The" *December 4*
Betrayal *April 14*
Beyond All Understanding *January 27*
Bible Without Tears, The *June 14*
Bigger Than Both of Us *August 29*
Birth of the Child *December 26*
Bitter Need *March 2*
Book About Us, A *November 16*
Books Like These *July 24*
Boredom *May 31*
Born Again *September 11*
By Letting Go *July 1*

Caiaphas *November 13*
Call to Prayer *February 15*
Calypso or Something *May 13*
Catching by Surprise *April 28*

Catechism *March 19*
Certainties *February 19*
Chanting *October 8*
Charismatic *May 16*
Child in Us, The *May 6*
Child or a Saint, A *May 24*
Christian *February 28*
Clack-Clack *May 12*
Communion of Saints *August 20*
Congenital Believer *April 5*
Crazy, Holy Grace, A *January 10*
Creation Is Underway *April 9*
"Creative" Writing *July 21*
Cripples All of Us *March 24*
Crux of the Matter *July 5*
"Cultured Despisers" *February 10*

Darkness *June 10, October 3*
David *September 16*
Decision *February 9*
Deepest Self, The *December 15*
Denominations *March 15*
Descent into Hell *August 23*
Doorway Opens, A *October 13*
Do This *May 25*
Dream *September 28*
Dreams *August 15*

Easter Thoughts *April 23*
Emmanuel *December 29*
Enter Leo Bebb *February 18*
Epiphany *January 6*
Eternity *October 4*
Every Wedding a Dream *October 29*
Evil *August 26*
Extraordinary Event *July 11*

Extraordinary Things *October 21*
Eyes of Faith *April 11*

Face of Christ, The *February 1*
Final Answers *June 29*
Final Secret, The *June 19*
Finding the Words *October 23*
Fool *November 7*
"Fool for Thee, A" *March 7*
"For Christ and His Kingdom" *November 10*
Forgiveness *November 20*
For the First Time *January 13*
Friends *November 4*
From Afar *October 15*
Funeral *November 14*

Game We Play, A *June 25*
Giving Prodigally *November 26*
Glimpse of Someone, A *August 14*
Glimpses of Joy *November 23*
Gluttony *September 22*
God *October 6*
God Is Mightily Present *December 11*
God Makes Himself Scarce *April 27*
God Pardon and Deliver You *May 11*
Godric's Love of God *March 14*
Godric's Musing *March 10*
Godric's View of Prayer *March 12*
Gods Are Dying, The *May 19*
God's Demands *November 2*
God's Grand Glory *March 23*
Goodbye *October 20*
Good Friday *April 16*

"Good Guy" *September 6*
Good Works *September 29*
Gospel World, The *May 5*
Grace *October 30*
Greater Freedom *August 27*
Great Laughter *January 26*

Hate *May 15*
Healing, A *March 3*
Healing Grace *May 14*
Heart of It, The *May 29*
Hell *September 15*
He Who Seeks, Finds *May 23*
Hidden Gifts *July 30*
Hidden Treasure *June 7*
His Living Presence *April 21*
History *September 20*
Holocaust *October 25*
Holy Dream, The *March 31*
Holy in the Commonplace, The *March 20*
How Far Do You Go? *February 8*
How They Do Live On *November 1*
Humanly Best *January 15*
Humility *July 31*

I Am My Secrets *December 14*
If God Speaks *January 2*
I Had Been Starving *November 11*
Immortality *September 2*
Incarnation *December 28*
In Search *May 30*
In the Midst *March 26*
Isaiah *October 2*
I Shall Not Want *July 8*
Is It True? *October 17*
It All Happened *August 12*

James Muilenburg *February 4*
Jobs *February 22*
Jogging *February 24*
John the Evangelist *September 21*
Jonathan *July 20*
Joseph and His Brethren *August 16*
Judgment *February 29*

Keeping Touch *December 13*
King Does Come, The *June 13*
Kingdom of God *August 17*
Kingdom, The *November 17*
King Lear *January 29*

Last Rose, The *December 7*
La Vie *September 3*
Lear Among the Young *January 30*
Lent *February 26*
Let Go *December 21*
Life-Giving Power *May 22*
Life Is *With* *January 7*
Life Itself Is Grace *January 1*
Like a Great Feast *June 5*
Like a Shepherd *July 7*
Like a·Thief *June 8*
Like a Uniform *December 3*
Like Flirting or Courting *March 22*
Limitations *April 2*
Listen for Him *January 4*
Living the Day Out *April 3*
Lord, Jesus Christ *December 31*
Lord's Prayer *March 27*
Love *September 10, November 15*
Love Each Other *November 8*

Man's Face, A *September 17*
Meditation *November 6*
Memorable Woman, A *February 14*
Memory *May 2*
Miracle *November 19*
Missing Art of Bliss, The *March 9*
More Than Intellect Involved *February 2*
More Than Symbol *September 30*
Morning Thoughts *April 7*
Music So Lovely *July 6*
"My God, My God" *April 15*
Myth *October 27*

Need to Praise, The *January 20*
Neighbor *July 27*
No Man Is an Island *May 28*
No Metaphor *April 19*
No Miracle Happens *June 22*
No Telling What You Might Hear *May 18*
No Theological Axe *September 9*
Not for the Wise *August 31*
No Time Lost? *January 5*
Not Just the Saints *October 31*
Not Suitable for Framing *November 29*
"Not What I Will" *April 13*
Novelist at Work *October 14*

Observance *August 18*
Old Age *August 4*
"Once Upon a Time" *November 25*
One Good Reason, The *September 14*
One Step Forward *March 17*
Only by Dying *April 12*
Only One Life *August 25*

"Open a Vein" *July 23*
Opening of a Door *February 5*
Our Own Story *June 23*
Our Pilot, Our Guide *January 8*
Our Richest Treasure *July 12*
Our Search *May 3*
Our Stories *December 10*
Out of the Silence *October 24*

Pains We Suffer Here, The *February 21*
Parable *July 26*
Paths of Trust, The *July 9*
Patriotism *July 4*
Patterns Were Set *July 25*
Peace *September 8*
Peace of the Mountain *February 13*
Pentecostal Fire *May 8*
Plain Sense, The *September 19*
Pluralism *December 19*
Point of No Return, A *May 27*
Possibility *September 24*
Possibility of Miracle *March 29*
Poverty *August 2*
Power from Beyond Time, A *January 22*
Power of Language, The *January 17*
Power of Words *June 28*
Praise, Praise *January 9*
Prayer *August 13*
Preaching the Gospel *April 30*
Pride *July 13*
Principles *July 2*
Psychotherapy *March 16*

Quality of Time *July 17*
Questions *May 17*

Racism *February 25*
Real Article, The *February 11*
Real People *November 28*
Real Tears *April 24*
Reinhold Niebuhr *February 3*
Rejoice Is the Last Word *October 12*
Re-living the Passion *March 6*
Remember *January 16*
"Remember Me" *October 5*
Remnant *April 17*
Resurrection, The *April 20*
Rinkitink *January 12*
Risen Christ, The *April 18*
Risky and Holy *June 1*
Ritual *February 27*

Saints and Sinners Alike *July 10*
Saying Grace *June 24*
Search for a Face *December 24*
Secret, A *December 6*
Secret Understood, A *November 9*
Shakespeare at His Greatest *June 27*
Shakespeare's Truth *May 4*
Shattering Revelation *January 25*
Silence and Random Sounds *March 30*
Silence of the Holy Place *December 23*
Sleep *October 19*
Sloth *November 18*
Small Events *December 16*
So Caught Up *December 27*
So Corny, the Prayers *May 9*
So Hallowed *December 25*
Something Better and Truer *January 23*
Something Dimly Seen *June 21*

So Much to Read *January 18*
So Now at Last *January 31*
Sound of God's Voice *May 20*
Stay Put *June 6*
Steward of the Wildest Mystery *May 7*
Stones Do Cry Out, The *October 22*
Such a Gift *June 2*
Sudden Snow *November 22*
Summing Up *December 8*
Sunset *May 26*

Take Care of Yourself *December 9*
Tears *September 4*
Tears for the Past *March 5*
Telling Silence, A *November 27*
That Deep Place Inside Us *December 5*
Theologian and the Poet, The *March 28*
Theology *November 5*
This Way *September 23*
Thomas *August 10*
Those Who Hear *April 29*
"Though He Dies" *October 9*
"Thoughts of Our Hearts, The" *December 20*
Threadbare Language *May 21*
Three Rules *November 3*
"Time Is Fulfilled, The" *August 7*
Time's Wingéd Chariot *June 9*
To Become a Human Being *August 28*
To Be Himself *April 25*
Tobias *May 1*
Today *September 1*
To Find What We Have Lost *June 11*

To Give Yourself *June 18*
To Go On Trying *September 26*
Tongue for Holy Things *March 21*
To Put It Quite Simply *June 3*
To Suffer in Love *September 7*
To Touch Godric *March 4*
Touched with Joy *October 28*
Tourist Preaching *August 30*
Transfiguration *August 6*
Trinity *June 15*
Truly Human *September 12*
Truly Ourselves *October 10*
Trust *December 17*
Truth of Our Stories, The *November 21*
Trying to Tell Us Something *April 8*
Two Answers *September 13*

Ultimate, The *November 24*
Unbelief *August 19*
Under a Delusion *April 10*
Unforeseen *January 28*
Unmemorable Moments *February 16*
Unthinkable *June 30*
Uses of Memory *December 12*

Vast Diversity *February 6*
Vernacular *March 8*
Virtue *October 18*
Vision, A *March 13*
Visit, A *November 30*
Visit We Remember, A *December 2*
Vocation *July 18, September 27*

We Catch Glimmers *June 26*
We Have It in Us *June 17*
What All of Us Want *May 10*
What Christ Meant *December 22*
What Preaching Is *December 18*
What's Good About Religion? *February 12*
When a Man Leaves Home *January 21*
Where We Started *June 16*
Where Your Feet Take You *April 1*
Who Jesus Is *November 12*
Wider World, A *January 19*
Wild Hope, The *December 30*
Wine *August 3*
Wishful Thinking *October 26*
Word and Deed *July 22*
Word of Great Power, A *September 5*
Words *February 17*
Words Without Knowledge *April 26*
Word, The *June 20*
Work *February 23*
Worship *July 14*
Worth Dying For *October 16*

X *August 5*

YHWH *August 11*
You *October 7*
Your Own Journey *January 11*

Zaccheus *August 1*